HANDBOOKS

❖

NUMBER TWO

Introduction to Inequalities

C J Bradley

Edited by James Gazet,
Gerry Leversha and Nick Lord

Introduction to Inequalities

Published by The United Kingdom Mathematics Trust.

Maths Challenges Office, School of Mathematics, University of Leeds, Leeds, LS2 9JT, United Kingdom

http://www.ukmt.org.uk

First published 2006
(as part of *Introduction to Number Theory and Inequalities*).

Second edition published 2010

Reprinted 2013, 2014, 2016, 2018

ISBN 978-1-906001-11-7

Printed in the UK for the UKMT by The Charlesworth Group, Wakefield.

http://www.charlesworth.com

Typographic design by Andrew Jobbings of Arbelos.

http://www.arbelos.co.uk

Typeset with LaTeX.

The books published by the United Kingdom Mathematics Trust are grouped into series.

The EXCURSIONS IN MATHEMATICS series consists of monographs which focus on a particular topic of interest and investigate it in some detail, using a wide range of ideas and techniques. They are aimed at high school students, undergraduates and others who are prepared to pursue a subject in some depth, but do not require specialised knowledge.

1. *The Backbone of Pascal's Triangle*, Martin Griffiths

2. *A Prime Puzzle*, Martin Griffiths

The HANDBOOKS series is aimed particularly at students at secondary school who are interested in acquiring the knowledge and skills which are useful for tackling challenging problems, such as those posed in the competitions administered by the UKMT and similar organisations.

1. *Plane Euclidean Geometry: Theory and Problems*, A D Gardiner and C J Bradley

2. *Introduction to Inequalities*, C J Bradley

3. *A Mathematical Olympiad Primer*, Geoff C Smith

4. *Introduction to Number Theory*, C J Bradley

5. *A Problem Solver's Handbook*, Andrew Jobbings

6. *Introduction to Combinatorics*, Gerry Leversha and Dominic Rowland

7. *First Steps for Problem Solvers*, Mary Teresa Fyfe and Andrew Jobbings

8. *A Mathematical Olympiad Companion*, Geoff C Smith

The PATHWAYS series aims to provide classroom teaching material for use in secondary schools. Each title develops a subject in more depth and in more detail than is normally required by public examinations or national curricula.

1. *Crossing the Bridge*, Gerry Leversha

2. *The Geometry of the Triangle*, Gerry Leversha

❖

The PROBLEMS series consists of collections of high-quality and original problems of Olympiad standard.

1. *New Problems in Euclidean Geometry*, David Monk

The CHALLENGES series is aimed at students at secondary school who are interested in tackling stimulating problems, such as those posed in the Mathematical Challenges administered by the UKMT and similar organisations.

1. *Ten Years of Mathematical Challenges: 1997 to 2006*

2. *Ten Further Years of Mathematical Challenges: 2006 to 2016*

3. *Intermediate Problems*, Andrew Jobbings

4. *Junior Problems*, Andrew Jobbings

5. *Senior Problems*, Andrew Jobbings

❖

The YEARBOOKS series documents all the UKMT activities, including details of all the challenge papers and solutions, lists of high scorers, accounts of the IMO and Olympiad training camps, and other information about the Trust's work during each year.

Contents

Series Editor's Foreword

This book is part of a series whose aim is to help young mathematicians prepare for competitions, such as the British Mathematical Olympiad, at secondary school level. Like other volumes in the Handbooks series, it provides cheap and ready access to directly relevant material. All these books are characterised by the large number of carefully constructed exercises for the reader to attempt.

In its original form, this was presented as part of the composite volume Introductions to Number Theory and Inequalities. It has now been extensively revised and reorganised, with more examples and exercises, and is now published as a single volume dedicated to Inequalities . This work has been undertaken by James Gazet, Nick Lord and myself, with the blessing of the original author C J Bradley.

I hope that every secondary school will have these books in its library. The prices have been set so low that many good students will wish to purchase their own copies. Schools wishing to give out large numbers of copies as these books as prizes should note that discounts may be negotiated with the UKMT office.

London, UK   GERRY LEVERSHA

About the author

C J Bradley   was a prolific author of questions for mathematics competitions, and played an important role on the Problems Selection Committee of IMO 2002 in Glasgow. He was formerly a University Lecturer in the University of Oxford and Official Fellow and Tutor at Jesus College. He was Deputy Leader of the UK Mathematical Olympiad Team from 1992 to

1995, and was involved in training the team for the annual International Mathematical Olympiad. He was for many years a teacher at Clifton College, Bristol.

About the editors

James Gazet   runs one of the Summer Schools for the UKMT as well as acting as a marker for both the BMO and IMOK Olympiad competitions. He is currently head of mathematics at Eton College.

Gerry Leversha   is Editor of *The Mathematical Gazette,* and taught at St Paul's School in London. He has been involved in the UKMT as Chair of Publications and on the setting panel for the BMO and IMOK Olympiads and has been involved in the training of the UK IMO squad.

Nick Lord   is Editor of the Problem Corner of *The Mathematical Gazette* and teaches at Tonbridge School in Kent. He has been involved in the UKMT as a member of Council and a marker for the IMOK Olympiads.

Preface

The subject of inequalities provides a rich source of material for mathematics competitions, and from that point of view is usually classed as algebra. However, many inequalities are more honestly thought of as part of mathematical analysis, and yet more are so-called geometric inequalities.

Many algebraic inequalities essentially reduce to the fact that a perfect square, or a sum of perfect squares, cannot be negative. For this reason, the book begins with a treatment of this sort of argument. Very often, nothing beyond this is needed to solve a particular problem. The next two chapters focus on celebrated inequalities such as the AM-GM inequality and Cauchy-Schwarz. The difficulty in problem-solving is usually that of knowing which sort of inequality to select and how to apply it, and I hope that we have succeeded in giving useful tips as to how to do this effectively. Two chapters then concentrate on miscellaneous methods which are sometimes appropriate and on a whole series of inequalities which arise from the consideration of sequences. We are grateful to Jack Shotton, a member of the UK IMO team in 2005 and 2006, for supplying material on Schur's and Muirhead's inequalities.

Mathematics competitions do not usually require the use of the calculus, and, indeed, there are dangers in employing calculus methods haphazardly. Often they only succeed in demonstrating the local nature of maxima or minima and do not deal with global inequalities. However, the result known as Jensen's inequality is a general and wide-ranging theorem which allows one to prove a large number of inequalities concerning particular functions of real variables, and should be in every problem-solvers toolkit. The theory of the roots of polynomial equations can also be a useful technique in demonstrating certain types of inequality.

Geometrical inequalities are very important and they form the subject-matter of the final lengthy chapter. Their source is, as the name would suggest, geometrical configurations, but they can often be reduced, by means of various manipulations, to an algebraic or trigonometrical form. Perhaps the most beautiful formula is that due to Euler which states that, if O and I are circumcentre and incentre of a triangle with circumradius R and inradius r, then $OI^2 = R(R - 2r)$, and this, of course, gives rise to the result that $2r \leq R$. There is also a brief treatment of areal coordinates.

We refer the serious student of inequalities to Hojoo Lee's notes [3].

We are indebted to Andrew Jobbings of Arbelos for many wise and ingenious suggestions which have helped to clarify the presentation of ideas in this book.

Bristol   C J Bradley
Windsor   James Gazet
London   Gerry Leversha
Tonbridge   Nick Lord

Chapter 1

Basic properties of inequalities

1.1 The ordering of the real numbers

We begin with what you have always taken for granted, namely that given any pair of real numbers a and b, then one of the following three relationships must hold:

$$\text{either } a > b, \text{ or } a = b \text{ or } a < b.$$

A symbol is used to combine either the first two or the last two of these; thus $a \geq b$ means that a is greater than or equal to b and $a \leq b$ means that a is less than or equal to b.

It is permissible to write $a < x < b$ if *both* $a < x$ and $x < b$ and then x lies in the *open interval* (a, b). Likewise it is permissible to write $a \leq x \leq b$ when x lies in the *closed interval* $[a, b]$. On the other hand if $x < -5$ or $x > 3$ it is not permissible to write $3 < x < -5$.

Subsets of the real numbers, such as the rational numbers and integers, are ordered and inherit their ordering from that of the real numbers. In addition, the positive integers are said to be *well-ordered* because, in addition to the ordering, it is the case that every subset of positive integers has a least member. This is not, however, true of the rational or real numbers. For example, the set of rationals between 0 and 1 does not have a least member.

1.2   How to manipulate inequalities

The ordering of real numbers obeys the following rules:

(1) If $a > b$ and c is any other real number then

$$a + c > b + c \quad \text{and} \quad a - c > b - c.$$

(2) If $a > b$ and $c > 0$ then

$$ac > bc \quad \text{and} \quad \frac{a}{c} > \frac{b}{c},$$

but if $c < 0$ then

$$ac < bc \quad \text{and} \quad \frac{a}{c} < \frac{b}{c}.$$

(3) If $a > b$ and $b > c$ then $a > c$.

Rule (2) says in words that if you multiply an inequality by a negative number then you have to reverse the direction of the inequality. Thus $5 > 3$, but $-10 < -6$.

Analogous rules apply when $>$ is exchanged with $<$ and when $>$ and $<$ are replaced by $\geq$ and $\leq$ respectively.

Example 1.1   If $a > b$ and $c > d$, is it true that $a + c > b + d$?

Yes. We have from rule (1) that $a + c > b + c$ and also from rule (1) that $b + c > b + d$. Then from rule (3) $a + c > b + d$.

Example 1.2   If $a > b$ and $c > d$, is it true that $a - c > b - d$?

No. Take $a = 5$, $b = 4$, $c = 3$, $d = 1$ as a counterexample.

Example 1.3   If $a > b$ and $c > d$, is it true that $ac > bd$?

No. Take $a = -7, b = -10, c = 3, d = -5$ as a counterexample.

However, if all of a, b, c are positive, then it is true that $ac > bd$. For then by rule (2) $ac > bc$ and by rule (2) $bc > bd$ and then by rule (3) $ac > bd$.

Example 1.4   If $x^2 \leq 16$, what can you say about x?

We have $16 - x^2 \geq 0$, so $(4 - x)(4 + x) \geq 0$ and, since the terms in brackets cannot both be negative, they must be non-negative and hence $-4 \leq x \leq 4$.

It is a common fallacy, but not amongst good mathematicians, that the solution to this inequality is $x \leq 4$.

Exercise 1a

1. (a) If $a > b$, under what conditions does it follow that $\frac{1}{a} < \frac{1}{b}$?

    (b) If $a > b$, under what conditions does it follow that $a^2 > b^2$?

    (c) If $a > b$, under what conditions does it follow that $a^3 > b^3$?

    (d) If $a > b$, under what conditions does it follow that $\log_k a > \log_k b$, where $k > 0$ and $k \neq 1$?

    (e) If $f(x)$ is a function, and if $a > b$, under what conditions does it follow that $f(a) > f(b)$?

    (f) If $f(x)$ is a function, and if $a > b$, under what conditions does it follow that $f(a) < f(b)$?

2. Solve the inequality $x^3 > 8$.

3. Solve the inequality $x^4 \geq 16$.

4. Solve the inequality $x^2 \leq 16x$.

1.3 Some numerical problems

We now give a few examples of the sort of numerical problems that are part of the syllabus in the final years at school in many countries, followed by a set of exercises. Of course school syllabuses vary widely around the world. Readers are advised to check that they are familiar with the ideas involved before proceeding to study new work.

Example 1.5 Find the values of x satisfied by the inequality

$$3(x - 1) - 2(4x + 5) > x + 5.$$

Tidying up we have $-5x - 13 > x + 5$ or $6x < -18$, so that $x < -3$.

Example 1.6 Solve the quadratic inequality $x^2 - 5x - 6 \leq 0$.
Factorising, we get

$$(x - 6)(x + 1) \leq 0.$$

Either one of the brackets is zero (and their product is zero) or the brackets have opposite signs (and their product is negative). Since $x + 1 > x - 6$ it follows that $x + 1 \geq 0$ and $x - 6 \leq 0$ and hence the solution is $-1 \leq x \leq 6$.

The following diagram illustrates the interval involved. Of course, we can see from the sketch that $y \leq 0$ when $-1 \leq x \leq 6$.

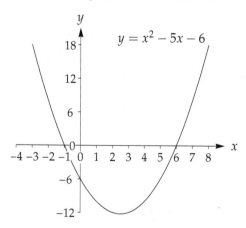

An alternative, which avoids drawing the whole graph but is essentially exactly the same technique, is to draw a number line with critical points marked on it and an indication of whether the function is positive or negative in each interval. In this case, the number line would look like this:

Example 1.7 Solve the quadratic inequality $x^2 - 5x + 6 > 0$.

Factorising, we get

$$(x - 3)(x - 2) > 0.$$

Both bracketed expressions are either negative or positive, and hence $x < 2$ or $x > 3$.

Example 1.8 For what values of x is

$$\frac{1}{x - 1} \geq \frac{1}{2x + 5}?$$

You cannot cross multiply as you would with an equation, because with unknown values in the denominators you do not know whether you are multiplying by a positive or negative quantity.

A neat way to deal with this is to multiply the inequality through by

$$(x - 1)^2(2x + 5)^2,$$

which cannot be negative. This gives

$$(x - 1)(2x + 5)^2 \geq (x - 1)^2(2x + 5).$$

Moving both terms onto the left-hand side and factorising, we have

$$(x - 1)(2x + 5)(x + 6) \geq 0$$

and this gives the solution as $-6 \leq x < -\frac{5}{2}$ or $x > 1$. Note that $x = -\frac{5}{2}$ and $x = 1$ are excluded since one of the expressions $\frac{1}{2x+5}$ and $\frac{1}{x-1}$ is not defined for each of these values.

Example 1.9   If $x \geq 0$, $y \geq 0$, $x + 2y \leq 20$, $3x + y \leq 30$ find the maximum value of $x + y$.

This is an example of what is called *linear programming*, in which the maximum or minimum of a linear function of several variables is required, subject to a number of linear inequalities in those variables. There is a vast literature on this topic, and in this book we only show how to deal with a simple two-variable problem by graphical means.

In such problems the linear function obtains its maximum or minimum at a vertex or on the boundary of the given region (or on or close to the boundary if there is a requirement that x and y have to be integers).

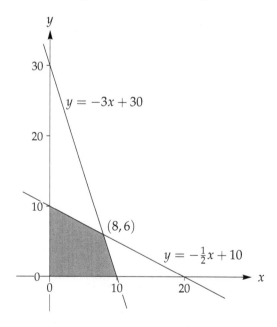

The region defined by the inequalities is shaded and the maximum value of $x + y$ is 14 at the vertex $(8,6)$. However, the maximum of

$4x + y$ is 40 at the vertex $(10, 0)$, which shows that the vertex required depends on the function to be maximised or minimised.

Example 1.10   Given

$$y = \frac{x - 1}{(x - 2)(x - 3)},$$

show that $y \leq -2\sqrt{2} - 3$ or $y \geq 2\sqrt{2} - 3$.

A problem such as this can be solved by calculus methods to determine the range of y by finding the turning points, but an algebraic method exists. On multiplying up we have

$$x^2 y - x(5y + 1) + (6y + 1) = 0.$$

For real values of x the discriminant must be non-negative, and hence

$$(5y + 1)^2 \geq 4y(6y + 1).$$

This quadratic inequality reduces to $(y + 3)^2 \geq 8$, which yields the required result.

This method works whenever the equation $y = f(x)$ can be rearranged into a quadratic in x.

Exercise 1b

1. Find all values of x for which $x^2 + 7x + 10 < 0$.

2. Find all values of x for which

$$\frac{4}{x - 2} < \frac{3}{x + 2}.$$

3. Find all values of x for which

$$\frac{3x}{x - 7} > \frac{1}{x - 3}.$$

4. Prove that, for all real x,

$$\frac{x-3}{(x-2)^2} \le \tfrac{1}{4}.$$

5. Find the maximum and minimum values of

$$\frac{x+4}{x^2+4x+9}$$

as x varies over all real values.

6. If $x \ge 0$, $y \ge 0$, $2x + 5y \le 34$ and $3x + 4y \le 37$ find the maximum value of $x + 2y$.

7. Show that, if $p > m > 0$, then

$$\frac{p-m}{p+m} \le \frac{x^2 - 2mx + p^2}{x^2 + 2mx + p^2} \le \frac{p+m}{p-m}$$

for all real values of x.

Chapter 2

Sums of squares

2.1 Some simple ideas

Most inequalities arise from the very simple idea that all squares are non-negative. In other words, for all real numbers x,

$$x^2 \geq 0$$

with equality if, and only if, $x = 0$.

For example, we can start with $(x - y)^2 \geq 0$ and deduce that

$$x^2 + y^2 \geq 2xy$$

with equality if, and only if, $x = y$.

In order to use this idea that squares are positive, we often have recourse to the process of 'completing the square'. For example, if you have to prove that $x^2 + x + 1 > 0$ for all x, it is enough to rewrite it as

$$\left(x + \tfrac{1}{2}\right)^2 + \tfrac{3}{4},$$

which is always positive. But, of course, you can do better than this since you can say that $x^2 + x + 1 \geq \tfrac{3}{4}$, with equality if, and only if, $x = -\tfrac{1}{2}$.

In general we have

$$Q(x) \equiv ax^2 + bx + c \equiv \frac{(2ax + b)^2 + 4ac - b^2}{4a}.$$

It follows that if $a > 0$ and $4ac \geq b^2$, then $Q(x) \geq 0$ for all real x, and equality holds if, and only if, $x = -\tfrac{b}{2a}$ and $b^2 = 4ac$.

Conversely, if $Q(x) \geq 0$ for all real x, it must be non-negative for very large values of x, and hence $a > 0$, and secondly it must be non-negative for $x = -\frac{b}{2a}$ and hence $4ac \geq b^2$. It is immediate that $Q(x) \leq 0$ for all real x if, and only if, $a < 0$ and $4ac \geq b^2$, with the same equality condition.

The simple idea that squares cannot be negative can obviously be extended to the idea that an expression which is a sum of squares is non-negative. One application of this is that

$$(x - y)^2 + (y - z)^2 + (z - x)^2 \geq 0$$

with equality if, and only if, $x = y = z$. This can be rearranged to give the useful inequality

$$x^2 + y^2 + z^2 \geq xy + yz + zx \tag{2.1}$$

with equality if, and only if, $x = y = z$.

Exercise 2a

1. Prove that $x^4 + x^2 - 2x + 3 > 0$.

2. Prove that $x^4 - 4x^3 + 5x^2 - 2x + 1 > 0$.

3. Prove that for all real x, y, z, w

$$x^2 + y^2 + z^2 + w^2 + 1 \geq x + y + z + w.$$

4. Find the range of values of k for which the function $f(x)$ is positive for all x, where $f(x) = x^2 + kx + 3$.

5. Find the range of values of k for which the function $f(x)$ is negative for all x, where $f(x) = kx^2 + 4x + k$.

6. Find the range of values of k for which the function $f(x)$ is positive for all x, where $f(x) = 2kx^2 + kx + 3$.

7. Find the range of values of k for which the function $f(x)$ has the same sign for all x, where $f(x) = 4kx^2 + 4x - 1$.

8. Prove that, if $a > 0$, then $1 + a \geq 2\sqrt{a}$, with equality if, and only if, $a = 1$.

9. Prove that, if $a, b > 0$, then $\sqrt{ab} \leq \frac{a+b}{2}$, with equality if, and only if, $a = b$.

10. Prove that $x^2 + y^2 + z^2 \geq xy - yz - zx$. When does equality hold?

11. Prove that $(a + b)^2 \leq 2(a^2 + b^2)$. When does equality hold?

12. Prove that, if $a, b > 0$, then $(a + b)(a^2 + b^2) \leq 2(a^3 + b^3)$. When does equality hold?

2.2 Algebraic manipulations

Often a new inequality can be derived by starting with a sum of squares and applying some simple algebraic manipulation. This has already been done in the last five questions of exercise 2a. In some cases, it is simply a matter of choosing the correct expressions to be squared and added.

Example 2.1   Prove that

$$2a^2 + 20b^2 + 5c^2 + 8ab - 4bc - 4ac \geq 0$$

and give conditions for equality.

This looks very much as if it comes from the sum of three squares, one involving each of the three pairs of variables.

Clearly there must be a term a^2 in two of these. To obtain $8ab$, we must have $(a + 4b)^2$ and to obtain $-4ac$ we must have $(a - 2c)^2$. What remains is $4b^2 - 4bc + c^2$ which is $(2b - c)^2$. Thus the original expression is

$$(a + 4b)^2 + (a - 2c)^2 + (2b - c)^2 \geq 0.$$

We must now check that equality is possible—this is not always the case! But here it is, so long as $a = -4b = 2c$.

When you have to prove that $P \geq Q$, it is often easier to try to show that $P - Q \geq 0$. It might be possible to factorise the expression which results.

Some factorisations which might turn out to be useful are

$$a^3 - b^3 \equiv (a - b)(a^2 + ab + b^2)$$
$$a^3 + b^3 \equiv (a + b)(a^2 - ab + b^2)$$
$$a^3 + b^3 + c^3 - 3abc \equiv (a + b + c)(a^2 + b^2 + c^2 - bc - ca - ab)$$

and the 'Sophie Germain identities'

$$a^4 + a^2b^2 + b^4 \equiv (a^2 + ab + b^2)(a^2 - ab + b^2)$$
$$a^4 + 4b^4 \equiv (a^2 + 2ab + 2b^2)(a^2 - 2ab + 2b^2),$$

which can be thought of as special cases of the difference of two squares since they are equivalent to the expressions

$$\left(a^2 + b^2\right)^2 - a^2b^2$$
$$\text{and} \quad \left(a^2 + 2b^2\right)^2 - 4a^2b^2.$$

Example 2.2   Prove that if $a, b, c > 0$ then $a^3 + b^3 + c^3 \geq 3abc$.

We have

$$a^3 + b^3 + c^3 - 3abc = (a + b + c)(a^2 + b^2 + c^2 - bc - ca - ab).$$

Since $a, b, c > 0$ we know $a + b + c > 0$. A rearrangement of result (2.1) on page 10 shows that $a^2 + b^2 + c^2 - bc - ca - ab \geq 0$, with equality if, and only if, $a = b = c$. Multiplying these two inequalities together yields the desired result.

Example 2.3   Prove that if $a, b, c, d > 0$ then

$$(a + b + c + d)(a^3 + b^3 + c^3 + d^3) \geq \left(a^2 + b^2 + c^2 + d^2\right)^2.$$

Multiplying out and subtracting, we see that this is equivalent to proving

$$\left(ab^3 + ac^3 + \cdots + bd^3 + cd^3\right) - 2\left(a^2b^2 + \cdots + c^2d^2\right) \geq 0,$$

where the first bracket contains twelve terms and the second bracket contains six terms. These can, in turn, be rearranged into six groups of three terms

$$\left(ab^3 + ba^3 - 2a^2b^2\right) + \cdots + \left(cd^3 + dc^3 - 2c^2d^2\right) \geq 0.$$

Each group can now be factorised, to produce expressions of the form $ab(a - b)^2$. We have now reorganised the original inequality into the form

$$ab(a - b)^2 + ac(a - c)^2 + \cdots + cd(c - d)^2 \geq 0,$$

which is true because $a, b, c, d \geq 0$. We have equality if, and only if, $a = b = c = d$.

Yet another useful technique is to multiply inequalities together.

Example 2.4   If $a, b, c > 0$ prove that

$$(b + c - a)(c + a - b)(a + b - c) \leq abc.$$

If any of the terms on the left-hand side is negative, then the inequality becomes trivially true. We therefore assume that all three terms are positive.

We have $(b + c - a)(c + a - b) = c^2 - (a - b)^2 \leq c^2$. Multiplying the three inequalities like this together and taking positive square roots provides the answer. We have equality if, and only if, $a = b = c$.

The most interesting case of this is when a, b, c are the sides of a triangle. Since the length of each side is less than the sum of the other two sides, the three brackets on the left-hand side are all positive. This is dealt with in more detail in chapter 9 on geometrical inequalities.

A final technique, with inequalities involving reciprocals, is to get rid of these by making a substitution.

Example 2.5   If $x, y > 0$ show that

$$\frac{1}{x} + \frac{1}{y} \geq \frac{4}{x+y}.$$

In this case, let $\frac{1}{x} = u$ and $\frac{1}{y} = v$, noting that you are allowed to do this because $x, y > 0$. The inequality is transformed into $(u + v)^2 \leq 4uv$, which follows immediately from $(u - v)^2 \geq 0$. Equality is achieved when $x = y$.

Exercise 2b

1. Prove that if $a, b, c > 0$ then $(a + b)(b + c)(c + a) \geq 8abc$. When does equality hold?

2. If $x, y, z > 0$ show that

$$\frac{1}{x} + \frac{1}{y} + \frac{1}{z} \geq \frac{9}{x+y+z}.$$

When does equality hold?

3. If $a, b, c > 0$ prove that

$$\frac{ab}{a+b} + \frac{bc}{b+c} + \frac{ca}{c+a} \leq \tfrac{1}{2}(a + b + c).$$

When does equality hold?

4. Prove that for all real values of a, b, c

$$a^4 + b^4 + c^4 \geq b^2c^2 + c^2a^2 + a^2b^2 \geq abc(a + b + c).$$

When does equality hold?

5. Prove that for all real values of a, b, c

$$b^8c^8 + c^8a^8 + a^8b^8 \geq a^4b^4c^4(a^4 + b^4 + c^4) \geq a^5b^5c^5(a + b + c).$$

When does equality hold?

6. Prove that $(a+b)(a^2+b^2)(a^3+b^3) \leq 4(a^6+b^6)$. When does equality hold?

7. Prove that $(p^2+q^2)(u^2+v^2) \geq 8qv(pu-qv)$. When does equality hold? [David Monk]

8. Prove that if $x > 1$ then

$$x + \frac{3}{x-1} - 2\sqrt{x+2} \geq 0.$$

When does equality hold?

9. Prove that if $z > 0$, then

$$\frac{3-z}{1+z} \leq \frac{1}{z}.$$

Hence deduce that if $a, b, c > 0$ then

$$\frac{a(3a-b)}{ca+bc} + \frac{b(3b-c)}{ab+ca} + \frac{c(3c-a)}{bc+ab} \leq \frac{a^3+b^3+c^3}{abc}.$$

When does equality hold?

10. If $a, b, c > 0$, prove that

(a) $4(a^3+b^3) \geq (a+b)^3$

(b) $9(a^3+b^3+c^3) \geq (a+b+c)^3$.

When does equality hold? [BMO1 Jan 1996, adapted]

11. If x, y, z are positive real numbers prove that

$$(x^2+y^2+z^2)(yz+zx+xy) \geq 3(x+y+z)xyz.$$

When does equality hold?

2.3 Inequalities with conditions

Often we are given an inequality which depends upon some stated condition, giving a relationship between the variables. Our general strategy here is to manipulate the material in such a way that the condition can be applied.

If the condition gives a numerical value for an expression, we try to recreate that expression and substitute.

Example 2.6   Show that if a, b, $c > 0$ and $(1+a)(1+b)(1+c) = 8$ then $abc \leq 1$.

By question 8 of exercise 2a, we have $(1+a) \geq 2\sqrt{a}$. Multiplying three such inequalities together we obtain

$$(1+a)(1+b)(1+c) \geq 8\sqrt{abc}.$$

Now we can replace the left-hand side of this inequality by 8, and, by squaring, obtain the required result. Equality is achieved if, and only if, $a = b = c = 1$.

Example 2.7   Given $xy + yz + zx = -1$ prove that

$$x^2 + 5y^2 + 8z^2 \geq 4.$$

When does equality hold? Does the expression have a greatest value subject to the same condition?   *[BMO1 Jan 1992, adapted]*

The expression $x^2 + 5y^2 + 8z^2$ suggests that we are going to need an approach similar to that in example 2.1, where it is written as a sum of squares. This, however, would involve terms of the type xy, yz and zx, and these will need to be eliminated using the given condition. A little experiment produces the identity

$$x^2 + 5y^2 + 8z^2 = (x + 2y + 2z)^2 + (y - 2z)^2 - 4(xy + yz + zx)$$

and the right-hand side of this is clearly no less than 4, as required. Equality holds when $x + 2y + 2z = 0$ and $y = 2z$, that is when $x = -6k$, $y = 2k$, $z = k$ for some constant k. But $xy + yz + zx = -1$ so $k = \pm\frac{1}{4}$. Then $(x, y, z) = \pm\left(-\frac{3}{2}, \frac{1}{2}, \frac{1}{4}\right)$.

Now

$$x = \frac{-1 - yz}{y + z}.$$

When $y = N + 1$, $z = -N$, $x = N^2 + N - 1$ then $x^2 + 5y^2 + 8z^2 > N^4$, so there is no greatest value.

Alternatively, we might manipulate the condition so that an inequality statement follows.

Example 2.8 Prove that if $0 < x, y, z < 1$ and

$$xyz = (1 - x)(1 - y)(1 - z)$$

then $xyz \leq \frac{1}{8}$.

We have

$$x^2 y^2 z^2 = x(1 - x)y(1 - y)z(1 - z).$$

Now $(2x - 1)^2 \geq 0$, so $x(1 - x) \leq \frac{1}{4}$. Multiplying three such inequalities together and taking positive square roots we obtain the required result. We have equality if, and only if, $x = y = z = \frac{1}{2}$.

In the next example, the required inequality $x^3 + y^3 \geq \sqrt{2}xy$ is said to be *non-homogeneous*, because the degree of the left-hand side is 3 and that of the right-hand side is 2. When this happens, it is often useful to try and make it homogeneous. This can be done by squaring both sides, to give expressions of degree 6 and 4, and then multiplying the right-hand side by the expression in the condition, which is of degree 2, and is equal to 1.

Example 2.9 If $x, y > 0$ and $x^2 + y^2 = 1$ prove that

$$x^3 + y^3 \geq \sqrt{2}xy.$$

Subtracting two expressions of the same degree, we have

$$
\begin{aligned}
\left(x^3 + y^3\right)^2 - 2x^2y^2\left(x^2 + y^2\right) &= x^6 - 2x^4y^2 + 2x^3y^3 - 2x^2y^4 + y^6 \\
&= (x - y)^2\left(x^4 + 2x^3y + x^2y^2 + 2xy^3 + y^4\right) \\
&\geq 0.
\end{aligned}
$$

Hence

$$
\begin{aligned}
\left(x^3 + y^3\right)^2 &\geq 2x^2y^2\left(x^2 + y^2\right) \\
&= 2x^2y^2
\end{aligned}
$$

and the result follows by taking positive square roots.

Equality is achieved if, and only if, $x = y = \frac{1}{\sqrt{2}}$.

Exercise 2c

1. Find the maximum and minimum values of $x^4 + y^4 - 2xy$ given that $x^2 + y^2 = 1$.

2. Find, with proof, the minimum value of $(x+y)(y+z)$ where x, y, z are positive real numbers satisfying the condition

$$xyz(x+y+z) = 1.$$

[BMO1 Jan 1991]

3. If $ad - bc = 1$ prove that $a^2 + b^2 + c^2 + d^2 + ac + bd \geq \sqrt{3}$.

4. Show that, if $7x^2 + 3xy + 3y^2 = 1$, then the least positive value of $\dfrac{x^2 + y^2}{y}$ is $\frac{1}{2}$.   [BMO1 Dec 1987]

5. Given $3(x^2 + y^2) + 4xy = 10$ find the maximum and minimum values of
$$f(x,y) \equiv (x^2 - 3)^2 + (y^2 - 3)^2.$$

Chapter 3

The inequality of the means

3.1 Different types of mean

In question 9 of exercise 2a we deduced the inequality: if $a, b > 0$, then

$$\sqrt{ab} \leq \frac{a+b}{2},$$

with equality if, and only if, $a = b$.

For two positive numbers a and b, $\frac{1}{2}(a+b)$ is known as the *arithmetic*[1] *mean* (AM) and $\sqrt{ab}$ is the *geometric mean* (GM). The inequality can be interpreted as saying that the arithmetic mean of two positive quantities is greater than or equal to their geometric mean.

Equality occurs when the numbers are equal. In other words, if you fix the sum of two numbers their product is maximised when the numbers are equal, or if the product of two numbers is fixed their sum is minimised when the two numbers are equal. Applications of this inequality and its generalisation to several variables are so frequent that we shall in future refer to it as the *AM-GM inequality*.

Applied to the positive numbers $\dfrac{1}{a}$ and $\dfrac{1}{b}$ the AM-GM inequality gives

$$\frac{1}{2}\left(\frac{1}{a} + \frac{1}{b}\right) \geq \sqrt{\frac{1}{ab}}$$

---

[1] When used adjectivally, the word arithmetic is stressed on the penultimate syllable, so it rhymes with *alphabetic*.

which simplifies to

$$\sqrt{ab} \geq h, \tag{3.1}$$

where

$$\frac{2}{h} = \frac{1}{a} + \frac{1}{b}.$$

The quantity h is called *harmonic mean* (HM) of a and b, which can be written as $\frac{2ab}{a+b}$. Inequality (3.1) tells us that the harmonic mean is less than or equal to the geometric mean: this is the *HM-GM inequality*.

In section 2.1 on page 9, we showed that, for any real numbers x, y,

$$x^2 + y^2 \geq 2xy,$$

with equality if, and only if, $x = y$. If we replace x by a and y by b, a little manipulation then produces the equivalent form

$$\frac{a+b}{2} \leq \sqrt{\frac{a^2 + b^2}{2}}.$$

The expression $\sqrt{\frac{a^2+b^2}{2}}$ is known as the *root mean square* (RMS), although the term *quadratic mean* is sometimes used. We have shown that the arithmetic mean of two numbers is always less than the root mean square: this is the *AM-RMS inequality*.

To summarise, we have shown that, for two positive numbers

$$\text{HM} \leq \text{GM} \leq \text{AM} \leq \text{RMS}.$$

Figure 3.1 on the next page illustrates $\text{HM} < \text{GM} < \text{AM} < \text{RMS}$ for two unequal positive numbers: it is worth spending time to check that the lengths are as shown.

It turns out that all four types of mean can be generalised to any number of variables, and that the same inequality

$$\text{HM} \leq \text{GM} \leq \text{AM} \leq \text{RMS}.$$

is still true. This is the theme of this chapter and, in part, chapter 6.

3.2   Using these inequalities

We first give some examples and exercises on how to use these inequalities in their simplest, two-variable, form. You may well recognise some of

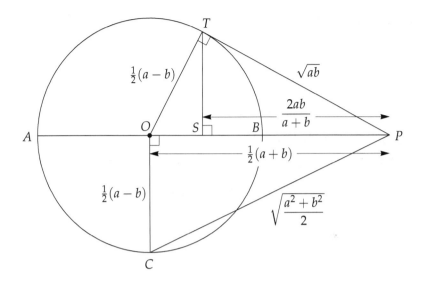

Figure 3.1:
$a = AP, b = BP,$
$HM = SP, GM = TP, AM = OP, RMS = CP$

these from chapter 2. This is not altogether surprising since we did, after all, use the methods there to derive the inequalities in the first place. But our new tools might well provide us with an efficient demonstration of old results. Please note that we have omitted units, such as metres and seconds, from the examples.

Example 3.1 Let k be a constant. Prove that, if $x > 0$, then

$$x + \frac{k^2}{x} \geq 2k.$$

When does equality hold?

Use the AM-GM inequality with $a = x$, $b = \frac{k^2}{x}$. Equality is achieved when $x = k$.

Example 3.2   What are the dimensions of a rectangle of perimeter 20 with the maximum area?

Let the width and height be a and b. Then we have $a + b = 10$, and the area A is ab. The AM-GM inequality then becomes

$$5 = \frac{a+b}{2} \geq \sqrt{ab} = \sqrt{A}.$$

Hence the maximum area is 25 and it occurs when $a = b = 5$, so the rectangle is a square.

Example 3.3   What are the dimensions of a rectangle of perimeter 20 with the minimum diagonal?

Let the width and height be a and b. Then we have $a + b = 10$, and the diagonal d is $\sqrt{a^2 + b^2}$. The AM-RMS inequality then becomes

$$5 = \frac{a+b}{2} \leq \sqrt{\frac{a^2 + b^2}{2}} = \frac{d}{\sqrt{2}}.$$

Hence the minimum diagonal is $5\sqrt{2}$ and it occurs when $a = b = 5$, so the rectangle is a square.

The last two examples illustrate an important point. If we want to show that something has a maximum value, we seek an inequality $P \leq Q$ where P represents (in some way) the thing we wish to maximise and Q is fixed. Conversely, if we want to show that something has a minimum value, we seek an inequality $P \leq Q$ where Q represents the thing we wish to minimise and P is fixed. We also need to make sure that the bound can be attained. In the two examples above, it is possible for a and b to be equal, but that might not always be true.

Exercise 3a

1. Prove that, for $x, y, z > 0$,

$$xz + \frac{y}{z} \geq 2\sqrt{xy}.$$

2. A farmer uses fencing of total length 30 to build three sides of a rectangular sheep-pen, where the fourth wall is created using an impenetrable hedge. How should he plan this to create the maximum area?

3. How can we split one million into two positive factors so that they have the smallest possible sum?

4. Two cyclists travel along the same road between two towns. Cyclist A travels half of the distance at speed x and the other half of the distance at speed y. Cyclist B travels half of the time at speed x and the other half of the time at speed y. In general, which cyclist arrives at the destination first, and under what circumstances do they arrive simultaneously?

5. Show that, in a right-angled triangle, the sum of the two shorter lengths can never exceed $\sqrt{2}$ times the length of the hypotenuse. In what circumstances is this bound achieved?

6. If $a, b > 0$, show that
$$\frac{ab}{a+b} \le \frac{a+b}{4}.$$
Deduce that, if $a, b, c > 0$,
$$\frac{ab}{a+b} + \frac{bc}{b+c} + \frac{ca}{c+a} \le \tfrac{1}{2}(a+b+c).$$

7. If $a, b > 0$, show that
$$\frac{a}{b} + \frac{b}{a} \ge 2.$$

8. Use the AM-GM inequality to find the maximum value of $\sin x \cos x$.

9. If $x, y > 0$, show that
$$\sqrt{x^2 + y^2} \le x + y \le \sqrt{2(x^2 + y^2)}$$
and interpret this result geometrically.

10. Use the AM-GM inequality twice to show that, if $a, b, c, d > 0$, then
$$\frac{a+b+c+d}{4} \ge (abcd)^{\frac{1}{4}}.$$

11. A farmer wishes to fence a rectangular enclosure cut in half by a fence down the middle.

He has 1200 metres of fencing and wants to maximise the area of the enclosure. What dimensions should be used for the enclosure?

Generalise to the cases where there are two internal fences cutting the enclosure into equal thirds, and so on.

12. Let $a, b > 0$. Find the maximum value of $\dfrac{x}{(x+a)(x+b)}$ for $x > 0$.

13. Let $a, b, c > 0$ and $x = \frac{1}{2}(b+c)$, $y = \frac{1}{2}(c+a)$, $z = \frac{1}{2}(a+b)$. Prove that $xyz \geq abc$.   *[BMO1 Jan 1965, adapted]*

14. A solid cuboid has base of dimensions $x \times y$ and height h. The perimeter of the base is 36 and the volume of the cuboid is 18. Find the minimum possible total surface area.

3.3 The AM-GM inequality for any number of variables

There are several proofs of this inequality, and in this book we give five of them; three in this section with two more to look out for in later chapters. The first proof is a curious form of induction; the second and third proofs are more direct and give more insight into the meaning of the inequality.

Arithmetic mean (AM) *The arithmetic mean of* $a_1, a_2, \ldots, a_n > 0$ *is*

$$\frac{a_1 + a_2 + \cdots + a_n}{n}.$$

Geometric mean (GM) *The geometric mean of* $a_1, a_2, \ldots, a_n > 0$ *is*

$$\sqrt[n]{a_1 a_2 \cdots a_n}.$$

Theorem 3.1 (AM-GM inequality) *Let a_1, a_2, ..., a_n be positive numbers. Then their arithmetic mean is not less than their geometric mean. That is,*

$$\frac{a_1 + a_2 + \cdots + a_n}{n} \geq (a_1 a_2 \cdots a_n)^{\frac{1}{n}}.$$

Moreover, there is equality if, and only if, $a_1 = a_2 = \cdots = a_n$.

PROOF 1 (INDUCTION)

The case $n = 1$ is trivial. The case $n = 2$ has been given in exercise 2a question 9 on page 11 and derives from $(\sqrt{a_1} - \sqrt{a_2})^2 \geq 0$.

We now make the induction hypothesis that the result (including the case of equality) is true for $n = 2^k$. Then take

$$b_1 = \frac{a_1 + a_2 + \cdots + a_n}{n}$$

$$\text{and} \quad b_2 = \frac{a_{n+1} + a_{n+2} + \cdots + a_{2n}}{n}$$

and from the case $n = 2$ we have

$$\frac{a_1 + a_2 + \cdots + a_{2n}}{2n} = \frac{b_1 + b_2}{2} \geq \sqrt{b_1 b_2}.$$

But, by the induction hypothesis,

$$b_1 \geq (a_1 a_2 \cdots a_n)^{\frac{1}{n}}$$

$$\text{and} \quad b_2 \geq (a_{n+1} a_{n+2} \cdots a_{2n})^{\frac{1}{n}}$$

and so

$$\sqrt{b_1 b_2} \geq (a_1 a_2 \cdots a_{2n})^{\frac{1}{2n}}$$

and the inequality is therefore true for $2n = 2^{k+1}$. Moreover, there is equality if, and only if, $a_1 = a_2 = \cdots = a_n$ and $a_{n+1} = a_{n+2} = \cdots = a_{2n}$ and $b_1 = b_2$ which forces $a_1, a_2, \ldots, a_{2n}$ to be equal. It follows by induction that the result is true for n equal to any integer power of 2.

It is now very easy to fill the gaps. For example, if we want to prove that

$$\frac{a_1 + a_2 + \cdots + a_6}{6} \geq (a_1 a_2 \cdots a_6)^{\frac{1}{6}}$$

we start from

$$\frac{a_1 + a_2 + \cdots + a_8}{8} \geq (a_1 a_2 \cdots a_8)^{\frac{1}{8}},$$

which we know to be true, and we set

$$a_7 = a_8 = m = \frac{a_1 + a_2 + \cdots + a_6}{6}.$$

Then

$$\frac{a_1 + a_2 + \cdots + a_8}{8} = \frac{6m + m + m}{8}$$

$$= m$$

$$\geq (a_1 a_2 \cdots a_6 mm)^{\frac{1}{8}}.$$

Hence

$$m^8 \geq a_1 a_2 \cdots a_6 m^2$$

and so

$$m \geq (a_1 a_2 \cdots a_6)^{\frac{1}{6}},$$

as required.

Again, there is equality if, and only if, $a_1 = a_2 = \cdots = a_6 = m$.

All other cases of filling the gaps follow similarly by taking redundant variables equal to the arithmetic mean of the given variables. ❑

PROOF 2 (FIXED GEOMETRIC MEAN g)

Either all the variables are equal to g, in which case AM = GM = g, or, since

$$a_1 a_2 \cdots a_n = g^n,$$

there must be two variables, say a_j and a_k such that $a_j < g < a_k$. If we now replace these variables by

$$b_j = g \quad \text{and} \quad b_k = \frac{a_j a_k}{g},$$

then the geometric mean of the new variables remains equal to g, but the arithmetic mean is changed from m to

$$m + \frac{1}{n}\left(g + \frac{a_j a_k}{g} - a_j - a_k\right) = m - \frac{(a_k - g)(g - a_j)}{ng}.$$

This is a decrease of

$$\frac{(a_k - g)(g - a_j)}{gn}.$$

Now, either all the variables are equal to g or we can repeat the process. At each turn the geometric mean remains the same, but the arithmetic mean is decreased. Furthermore, at each turn a new variable is introduced which is equal to g. The process therefore terminates after at most $(n-1)$ turns. At this point we know that AM = GM, so at the start AM $\geq$ GM. The attraction of this particular proof is the clear demonstration that if a number of positive variables have a fixed product then their arithmetic mean is minimised when the variables are equal. $\square$

PROOF 3 (FIXED ARITHMETIC MEAN m)
Either all the variables are equal to m, or, since

$$a_1 + a_2 + \cdots + a_n = nm,$$

there must be two variables, say a_j and a_k, such that $a_j < m < a_k$. If we now replace these variables by $y_j = m$ and $y_k = a_j + a_k - m$, then the arithmetic mean of the new variables remains the same, but the nth power of the geometric mean is increased by a factor

$$\frac{m(a_j + a_k - m)}{a_j a_k}.$$

This factor is indeed greater than 1, indicating an increase, since

$$m(a_j + a_k - m) - a_j a_k = (m - a_j)(a_k - m) > 0.$$

Now, either all the variables are equal to m or we can repeat the process. At each turn the arithmetic mean remains the same and the geometric mean increases. Furthermore, at each turn a new variable is introduced, which is equal to m. The process therefore terminates after at most $(n-1)$ turns. At this point we know that AM = GM, so that at the start AM $\geq$ GM. The attraction of this particular proof is the clear demonstration that if a number of positive variables have a fixed sum their geometric mean is maximised when they are equal. $\square$

It is worth noting that the inequality of the means is still valid if $a_1, \ldots, a_n$ are non-negative numbers, but it loses its power once one of the numbers is 0 (because the right-hand side is then 0). Note also that example 2.2 on page 12 gives a stand-alone proof of the AM-GM inequality for $n = 3$.

Harmonic mean (HM) *The* harmonic mean *of $a_1, a_2, \ldots, a_n > 0$ is defined by*

$$\frac{1}{h} = \frac{1}{n}\left(\frac{1}{a_1} + \frac{1}{a_2} + \cdots + \frac{1}{a_n}\right).$$

Now by AM-GM on the variables $\frac{1}{a_1}, \frac{1}{a_2}, \ldots, \frac{1}{a_n}$ we have

$$\frac{1}{\text{HM}} = \frac{1}{h} = \frac{1}{n}\left(\frac{1}{a_1} + \frac{1}{a_2} + \cdots + \frac{1}{a_n}\right) \geq \left(\frac{1}{a_1 a_2 \cdots a_n}\right)^{\frac{1}{n}} = \frac{1}{\text{GM}}.$$

It follows that for n variables also

$$\text{HM} \leq \text{GM} \leq \text{AM}.$$

The relation $\text{HM} \leq \text{AM}$ is worth quoting as a theorem, because of its significance.

Theorem 3.2 (HM-AM inequality) *If $a_1, a_2, \ldots, a_n$ are n positive variables then*

$$\frac{1}{a_1} + \frac{1}{a_2} + \cdots + \frac{1}{a_n} \geq \frac{n^2}{a_1 + a_2 + \cdots + a_n},$$

with equality if, and only if, $a_1 = a_2 = \cdots = a_n$.

3.4   Applications of the AM-GM inequality

We conclude this chapter by giving several illustrative examples of the applications of the AM-GM inequality and a lengthy set of exercises. It is clear that a great deal of ingenuity has been put into devising problems in this area, and it is for this reason we give such a comprehensive selection of problems.

Example 3.4   If $a, b, c > 0$ prove that

$$a^2 b + b^2 c + c^2 a + b^2 a + c^2 b + a^2 c \geq 6abc.$$

This is an immediate application of AM-GM to the six variables on the left.

Example 3.5   Find the maximum value of $x^2(6-x)$ on the interval $0 < x < 6$.

Typically, we would use differentiation to do this. The AM-GM inequality gives a neat alternative. We are trying to maximise a product, so we are on the look-out for a constant sum. Since $\frac{1}{2}x + \frac{1}{2}x + (6-x) = 6$ we apply AM-GM to the three variables $\frac{1}{2}x$, $\frac{1}{2}x$, $6-x$. Since their AM is 2 we have

$$2 \geq \left(\tfrac{1}{4}x^2(6-x)\right)^{\frac{1}{3}},$$

so the maximum value is 32 with equality when $\frac{1}{2}x = 6-x$, that is, when $x = 4$.

The crucial point is the constant sum: the more obvious choice x, x, $6-x$ has sum $6+x$ so will not work.

Note that in such a problem the maximum becomes an upper bound that is not achieved if the variables used cannot be made equal to one another: this is why choices such as $\frac{1}{3}x$, $\frac{2}{3}x$, $6-x$ do not work.

Also note how using $\frac{1}{2}x$, $\frac{1}{2}x$ just introduces numerical factors into the calculation which come out in the wash.

Example 3.6   Find the maximum value of $(2x+1)^3(5-x)^2$ for $-\frac{1}{2} < x < 5$.

Notice that $2x+1$ and $5-x$ are both positive when $-\frac{1}{2} < x < 5$. With AM-GM in mind, we seek a constant sum from multiples of $2x+1$ and $5-x$, such as $3(2x+1) + 2(15-3x) = 33$. So

$$(2x+1)^3(15-3x)^2 \leq \left(\frac{33}{5}\right)^5$$

and

$$(2x+1)^3(5-x)^2 \leq \frac{11^5 \times 3^3}{5^5}$$

with equality if, and only if, $2x+1 = 15-3x$, that is, $x = \frac{14}{5}$.

Example 3.7   Find the maximum value of $y(y+1)(5-3y)$ for $0 < y < \frac{5}{3}$.

Here, we seek multiples of y, $y+1$ and $5-3y$ with a constant sum. The obvious candidates are $2y$, $y+1$, $5-3y$ and y, $2(y+1)$, $5-3y$; there is equality of each factor if $y = 1$ in the former, but no chance of equality of each factor in the latter. We thus apply AM-GM to $2y$, $y+1$, $5-3y$ to obtain $2y(y+1)(5-3y) \leq 2^3$, so the maximum value sought is 4, attained if $y = 1$.

Example 3.8   Find the minimum value of $x^6 + y^6 + z^6 - 6xyz$.

By AM-GM,

$$x^6 + y^6 + z^6 - 6xyz \geq 3(xyz)^2 - 6xyz,$$

with equality if, and only if, $x = y = z$. Putting $xyz = u$ this is equal to

$$3u^2 - 6u = 3\{(u-1)^2 - 1\} \geq -3,$$

with equality if, and only if, $u = 1$. So the minimum is -3, when $x = y = z = 1$.

Exercise 3b

1. Find the maximum value of xy^2z^3 given $x^2 + y^2 + z^2 = 1$.

2. Find the maximum value of xy^3z^4 subject to $x, y, z > 0$ and $x^3 + y^3 + z^3 = 1$.

3. Suppose that p, q are positive integers. Show that the maximum value of $\sin^{2p} \theta \cos^{2q} \theta$ is

$$\frac{p^p q^q}{(p+q)^{p+q}}.$$

4. Find the maximum value of $(2x + 5)^5(7 - x)^2$ on the interval $-\frac{5}{2} < x < 7$.

5. Prove that if $0 < x < 1$ then

$$1 - x^n > n(1 - x)x^{\frac{1}{2}(n-1)}.$$

6. Find the minimum surface area of a solid cylinder of given volume V.

7. Find the maximum volume of a right circular cone inscribed in a sphere of radius r.

8. If $a, b, c, x, y, z > 0$ and $ax + by + cz = N$ find the maximum value of xyz and the corresponding values of x, y, z.

9. If $a, b, c, x, y, z > 0$ and

$$\frac{ax^2}{y} + \frac{by^2}{z} + \frac{cz^2}{x} = N$$

find the maximum value of xyz.

10. Suppose that $a, b, c, x, y, z > 0$, with $ax + by + cz = N$, and that p, q, r are positive integers. Find the maximum value of $x^p y^q z^r$ and the corresponding values of x, y, z.

11. Prove that if π is any permutation of the numbers $1, 2, \ldots, n$ then

$$\sum \frac{k}{\pi(k)} \geq n.$$

12. If $x, y, z > 0$ prove that

$$(x + y + z)^3 \geq 27(y + z - x)(z + x - y)(x + y - z).$$

13. Give a direct proof of theorem 3.2 on page 28 by multiplying out

$$(a_1 + a_2 + \cdots + a_n)\left(\frac{1}{a_1} + \frac{1}{a_2} + \cdots + \frac{1}{a_n}\right)$$

and pairing terms.

3.5   Harder applications of the AM-GM inequality

The following examples and exercises either involve more than one application of the AM-GM inequality or a less obvious choice of variables.

Example 3.9   If $a, b, c, d > 0$ prove that

$$\frac{a+b+c+d}{4} \geq \frac{ab}{a+b} + \frac{cd}{c+d} \geq \frac{16abcd}{(a^2+b^2+c^2+d^2)(a+b+c+d)}.$$

For the left-hand inequality,

$$\frac{ab}{a+b} \leq \frac{a+b}{4} \quad \text{and} \quad \frac{cd}{c+d} \leq \frac{c+d}{4}$$

since both are immediate from $(a-b)^2 \geq 0$ and $(c-d)^2 \geq 0$.
For the right-hand inequality, since

$$\frac{ab}{a+b} + \frac{cd}{c+d} \geq \frac{2\sqrt{abcd}}{\sqrt{(a+b)(c+d)}},$$

by AM-GM, it is sufficient to prove that

$$8\sqrt{abcd}\sqrt{(a+b)(c+d)} \leq (a^2+b^2+c^2+d^2)(a+b+c+d).$$

This is so since, by AM-GM, we have

$$(a+b) + (c+d) \geq 2\sqrt{(a+b)(c+d)}$$

and $\quad a^2+b^2+c^2+d^2 \geq 4\sqrt{abcd}$.

Example 3.10   Find all the possible values of $a, b, c, d, \geq 0$ satisfying

$$a+b+c+d = 12$$

and $abcd = 27 + ab + bc + ca + ad + bd + cd.$

[BMO1 Feb 1996]

We have
$$3 = \frac{a+b+c+d}{4} \geq (abcd)^{\frac{1}{4}}$$
so $abcd \leq 81$ with equality if, and only if, $a = b = c = d = 3$. Also,

$$abcd = 27 + ab + bc + ca + ad + bd + cd \geq 27 + 6(abcd)^{\frac{1}{2}}.$$

Putting $abcd = u^2$ this means $u^2 \geq 27 + 6u$, that is, $(u+3)(u-9) \geq 0$, so $u \geq 9$ and $abcd \geq 81$. Hence $abcd = 81$ and $a = b = c = d = 3$ is the only solution.

Example 3.11 Prove that for positive integral $n > 2$

$$\left(\frac{n+1}{2}\right)^n > n! > n^{\frac{1}{2}n}.$$

The left-hand inequality is proved by AM-GM on $1, 2, 3, \ldots, n$. Note that equality is impossible here, so the inequality is strict. The right-hand inequality is equivalent to $(n!)^2 > n^n$. And

$$(n!)^2 = (1 \times n)(2 \times (n-1)) \cdots (n \times 1) > n^n$$

since $x(n+1-x) - n = (n-x)(x-1) \geq 0$ for $1 \leq x \leq n$ and, since $n > 2$, at least one of these terms is greater than 0 so this inequality is also strict.

Example 3.12 If $x, y, z > 0$ and a, b, c are positive integers prove that

$$\frac{(x+y+z)^{a+b+c}}{x^a y^b z^c} \geq \frac{(a+b+c)^{a+b+c}}{a^a b^b c^c}.$$

This is equivalent to

$$\frac{x+y+z}{a+b+c} \geq \left[\left(\frac{x}{a}\right)^a \left(\frac{y}{b}\right)^b \left(\frac{z}{c}\right)^c\right]^{\frac{1}{a+b+c}},$$

which gives the AM-GM clue: apply the AM-GM inequality with $n = a + b + c$ to $\frac{x}{a}$ (a times), $\frac{y}{b}$ (b times) and $\frac{z}{c}$ (c times).

In fact, the result is still true if a, b, c are positive rational numbers, for if $a = \frac{a_1}{a_2}, b = \frac{b_1}{b_2}, c = \frac{c_1}{c_2}$, where $a_1, a_2, b_1, b_2, c_1, c_2$ are integers then the required inequality is identical to that already proved with a replaced by $a_1 b_2 c_2$ etc.

Example 3.13   Show that for all integers $n \geq 1$

$$\left(1 + \frac{1}{n+1}\right)^{n+1} > \left(1 + \frac{1}{n}\right)^{n}.$$

Use AM-GM with $\frac{n+1}{n}$ n times and 1 once to give

$$\frac{n+2}{n+1} > \left(\frac{n+1}{n}\right)^{\frac{n}{n+1}},$$

from which the result follows immediately.

In fact, the sequence $\left(1 + \frac{1}{n}\right)^{n}$ increases monotonically to e.

Exercise 3c

1. If $a, b, c, d > 0$ and $abcd = 2$ prove that

$$a^2 + b^2 + c^2 + d^2 + ab + bc + ca + ad + bd + cd > 14.$$

2. Prove that if $a, b, c > 0$ then $(1 + a^3)(1 + b^3)(1 + c^3) \geq (1 + abc)^3$. Generalise.

3. Given $a, b, c > -1$ prove that

$$(1+a)(1+b)(1+c) \leq \left\{1 + \tfrac{1}{4}(a+b+c)\right\}^4.$$

4. Given that $x, y, z > 0$ and $xyz = 32$, find the minimum value of $x^2 + 4xy + 4y^2 + 2z^2$. *[BMO1 Feb 2000]*

5. Prove that if $x_j > 0$, $j = 0, 1, 2, \ldots, n$, then

$$x_0^n + x_1^n + \cdots + x_n^n \geq x_0 x_1 \cdots x_n \left(\frac{1}{x_0} + \frac{1}{x_1} + \cdots + \frac{1}{x_n} \right).$$

6. Let n, x be positive integers. Prove that

$$\left(1 + \frac{x}{n+x} \right)^{n+x} > \left(1 + \frac{x}{n} \right)^n.$$

7. Prove that for all positive integers

$$\left(1 + \frac{1}{n+1} \right)^{n+2} < \left(1 + \frac{1}{n} \right)^{n+1}.$$

8. If $x, y, z > 0$ and $\frac{1}{3} \leq xy + yz + zx \leq 3$ determine the ranges for xyz and $(x + y + z)$. *[BMO1 Jan 1993]*

9. If $a, b, c, d > 0$ prove that

$$4 (a^4 + b^4 + c^4 + d^4) \geq (a + b + c + d)(a^3 + b^3 + c^3 + d^3)$$
$$\geq (a^2 + b^2 + c^2 + d^2)^2$$
$$\geq 16abcd.$$

10. Given $x^2 + y^2 + z^2 + 2xyz = 1$ prove that $x^2 + y^2 + z^2 \geq \frac{3}{4}$.

11. Let $x_1, x_2, \ldots, x_n$ be n positive quantities, and define S_r to be the sum of their rth powers and P_r to be the sum of all their products taken r at a time. Prove that

$$(n-1)! S_r \geq r!(n-r)! P_r.$$

12. Let $x_j > 0$, for $j = 1$ to n, and $\sum x_j = s$. Prove that

$$\sum \frac{1}{x_j} \geq \sum \frac{n-1}{s - x_j}.$$

13. If $s, t, u, v > 0$ and $\frac{1}{u} + \frac{1}{v} = 1$ (u and v being rational) prove that

$$\frac{s^u}{u} + \frac{t^v}{v} \geq st.$$

14. Prove that if $x_j > 0$ and q_j are positive rational numbers, $j = 1$ to n, then

$$\left(\frac{q_1 x_1 + q_2 x_2 + \cdots + q_n x_n}{q_1 + q_2 + \cdots + q_n} \right)^{q_1 + q_2 + \cdots + q_n} \geq x_1^{q_1} x_2^{q_2} \cdots x_n^{q_n}.$$

15. Prove that if n is any positive integer

$$n^{\frac{1}{n}} + n^{\frac{1}{n+1}} + \cdots + n^{\frac{1}{2n-1}} \geq n^k,$$

where $k = 2^{\frac{1}{n}}$.

16. Prove that, if $x, y, z > 0$, then

$$\frac{x}{y+z} + \frac{y}{z+x} + \frac{z}{x+y} \geq \frac{3}{2}.$$

[BMO1 Jan 1996]

17. Let $a, b, c > 0$. Prove that

(a) $a^3 + b^3 + c^3 \geq a^2 b + b^2 c + c^2 a$

(b) $abc \geq (a + b - c)(b + c - a)(c + a - b)$.   *[BMO1 Jan 1981]*

18. If $x, y, z > 0$, find the maximum value of

$$\frac{xyz}{(1+x)(x+y)(y+z)(z+16)}.$$

[BMO1 Jan 1987]

Chapter 4

The Cauchy-Schwarz inequality

4.1 The Cauchy-Schwarz inequality

As has been seen in the previous chapters, many useful inequalities can be manufactured by taking identities involving squares and then applying the simple principle that squares are always positive. The Cauchy-Schwarz inequality also arises in this way, though we shall see that this is not the most natural way of looking at it.

Consider the identity

$$(ax + by)^2 + (ay - bx)^2 = (a^2 + b^2)(x^2 + y^2),$$

which is valid for all real numbers a, b, x and y. A little relabelling transforms the identity into

$$(x_1y_1 + x_2y_2)^2 + (x_1y_2 - x_2y_1)^2 = (x_1^2 + x_2^2)(y_1^2 + y_2^2) \qquad (4.1)$$

which suggests there is a generalisation. The expressions on the right-hand side and the first term on the left-hand side are easiest to generalise, so subtract the latter from the former to give, after a little algebra,

$$
\begin{aligned}
(x_1^2 + x_2^2 + x_3^2)(y_1^2 + y_2^2 + y_3^2) &- (x_1y_1 + x_2y_2 + x_3y_3)^2 \\
&= (x_1y_2 - x_2y_1)^2 + (x_2y_3 - x_3y_2)^2 + (x_3y_1 - x_1y_3)^2 \quad (4.2)
\end{aligned}
$$

You should check this identity yourself.

Now for the inequality. In identity (4.1), since $(x_1y_2 - x_2y_1)^2 \geq 0$ we have

$$(x_1y_1 + x_2y_2)^2 \leq \left(x_1^2 + x_2^2\right)\left(y_1^2 + y_2^2\right)$$

with equality if, and only if, $x_1y_2 = x_2y_1$. Also, in identity (4.2), since $(x_1y_2 - x_2y_1)^2 \geq 0$, $(x_2y_3 - x_3y_2)^2 \geq 0$ and $(x_3y_1 - x_1y_3)^2 \geq 0$ we have

$$(x_1y_1 + x_2y_2 + x_3y_3)^2 \leq \left(x_1^2 + x_2^2 + x_3^2\right)\left(y_1^2 + y_2^2 + y_3^2\right)$$

with inequality if, and only if, $x_1y_2 = x_2y_1$, $x_2y_3 = x_3y_2$ and $x_3y_1 = x_1y_3$.

We can produce a similar result for $x_1, x_2, \ldots, x_n$ and $y_1, y_2, \ldots, y_n$. Indeed, consider

$$\left(x_1^2 + x_2^2 + \cdots + x_n^2\right)\left(y_1^2 + y_2^2 + \cdots + y_n^2\right) - (x_1y_1 + x_2y_2 + \cdots + x_ny_n)^2.$$

After multiplying out, we may eliminate each term of the form $x_i^2 y_i^2$ (for $1 \leq i \leq n$). We are left with all the terms $x_i^2 y_j^2$ and $x_j^2 y_i^2$ from the first expression and $-2x_i y_i x_j y_j$ from the second squared expression (for $1 \leq i < j \leq n$). These terms can be combined to give $(x_i y_j - x_j y_i)^2$. Hence

$$\left(x_1^2 + x_2^2 + \cdots + x_n^2\right)\left(y_1^2 + y_2^2 + \cdots + y_n^2\right)$$
$$= (x_1y_1 + x_2y_2 + \cdots + x_ny_n)^2 + \sum_{1 \leq i < j \leq n}(x_i y_j - x_j y_i)^2$$

This gives us

Theorem 4.1 (Cauchy-Schwarz inequality) *Let* $x_1, x_2, \ldots, x_n, y_1, y_2, \ldots, y_n$ *be real numbers. Then*

$$(x_1y_1 + x_2y_2 + \cdots + x_ny_n)^2 \leq \left(x_1^2 + x_2^2 + \cdots + x_n^2\right)\left(y_1^2 + y_2^2 + \cdots + y_n^2\right).$$

Equality holds if, and only if, $x_i y_j = x_j y_i$ *for all* $1 \leq i < j \leq n$.

Before we examine a more geometrical explanation of this inequality, we exhibit two straightforward applications.

Example 4.1 Let $a_1, a_2, \ldots, a_n$ all be positive. Setting $x_i = \sqrt{a_i}$ and $y_i = \frac{1}{\sqrt{a_i}}$ into the Cauchy-Schwarz inequality gives

$$(1 + 1 + \cdots + 1)^2 \le (a_1 + a_2 + \cdots + a_n)\left(\frac{1}{a_1} + \frac{1}{a_2} + \cdots + \frac{1}{a_n}\right),$$

that is,

$$\frac{n}{\frac{1}{a_1} + \frac{1}{a_2} + \cdots + \frac{1}{a_n}} \le \frac{a_1 + a_2 + \cdots + a_n}{n},$$

which is theorem 3.2 on page 28.

Note the equality condition here is

$$\frac{\sqrt{a_i}}{\sqrt{a_j}} = \frac{\sqrt{a_j}}{\sqrt{a_i}}$$

that is, $a_i = a_j$, for all $1 \le i < j \le n$.

Root mean square (RMS) *The root mean square of $a_1, a_2, \ldots, a_n > 0$ is*

$$\sqrt{\frac{a_1^2 + a_2^2 + \cdots + a_n^2}{n}}.$$

Example 4.2 Again let $a_1, a_2, \ldots, a_n$ all be positive. Setting $x_i = a_i$ and $y_1 = 1$ into the Cauchy-Schwarz inequality gives

$$(a_1 \times 1 + a_2 \times 1 + \cdots + a_n \times 1)^2 \le (a_1^2 + a_2^2 + \cdots + a_n^2)(1 + 1 + \cdots + 1),$$

that is,

$$\frac{a_1 + a_2 + \cdots + a_n}{n} \le \sqrt{\frac{a_1^2 + a_2^2 + \cdots + a_n^2}{n}},$$

which is the AM-RMS inequality mentioned in chapter 3.

Note the equality condition here is $\frac{a_i}{1} = \frac{a_j}{1}$, that is, $a_i = a_j$, for all $1 \le i < j \le n$.

It is worth remarking that it is not surprising that we can prove these two inequalities from the Cauchy-Schwarz inequality. After all, they all come simply from the fact that sums of squares cannot be negative!

The following questions can be solved using other methods, but they are all intended to be done as applications of the Cauchy-Schwarz inequality.

Exercise 4a

1. Prove that, for a, b and c all non-negative,

$$\left(a^3 + b^3 + c^3\right)^2 \le \left(a^2 + b^2 + c^2\right)\left(a^4 + b^4 + c^4\right)$$

and write down the equality condition.

2. Prove that, for a, b and c all positive,

$$(a + b + c)^2 \le \left(a^3 + b^3 + c^3\right)\left(\frac{1}{a} + \frac{1}{b} + \frac{1}{c}\right)$$

and write down the equality condition.

3. Show that

$$\frac{a_1 + 2a_2 + \cdots + na_n}{n(2n + 1)} < \sqrt{\frac{a_1^2 + a_2^2 + \cdots + a_n^2}{6n}}$$

for all $a_i > 0$.

4. Here is another proof of the Cauchy-Schwarz inequality for the case $n = 2$. It can be extended to the general case in the obvious manner. Let $P(t) = (x_1 - ty_1)^2 + (x_2 - ty_2)^2$.

    (a) Explain why $P(t) \ge 0$ for all real values of t and hence state the range of values of its discriminant.

    (b) By writing $P(t)$ explicitly as a quadratic in t and using its discriminant, prove the Cauchy-Schwarz inequality.

    (c) How do we get equality here?

4.2 A geometric interpretation

The equality condition we have given for the Cauchy-Schwarz inequality is a little unwieldy, and an examination of it soon reveals a useful geometric insight into the inequality.

First of all, we need to recast our equality conditions into a more useful form.

We may assume that not all the x_i are equal to zero and that not all the y_i are equal to zero, otherwise the inequality reduces to the trivial equality $0 = 0$.

To begin with, in the Cauchy-Schwarz inequality, let us assume that all the x and y terms are non-zero. Then the condition $x_i y_j = x_j y_i$ is the same as the condition

$$\frac{x_i}{y_i} = \frac{x_j}{y_j}$$

for *every* pair of non-equal i and j. If we call this ratio λ, we have $x_i = \lambda y_i$ for all i.

What if $x_i = 0$? Then $0 = x_j y_i$ for all $j \neq i$ and so, as not all the x_j can be zero, it follows that $y_i = 0$. This argument is symmetrical in x and y, therefore in the equality condition we have $x_i = 0$ if, and only if, $y_i = 0$. So the condition $x_i = \lambda y_i$ remains valid here too.

Thus the equality condition for the Cauchy-Schwarz inequality merely says that we get

$$(x_1 y_1 + x_2 y_2 + \cdots + x_n y_n)^2 = \left(x_1^2 + x_2^2 + \cdots + x_n^2\right)\left(y_1^2 + y_2^2 + \cdots + y_n^2\right)$$

if, and only if, $x_i = \lambda y_i$ for all i, that is, the x_i and y_i are proportional.

Now for the geometric interpretation. We consider the special case when $n = 2$ where the Cauchy-Schwarz inequality becomes

$$(x_1 y_1 + x_2 y_2)^2 \leq \left(x_1^2 + x_2^2\right)\left(y_1^2 + y_2^2\right)$$

with equality if, and only if, the x_i and y_i are proportional. In the language of vectors, the equality condition is nothing other than requiring that the vectors

$$\mathbf{x} = \begin{pmatrix} x_1 \\ x_2 \end{pmatrix} \quad \text{and} \quad \mathbf{y} = \begin{pmatrix} y_1 \\ y_2 \end{pmatrix}$$

are parallel, and the right-hand side of the inequality looks suspiciously like the product of the squared lengths of these vectors.

So consider these two vectors and use | | to denote the length of a vector. Either the two vectors are parallel in the same direction, in which case

$$|\mathbf{x} + \mathbf{y}| = |\mathbf{x}| + |\mathbf{y}| \quad \text{and} \quad |\mathbf{x} - \mathbf{y}| < |\mathbf{x}| + |\mathbf{y}|,$$

or parallel in the opposite direction (so that $\mathbf{x}$ and $-\mathbf{y}$ have the same direction), in which case

$$|\mathbf{x} + \mathbf{y}| < |\mathbf{x}| + |\mathbf{y}| \quad \text{and} \quad |\mathbf{x} - \mathbf{y}| = |\mathbf{x}| + |\mathbf{y}|,$$

or they are not parallel, in which case

$$|\mathbf{x} + \mathbf{y}| < |\mathbf{x}| + |\mathbf{y}| \quad \text{and} \quad |\mathbf{x} - \mathbf{y}| < |\mathbf{x}| + |\mathbf{y}|.$$

Hence in all cases we have

Result 4.1 (Triangle inequality) *Let* $\mathbf{x}$ *and* $\mathbf{y}$ *be two vectors. Then*

$$|\mathbf{x} + \mathbf{y}| \le |\mathbf{x}| + |\mathbf{y}| \quad \text{and} \quad |\mathbf{x} - \mathbf{y}| \le |\mathbf{x}| + |\mathbf{y}|.$$

Figure 4.1 illustrates the general case and figure 4.2 shows how equality arises when $\mathbf{x}$ and $\mathbf{y}$ are parallel.

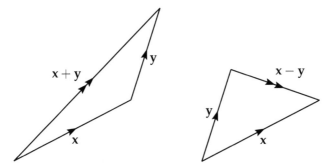

Figure 4.1: Triangle inequality: $\mathbf{x}$ and $\mathbf{y}$ not parallel

Since all the lengths here are non-negative we have

$$|\mathbf{x} \pm \mathbf{y}| \le (|\mathbf{x}| + |\mathbf{y}|)^2$$

and so, using the fact that

$$\mathbf{x} \pm \mathbf{y} = \begin{pmatrix} x_1 \pm y_1 \\ x_2 \pm y_2 \end{pmatrix},$$

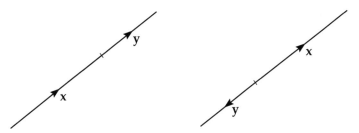

Figure 4.2: Triangle inequality: **x** and **y** parallel

we have

$$(x_1 \pm y_1)^2 + (x_2 \pm y_2)^2 \le |\mathbf{x}|^2 + 2|\mathbf{x}||\mathbf{y}| + |\mathbf{y}|^2,$$

that is,

$$x_1^2 + x_2^2 \pm 2(x_1y_2 + x_2y_1) + y_1^2 + y_2^2 \le |\mathbf{x}|^2 + 2|\mathbf{x}||\mathbf{y}| + |\mathbf{y}|^2,$$

that is,

$$|\mathbf{x}|^2 \pm 2(x_1y_2 + x_2y_1) + |\mathbf{y}|^2 \le |\mathbf{x}|^2 + 2|\mathbf{x}||\mathbf{y}| + |\mathbf{y}|^2.$$

Hence

$$\pm(x_1y_2 + x_2y_1) \le |\mathbf{x}||\mathbf{y}|$$
$$= \sqrt{x_1^2 + x_2^2}\sqrt{y_1^2 + y_2^2}.$$

Since both the $+$ case and the $-$ case hold we have

$$(x_1y_1 + x_2y_2)^2 \le \left(x_1^2 + x_2^2\right)\left(y_1^2 + y_2^2\right),$$

which is the Cauchy-Schwarz inequality.

Furthermore, we have equality if, and only if,

$$|\mathbf{x} - \mathbf{y}| = |\mathbf{x}| + |\mathbf{y}| \quad \text{or} \quad |\mathbf{x} + \mathbf{y}| = |\mathbf{x}| + |\mathbf{y}|,$$

that is,

the vectors **x** and **y** are parallel,

that is,

there is a real λ such that $x_1 = \lambda y_1$ and $x_2 = \lambda y_2$.

It should be clear that essentially the same argument works in the case $n = 3$, and that, with a little imagination, it extends to n-dimensional vectors.

Remarks

1. In this discussion, we have taken it to be obvious from a geometric point of view that the triangle inequality is true. Is this fair? In a sense no: if we wanted to prove it, we would have to reverse our argument here and use the Cauchy-Schwarz inequality in the proof. However, when a distance function is defined in higher mathematics, the triangle inequality is usually taken as an axiom.

2. Readers who have met the scalar (dot) product may well recognise that

$$\mathbf{x} \cdot \mathbf{y} = x_1 y_1 + x_2 y_2,$$

in which case the Cauchy-Schwarz inequality becomes

$$(\mathbf{x} \cdot \mathbf{y})^2 \leq |\mathbf{x}|^2 |\mathbf{y}|^2.$$

This says nothing more than $\cos^2 \theta \leq 1$, where θ is the angle between the two vectors.

3. Readers who have met the product moment correlation coefficient in statistics may recognise it to be

$$r = \frac{\mathbf{x} \cdot \mathbf{y}}{|\mathbf{x}||\mathbf{y}|}$$

in the case where the xs and ys both have mean 0. In this context, all the Cauchy-Schwarz inequality says is that the product moment correlation coefficient lies between -1 and 1, inclusive.

4.3 Applications

As with the AM-GM inequality, it is the ingenuity of the ways that one can apply the Cauchy-Schwarz inequality that provides the real challenge in solving inequalities. Part of that challenge is knowing when one should use the Cauchy-Schwarz inequality. Of course, in this chapter this part of the challenge has been removed since presumably all the exercises here can be done using Cauchy-Schwarz, or they wouldn't be included in this chapter! Instead we shall focus on a few ideas which might be useful in recognising how the Cauchy-Schwarz inequality can be used.

Successful applications of the Cauchy-Schwarz inequality usually use one of the following techniques:

(a) creating an upper bound on a sum by considering it as a sum of products;
(b) creating a lower bound on a sum of squares by considering it as one of two sets of sums of squares.

Example 4.3   Find the maximum value of $x + 2y + 4z$ given that $x^2 + y^2 + 2z^2 = 1$.

The obvious way of rewriting $x + 2y + 4z$ and then using the Cauchy-Schwarz inequality is to say

$$\begin{aligned}(x + 2y + 4z)^2 &= (1 \times x + 2 \times y + 4 \times z)^2 \\ &\le \left(1^2 + 2^2 + 4^2\right)\left(x^2 + y^2 + z^2\right) \\ &= 21\left(x^2 + y^2 + z^2\right),\end{aligned}$$

but this does not help since we do not know the value of $x^2 + y^2 + z^2$.

To use the information about $x^2 + y^2 + 2z^2$, we want this expression to appear on the right-hand side of the inequality, and this suggests that instead we rewrite $x + 2y + 4z$ as $1 \times x + 2 \times y + \frac{4}{\sqrt{2}} \times \sqrt{2}z$ to get

$$\begin{aligned}(x + 2y + 4z)^2 &\le \left(1^2 + 2^2 + \left[\frac{4}{\sqrt{2}}\right]^2\right)\left(x^2 + y^2 + 2z^2\right) \\ &= 13\left(x^2 + y^2 + 2z^2\right)\end{aligned}$$

and so the maximum value of $x + 2y + 4z$ is $\sqrt{13}$.

This maximum occurs when

$$\frac{x}{1} = \frac{y}{2} = \frac{\sqrt{2}z}{\frac{4}{\sqrt{2}}},$$

that is, when $2x = y = z$. Using the condition $x^2 + y^2 + 2z^2 = 1$ gives $x = \frac{1}{\sqrt{13}}$ and $y = z = \frac{2}{\sqrt{13}}$.

Example 4.4   If $0 \le x_j \le 1$ for $j = 1$ to 6 and

$$x_1 x_2 + x_2 x_3 + x_3 x_4 + x_4 x_5 + x_5 x_6 + x_6 x_1 = 1$$

find the minimum value of $x_1^2 + x_2^2 + \cdots + x_6^2$.

We can use the same method as in the previous example:

$$x_1 x_2 + x_2 x_3 + x_3 x_4 + x_4 x_5 + x_5 x_6 + x_6 x_1$$
$$\le \left(x_1^2 + x_2^2 + \cdots + x_6^2 \right) \left(x_2^2 + x_3^2 + \cdots + x_6^2 + x_1^2 \right)$$

and so $\left(x_1^2 + x_2^2 + \cdots + x_6^2 \right)^2 \ge 1$. Hence the minimum value is 1 and it occurs when $x_j = \frac{1}{\sqrt{6}}$ for $j = 1$ to 6.

Example 4.5   Prove that, if $a, b, c > 0$, then

$$\frac{a}{b+c} + \frac{b}{c+a} + \frac{c}{a+b} \ge \frac{3}{2}.$$

It is less obvious here that the Cauchy-Schwarz inequality will work, but the direction of the inequality suggests that, if it does, then we want to rewrite the right-hand side as the product of two sums of squares, in the form

$$\left(\left[\sqrt{\frac{a}{b+c}} \right]^2 + \left[\sqrt{\frac{b}{c+a}} \right]^2 + \left[\sqrt{\frac{c}{a+b}} \right]^2 \right) \left([\ldots]^2 + [\ldots]^2 + [\ldots]^2 \right).$$

What could the second set of squares be? It is pretty clear we do not want it to be $1^2 + 1^2 + 1^2$ since the Cauchy-Schwarz inequality would then give us

$$\left(\left[\sqrt{\frac{a}{b+c}} \right]^2 + \left[\sqrt{\frac{b}{c+a}} \right]^2 + \left[\sqrt{\frac{c}{a+b}} \right]^2 \right) \times 3$$

$$\ge \left(\sqrt{\frac{a}{b+c}} + \sqrt{\frac{b}{c+a}} + \sqrt{\frac{c}{a+b}} \right)^2,$$

which is worse than what we started with. To get a "nice" product on the left-hand side of the Cauchy-Schwarz inequality, we would like to end up without fractions or square roots, in which case we would like to multiply $\sqrt{\frac{a}{b+c}}$ by $\sqrt{a(b+c)}$ to get just a. Hence by symmetry we try

$$\left(\left[\sqrt{\frac{a}{b+c}} \right]^2 + \left[\sqrt{\frac{b}{c+a}} \right]^2 + \left[\sqrt{\frac{c}{a+b}} \right]^2 \right)$$
$$\times \left(\left[\sqrt{a(b+c)} \right]^2 + \left[\sqrt{b(c+a)} \right]^2 + \left[\sqrt{c(a+b)} \right]^2 \right)$$
$$\geq (a+b+c)^2,$$

which gives

$$\left(\frac{a}{b+c} + \frac{b}{c+a} + \frac{c}{a+b} \right) (2ab + 2bc + 2ca) \geq (a+b+c)^2.$$

Thus

$$\frac{a}{b+c} + \frac{b}{c+a} + \frac{c}{a+b} \geq \frac{(a+b+c)^2}{2(ab+bc+ca)}$$
$$\geq 1 + \frac{a^2 + b^2 + c^2}{2(ab+bc+ca)}$$
$$\geq \frac{3}{2},$$

where the last inequality $ab + bc + ca \leq a^2 + b^2 + c^2$ follows from inequality (2.1) on page 10.

Example 4.5 already appeared as question 16 of exercise 3c. We shall also meet it as example 6.3 on page 70 and example 6.13 on page 88.

The Cauchy-Schwarz inequality can also be used to find the ranges of variables defined by equations, as illustrated by the following example.

Example 4.6   Given that $a + b + c + d = 6$ and $a^2 + b^2 + c^2 + d^2 = 12$, find the range of values of each of a, b, c, d.

We have, by the Cauchy-Schwarz inequality,

$$(a + b + c)^2 \le 3(a^2 + b^2 + c^2)$$

and so $(6 - d)^2 \le 3(12 - d^2)$, from which $0 \le d \le 3$. When $d = 0$, $a = b = c = 2$ and when $d = 3$, $a = b = c = 1$. By symmetry, the other variables will also have the same range as that of d.

Exercise 4b

1. Show that, if $x, y, z > -1$ and $x + y + z = 1$, then

$$\sqrt{1+x} + \sqrt{1+y} + \sqrt{1+z} \le 2\sqrt{3}$$

and find the values of x, y and z for which equality occurs.

2. Find the maximum of $2x + 3y + 6z$ subject to the constraint $x^2 + y^2 + z^2 = 1$.

3. Minimise $x^2 + y^2 + z^2$ subject to $x + 2y + 3z = 4$.

4. (a) Find the maximum value of $a_1 x_1 + a_2 x_2 + \cdots + a_n x_n$ subject to the constraint $x_1^2 + x_2^2 + \cdots + x_n^2 = 1$.

    (b) Find the minimum value of $x_1^2 + x_2^2 + \cdots + x_n^2$ subject to the constraint $a_1 x_1 + a_2 x_2 + \cdots + a_n x_n = 1$.

5. Find the minimum value of $2x^2 + y^2 + z^2$ subject to $x + y + z = 10$.

6. If $a, b, c > 0$ and $a \cos^2 \theta + b \sin^2 \theta < c$, prove that

$$\sqrt{a} \cos^2 \theta + \sqrt{b} \sin^2 \theta < \sqrt{c}.$$

7. Suppose that $x, y, z > 0$ and that $\dfrac{1}{x} + \dfrac{1}{y} + \dfrac{1}{z} = 1$. Prove that

$$\sqrt{x+1} + \sqrt{y+1} + \sqrt{z+1} \le 2\sqrt{x+y+z}.$$

8. Suppose that $x, y, z > 1$ and $\frac{1}{x} + \frac{1}{y} + \frac{1}{z} = 2$. Prove that

$$\sqrt{x-1} + \sqrt{y-1} + \sqrt{z-1} \le \sqrt{x+y+z}.$$

9. Suppose that $x, y, z > 0$. Prove that

$$\frac{2}{x+y} + \frac{2}{y+z} + \frac{2}{z+x} \ge \frac{9}{x+y+z}.$$

10. Suppose that $a, b, c > 0$. Prove that

$$abc(a+b+c) \le a^3 b + b^3 c + c^3 a.$$

11. Suppose that $a, b, x, y, z > 0$. Prove that

$$\frac{x}{ay+bz} + \frac{y}{az+bx} + \frac{z}{ax+by} \ge \frac{3}{a+b}.$$

12. Suppose that $p(x)$ is a polynomial with positive coefficients. Given that $p(1) = 1$ and $x > 0$, show that

$$p\left(\frac{1}{x}\right) \ge \frac{1}{p(x)}.$$

13. Suppose that $a, b, c > 0$ and $abc = 1$. Prove that

$$\frac{1}{a^3(b+c)} + \frac{1}{b^3(c+a)} + \frac{1}{c^3(a+b)} \ge \frac{3}{2}.$$

[IMO 1995]

4.4 Geometric applications

The Cauchy-Schwarz inequality can also be used in geometric questions.

Example 4.7   The vertices of a fixed triangle are A, B and C, and P, Q and R lie on the line segments BC, CA and AB respectively. If $[XYZ]$ denotes the area of the triangle XYZ , prove that

$$\sqrt{[AQR]} + \sqrt{[BRP]} + \sqrt{[CPQ]} \leq \tfrac{3}{2}\sqrt{[ABC]}.$$

Without loss of generality, we may assume that the area of ABC is 1. If P, Q and R divide the line segments BC, CA and AB respectively in the ratios $\ell : 1 - \ell$, $m : 1 - m$ and $n : 1 - n$, it follows that the areas of the triangles AQR, BRP and CPQ are $n(1 - m)$, $\ell(1 - n)$ and $m(1 - \ell)$ respectively. Hence the inequality that needs to be proved is

$$\sqrt{n(1 - m)} + \sqrt{\ell(1 - n)} + \sqrt{m(1 - \ell)} \leq \frac{3}{2}.$$

However, the Cauchy-Schwarz inequality gives

$$\sqrt{n(1 - m)} + \sqrt{\ell(1 - n)} + \sqrt{m(1 - \ell)}$$
$$\leq \sqrt{n + \ell + m}\, \sqrt{1 - m + 1 - n + 1 - \ell}$$
$$= \sqrt{(l + m + n)\big(3 - (l + m + n)\big)}$$
$$\leq \frac{3}{2},$$

where the last inequality comes from the AM-GM inequality.

Exercise 4c

1. Let P be a point in the interior of a triangle ABC and let d, e, f be the distances from P to the sides a, b, c of the triangle. Show that the minimum value of $\frac{a}{d} + \frac{b}{e} + \frac{c}{f}$ occurs when P is the incentre of the triangle.

2. If a, b, c are the sides of a triangle and $ab + bc + ca = 27$, between what bounds does $p = a + b + c$ lie?

3. Suppose that a, b, c and x, y, z are the sides of two triangles. What can be said about the triangles if

$$\sqrt{ax} + \sqrt{by} + \sqrt{cz} = \sqrt{(a+b+c)(x+y+z)}?$$

4. Let P be an internal point of triangle ABC. The line through P parallel to AB meets BC at L, the line through P parallel to BC meets CA at M, and the line through P parallel to CA meets AB at N. Prove that

$$\frac{BL}{LC} + \frac{CM}{MA} + \frac{AN}{NB} \geq \frac{3}{2}.$$

4.5   A generalisation

One of the delights of mathematics is discovering that a result can be put into a more general framework. The Cauchy-Schwarz inequality can be generalised in this way. The way forward is to look at the vector form of the inequality in an n-dimensional setting.

Let

$$\mathbf{x} = \begin{pmatrix} x_1 \\ x_2 \\ \vdots \\ x_n \end{pmatrix} \quad \text{and} \quad \mathbf{y} = \begin{pmatrix} y_1 \\ y_2 \\ \vdots \\ y_n \end{pmatrix},$$

with vector addition and multiplication by a scalar defined as one might expect:

$$\mathbf{x} + \lambda\mathbf{y} = \begin{pmatrix} x_1 + \lambda y_1 \\ x_2 + \lambda y_2 \\ \vdots \\ x_n + \lambda y_n \end{pmatrix}.$$

Define $\langle \mathbf{x}, \mathbf{y} \rangle$ by

$$\langle \mathbf{x}, \mathbf{y} \rangle = x_1 y_1 + x_2 y_2 + \cdots + x_n y_n. \tag{4.3}$$

Then $\langle \mathbf{x}, \mathbf{y} \rangle$ has the following properties which you should verify:

1. $\langle \mathbf{x}, \mathbf{y} \rangle = \langle \mathbf{y}, \mathbf{x} \rangle$ for all vectors $\mathbf{x}$ and $\mathbf{y}$.
2. $\langle \lambda\mathbf{x}, \mathbf{y} \rangle = \langle \mathbf{x}, \lambda\mathbf{y} \rangle = \lambda\langle \mathbf{x}, \mathbf{y} \rangle$ if λ is real.

3. $\langle \mathbf{x}, \mathbf{y} + \mathbf{z} \rangle = \langle \mathbf{x}, \mathbf{y} \rangle + \langle \mathbf{x}, \mathbf{z} \rangle$ for all vectors $\mathbf{x}$, $\mathbf{y}$ and $\mathbf{z}$.

4. $\langle \mathbf{x}, \mathbf{x} \rangle \geq 0$, with equality if, and only if, $\mathbf{x}$ is the zero vector.

Now consider $f(\lambda) = \langle \mathbf{x} + \lambda \mathbf{y}, \mathbf{x} + \lambda \mathbf{y} \rangle$. Then

$$
\begin{aligned}
f(\lambda) &= \langle \mathbf{x} + \lambda \mathbf{y}, \mathbf{x} + \lambda \mathbf{y} \rangle \\
&= \langle \mathbf{x} + \lambda \mathbf{y}, \mathbf{x} \rangle + \langle \mathbf{x} + \lambda \mathbf{y}, \lambda \mathbf{y} \rangle \\
&= \langle \mathbf{x}, \mathbf{x} + \lambda \mathbf{y} \rangle + \lambda \langle \mathbf{x} + \lambda \mathbf{y}, \mathbf{y} \rangle \\
&= \langle \mathbf{x}, \mathbf{x} \rangle + \langle \mathbf{x}, \lambda \mathbf{y} \rangle + \lambda \langle \mathbf{y}, \mathbf{x} + \lambda \mathbf{y} \rangle \\
&= \langle \mathbf{x}, \mathbf{x} \rangle + \lambda \langle \mathbf{x}, \mathbf{y} \rangle + \lambda \langle \mathbf{y}, \mathbf{x} \rangle + \lambda \langle \mathbf{y}, \lambda \mathbf{y} \rangle \\
&= \langle \mathbf{x}, \mathbf{x} \rangle + 2\lambda \langle \mathbf{x}, \mathbf{y} \rangle + \lambda^2 \langle \mathbf{y}, \mathbf{y} \rangle
\end{aligned}
$$

where each expression is derived from the previous one *only* using one of the properties 1 to 3. (You should check this too.)

Suppose first that $\mathbf{y}$ is not the zero vector. By property 4, $\langle \mathbf{y}, \mathbf{y} \rangle > 0$, hence $f(\lambda)$ is a quadratic in λ. Furthermore, again because of property 4, $f(\lambda) \geq 0$ for all values of λ. Hence the discriminant of the quadratic expression is less than or equal to 0, that is,

$$
4\langle \mathbf{x}, \mathbf{y} \rangle^2 - 4\langle \mathbf{x}, \mathbf{x} \rangle \langle \mathbf{y}, \mathbf{y} \rangle \leq 0,
$$

which gives

$$
\langle \mathbf{x}, \mathbf{y} \rangle^2 \leq \langle \mathbf{x}, \mathbf{x} \rangle \langle \mathbf{y}, \mathbf{y} \rangle. \tag{4.4}
$$

Now we only get equality if $f(\lambda) = 0$ has exactly one solution, that is, if there is exactly one value of λ for which $\langle \mathbf{x} + \lambda \mathbf{y}, \mathbf{x} + \lambda \mathbf{y} \rangle = 0$, which implies, again by property 4, that $\mathbf{x} + \lambda \mathbf{y}$ is the zero vector, in other words, $\mathbf{x}$ and $\mathbf{y}$ are parallel.

Substituting from the formula (4.3) for $\langle \mathbf{x}, \mathbf{y} \rangle$ into inequality (4.4) gives us the Cauchy-Schwarz inequality in the form already stated on page 38. (This inequality is obviously also true if $\mathbf{y} = \mathbf{0}$.) So where is the gain?

The point is we have only used our definition of $\langle \mathbf{x}, \mathbf{y} \rangle$ in the last sentence: the inequality (4.4) and its equality condition only depended on the four properties of $\langle \mathbf{x}, \mathbf{y} \rangle$. Thus if we ever come across a function of two vectors which satisfy those four properties, it will satisfy a Cauchy-Schwarz type of inequality. This is our generalisation.

Remark

The full extent of our generalisation becomes clear if we realise that we can also generalise our notion of what a vector is. In more advanced mathematics, a vector, rather than being a "quantity with a magnitude and direction", becomes any type of object that can be "added" and "multiplied by a scalar", where this "addition" and "scalar multiplication" satisfy certain rules or axioms. As a simple example consider polynomials, or indeed real-valued functions with the same domain: these can be added or multiplied by real numbers and as such can be treated as vectors.

Now if, for a set of vectors, we come up with a bracket $\langle\,,\,\rangle$ defined for any pair of vectors which satisfies our properties 1 to 4, then $\langle\,,\,\rangle$ is called an *inner product*. What we have really proved in this section is that, irrespective of what our vectors are and irrespective of the actual formula for the inner product, an inner product satisfies the Cauchy-Schwarz inequality in the form of (4.4).

Example 4.8　　Consider any two continuous functions $f(x)$ and $g(x)$ defined for $0 \le x \le 1$, and define

$$\langle f,g\rangle = \int_0^1 f(x)g(x)dx.$$

Then $\langle f,g\rangle$ satisfies properties 1 to 4 and so we immediately have

$$\left(\int_0^1 f(x)g(x)dx\right)^2 \le \int_0^1 f^2(x)dx \int_0^1 g^2(x)dx.$$

Chapter 5

Miscellaneous methods

In this chapter, we introduce some new elementary techniques which do not fit into the preceding chapters, and then attempt to summarise what has been covered so far.

5.1 Schur's inequality

In examples 1.6 and 1.7 on pages 4–5 we drew conclusions depending on whether the terms in a product of factors were of positive or negative sign. This idea is sometimes useful for harder problems, particularly when the variables are positive real numbers and the expressions are symmetrical. In such situations, it is often a good idea to assume, without loss of generality, something about the relative magnitudes of the variables.

Example 5.1   Prove that if $a, b, c > 0$ then

$$a^3 + b^3 + c^3 + 3abc \geq b^2c + bc^2 + c^2a + ca^2 + a^2b + ab^2.$$

The left-hand side minus the right-hand side simplifies to

$$a(a - b)(a - c) + b(b - c)(b - a) + c(c - a)(c - b).$$

Assume, without loss of generality, that $a \geq b \geq c > 0$. The final bracket is clearly non-negative since it has one positive and two non-positive terms. Now we combine the first two brackets to give

$$(a - b)^2 (a + b - c),$$

which is also non-negative.

We have equality if, and only if, $a = b = c$.

In fact, the result used in this example can be generalised.

Theorem 5.1 (Schur's inequality) *Let x, y, z be non-negative real numbers and let t be a positive real number. Then*

$$x^t(x - y)(x - z) + y^t(y - z)(y - x) + z^t(z - x)(z - y) \geq 0.$$

Equality holds if, and only if, one of the following four conditions holds:

   (i) $x = y = z$;

  (ii) $x = y$ *and* $z = 0$;

 (iii) $y = z$ *and* $x = 0$;

 (iv) $z = x$ *and* $y = 0$.

PROOF Assume, without loss of generality, that $x \geq y \geq z \geq 0$. Then $x^t > y^t$ and $x - z \geq y - z$ and so

$$x^t(x - y)(x - z) + y^t(y - z)(y - x) = (x - y)\left(x^t(x - z) - y^t(y - z)\right)$$
$$\geq 0$$

and also $z^t(z - x)(z - y) \geq 0$ since two of the terms are negative or one is zero. Adding, we have proved the inequality.

In order to be zero, both of these expressions must be zero, and that can only happen if one (or more) of the conditions holds. It is also clear that, if any of the conditions holds, the expression on the left-hand side of the inequality is equal to zero. ❑

5.2 Trigonometrical substitutions

Since both the sine and cosine functions can only take values between -1 and $+1$ it is sometimes possible to prove an inequality by making a substitution and converting an algebraic statement into a trigonometrical expression. The appropriateness of this substitution is often indicated by a condition which suggests a trigonometrical identity, such as $\sin^2 \theta + \cos^2 \theta = 1$.

Example 5.2   Find the maximum and minimum values of $x^4 + y^4 - 2xy$ given that $x^2 + y^2 = 1$.

An alternative approach to the algebraic method suggested for question 1 of exercise 2c on page 18 is to substitute $x = \sin\theta$, $y = \cos\theta$. The expression then becomes

$$\sin^4\theta + \cos^4\theta - 2\sin\theta\cos\theta$$

$$= (\sin^2\theta + \cos^2\theta)^2 - 2\sin^2\theta\cos^2\theta - 2\sin\theta\cos\theta$$
$$= 1 - \tfrac{1}{2}\sin^2 2\theta - \sin 2\theta$$
$$= \tfrac{3}{2} - \tfrac{1}{2}(\sin 2\theta + 1)^2,$$

with a maximum of $\tfrac{3}{2}$ when

$$(x,y) = \pm\left(\tfrac{\sqrt{2}}{2}, -\tfrac{\sqrt{2}}{2}\right)$$

and a minimum of $-\tfrac{1}{2}$ when

$$(x,y) = \pm\left(\tfrac{\sqrt{2}}{2}, \tfrac{\sqrt{2}}{2}\right).$$

5.3 Fixing one variable

If we wish to maximise or minimise a function $f(x)$ we would normally use calculus. In the case of two or more variables, we would analyse a function such as $f(x,y,z)$ by using partial differentiation. This amounts to keeping one or more of the variables constant and seeing what happens when the remaining variable is allowed to change. This sort of approach can equally be employed even when calculus itself is not used.

Example 5.3

(a) Find the maximum value of $x^2y - y^2x$ when $0 \le x \le 1$ and $0 \le y \le 1$.

(b) Find the maximum value of $x^2y - y^2x + y^2z - z^2y + z^2x - x^2z$
when $0 \le x \le 1, 0 \le y \le 1, 0 \le z \le 1$.   *[BMO1 Jan 1995]*

In part (a), $f(x,y) = x^2y - xy^2 = xy(x-y)$. We treat y as if it were constant, noting that $0 \le y \le 1$. Then $f(x,y)$ takes its greatest value when $x = 1$ since both the first and third factor are increasing over the interval $0 \le x \le 1$. Now we allow y to vary, and consider

$$f(1,y) = y(1-y) = \tfrac{1}{4} - (y - \tfrac{1}{2})^2 \le \tfrac{1}{4}.$$

Thus we see that $f(x,y)$ takes its maximum value of $\tfrac{1}{4}$ when $(x,y) = (1, \tfrac{1}{2})$.

In part (b), $f(x,y,z) = (x-y)(y-z)(x-z)$. Again, we fix y and $f(x,y,z)$ takes its greatest value when $x = 1$ and $z = 0$ since this makes each bracket as large as possible. Again we have $f(1,y,0) = y(1-y)$ and consequently we see that $f(x,y,z)$ takes its maximum value of $\tfrac{1}{4}$ when $(x,y,z) = (1, \tfrac{1}{2}, 0)$.

Exercise 5a

1. (a) Prove that, if $x, y, z \ge 0$, then

   $$x(x-y)(x-z) + y(y-z)(y-x) + z(z-x)(z-y) \ge 0.$$

   (b) Hence or otherwise, show that, for any real numbers a, b, c,

   $$a^6 + b^6 + c^6 + 3a^2b^2c^2 \ge 2(b^3c^3 + c^3a^3 + a^3b^3).$$

   [BMO1 Jan 1978]

2. If $a, b, c > 0$ prove that

   $$a^4 + b^4 + c^4 + 2abc(a+b+c) \ge (ab + bc + ca)(a^2 + b^2 + c^2).$$

   When does equality hold?

3. Use example 2.2 on page 12 and example 5.1 to show that if $a, b, c > 0$ then

   $$5(a^3 + b^3 + c^3) + 3abc \ge 3(b^2c + bc^2 + c^2a + ca^2 + a^2b + ab^2).$$

4. Maximise
$$f(x,y,z) \equiv x^4 + y^4 - 2z^4 - 3\sqrt{2}xyz$$
subject to the side condition $x^2 + y^2 + z^2 = 1$.

5. Find the minimum value of $x^2 + y^2$ given that $xy(x^2 - y^2) = x^2 + y^2$ and $x \neq 0$. [BMO2 Jan 2006]

6. Find the maximum value of
$$\frac{a + x}{\sqrt{b^2 + x^2}}$$
for real values of x, where $a, b > 0$.

5.4 Strict inequalities

When we are asked to prove that $P < Q$, the techniques are sometimes rather different. This is because we do not need to establish conditions for equality, and, indeed, this is usually not possible. The methods are cruder, in the sense that we lose precision, sometimes by deliberately ignoring terms in expressions. One technique which is often useful here is mathematical induction.

Example 5.4 Prove that $2^{n-1} < n!$ for $n \geq 3$.

We use mathematical induction on n.

BASE STEP For $n = 3$, the left-hand side is 4 and the right-hand side is 6, so the inequality is true.

INDUCTION STEP Now assume that the statement is true for some $n = k \geq 3$, so that $2^{k-1} < k!$. Then

$$2^k = 2 \times 2^{k-1} < 2(k!) < (k+1)k! = (k+1)!$$

so the statement is true for $n = k + 1$. Hence, by induction, the statement is true for all n.

Note, in passing, that it would be an equality for $n = 1, 2$. Inequalities such as this are often only strict inequalities when n becomes sufficiently large. For smaller values of n they might be equalities, or they might not even be true; consider, for example, the inequality $3^{n-1} < n!$ for $n \geq 5$.

Fractional expressions often lead to strict inequalities. One useful observation is that, if you have a fraction between 0 and 1 and add the same positive value to numerator and denominator, then you increase the fraction. The reverse occurs if you have an improper fraction greater than 1.

This can be be formally stated as:

Lemma 5.1 *If a, b, c are positive real numbers such that $a < b$, then*

$$\frac{a}{b} < \frac{a+c}{b+c}.$$

Also, if $a > b$, then

$$\frac{a}{b} > \frac{a+c}{b+c}.$$

The proof is trivial and left to the reader.

The lemma can be extended to give the following result.

Theorem 5.2 *Suppose $a_j, b_j, j = 1$ to n are positive real numbers such that*

$$\frac{a_1}{b_1} < \frac{a_2}{b_2} < \cdots < \frac{a_n}{b_n},$$

then

$$\frac{a_1}{b_1} < \frac{a_1 + a_2 + \cdots + a_n}{b_1 + b_2 + \cdots + b_n} < \frac{a_n}{b_n}.$$

PROOF The proof is by induction on n. For the case $n = 2$ we are required to prove

$$\frac{a_1}{b_1} < \frac{a_1 + a_2}{b_1 + b_2} < \frac{a_2}{b_2}.$$

For the left-hand inequality we need to prove $a_1(b_1 + b_2) < b_1(a_1 + a_2)$, which is true since $a_1 b_2 < b_1 a_2$. The right-hand inequality is proved in the same way.

Now put

$$\frac{a_1 + a_2}{b_1 + b_2} = \frac{c_1}{d_1}$$

then by the same argument repeated several times we have

$$\frac{a_1}{b_1} < \frac{c_1}{d_1} < \frac{c_1 + a_3}{d_1 + b_3} < \frac{a_3}{b_3}$$

since

$$\frac{c_1}{d_1} < \frac{a_2}{b_2} < \frac{a_3}{b_3}.$$

Though the inductive step has only been argued from $n = 2$ to $n = 3$, it is easy to see that it may be repeated. ❏

Perhaps the most common technique of all is 'to give something away' of which the theorems on fractions above are examples. Another context in which this may take place is to replace a series that cannot be summed by an easier one that can. For example,

$$1 + \frac{1}{4} + \frac{1}{9} + \cdots + \frac{1}{n^2} < 1 + \frac{1}{2} + \frac{1}{6} + \cdots + \frac{1}{n(n-1)}$$

$$= 1 + \left(1 - \frac{1}{2}\right) + \left(\frac{1}{2} - \frac{1}{3}\right) + \cdots + \left(\frac{1}{n-1} - \frac{1}{n}\right)$$

$$= 2 - \frac{1}{n}$$

for $n \geq 2$. In the limit as $n \to \infty$ this gives $1 + \frac{1}{4} + \frac{1}{9} + \cdots + \frac{1}{n^2} + \cdots \leq 2$. In fact $1 + \frac{1}{4} + \frac{1}{9} + \cdots + \frac{1}{n^2} + \cdots = \frac{\pi^2}{6}$ so $\pi^2 \leq 12$, which is true, but not very interesting. Too much has been given away to provide a nice inequality.

Example 5.5   If $x, y, z > 0$ prove that

$$\frac{x}{x+y} + \frac{y}{y+z} + \frac{z}{z+x} < 2.$$

By lemma 5.1 the left-hand side is less than

$$\frac{x+z}{x+y+z} + \frac{y+x}{x+y+z} + \frac{z+y}{x+y+z} = 2.$$

Example 5.6   Prove that for positive integers n we have

$$\frac{(2n)!}{2^{2n}(n!)^2} < \frac{1}{\sqrt{2n}}.$$

The square of the left-hand side is

$$\left(\frac{1}{2} \times \frac{3}{4} \times \ldots \times \frac{2n-1}{2n} \right)^2$$

$$< \frac{1}{2} \times \frac{2}{3} \times \frac{3}{4} \times \frac{4}{5} \times \cdots \times \frac{2n-1}{2n} \times \frac{2n}{2n+1}$$

$$= \frac{1}{2n+1} < \frac{1}{2n}.$$

Now take positive square roots.

Example 5.7   Prove that for $n \geq 1$ we have

$$\left(\frac{n}{e}\right)^n < n! < e\left(\frac{n}{2}\right)^n.$$

For the left-hand inequality the case $n = 1$ is true since $\frac{1}{e} < 1$.
Suppose the inequality is true for $n = k$, that is $k! > k^k e^{-k}$. Then

$$(k+1)! > (k+1)k^k e^{-k} > (k+1)^{k+1} e^{-(k+1)}$$

since $e > \left(1 + \frac{1}{k}\right)^k$ as mentioned in example 3.13 on page 34. The result now follows by induction.

For the right-hand inequality the case $n = 1$ is true because $1 < \frac{e}{2}$.
Likewise the case $n = 2$ is true since $2 < e$.
Suppose the inequality is true for $n = k$, that is $k! < e\left(\frac{k}{2}\right)^k$. Then

$$(k+1)! < e(k+1)\left(\frac{k}{2}\right)^k < e\left(\frac{k+1}{2}\right)^{k+1}$$

because $2k^k < (k+1)^k$ for $k \geq 2$. The result now follows by induction.

Exercise 5b

1. Prove that $2^n < n!$ for all $n \geq 4$.

2. Prove that $n^2 < 2^{n-1}$ for all $n \geq 7$.

3. Prove that

$$\sum_{i=1}^{n} \frac{1}{i^2} > \frac{3n}{2n+1}$$

for all $n \geq 2$.

4. Prove that $n! < [i!(n-i)!]^2$ for all $n \geq 5$ and $1 \leq i < n$.

5. Prove that $(n+1)^{n-1}(n+2)^n > 3^n(n!)^2$ for all $n \geq 2$.

6. Prove that for all positive integers $n \geq 2$

$$\frac{1}{\sqrt{4n+1}} < \frac{1}{2} \times \frac{3}{4} \times \frac{5}{6} \times \cdots \times \frac{2n-1}{2n} < \frac{1}{\sqrt{3n+1}}.$$

7. Prove that if $a_j > 1$, $j = 1$ to n and $n \geq 2$, then

$$2^{n-1}(a_1 a_2 \cdots a_n + 1) > (a_1 + 1)(a_2 + 1) \cdots (a_n + 1).$$

8. Prove that if $\frac{p}{m} < \frac{q}{n}$ then

$$\frac{p}{p+m} < \frac{p+q}{p+q+m+n} < \frac{q}{q+n}.$$

9. Prove that $\sqrt{n} + \sqrt{n+1} < \sqrt{4n+2}$ for all positive integers n.
Can there exist an integer N such that

$$\sqrt{n} + \sqrt{n+1} < N < \sqrt{4n+2}?$$

10. If a, b, c are the sides of a triangle prove that

$$\frac{a}{b+c} + \frac{b}{c+a} + \frac{c}{a+b} < 2.$$

11. Given a, b, c, d are positive real numbers, find all the possible values of the sum

$$\frac{a}{a+b+d} + \frac{b}{a+b+c} + \frac{c}{b+c+d} + \frac{d}{a+c+d}.$$

[IMO 1974]

12. Prove that

$$\frac{1}{31} + \frac{1}{81} + \frac{1}{151} + \cdots + \frac{1}{10N^2 + 20N + 1} + \cdots < \frac{3}{40}.$$

13. Prove that for all positive integers n

$$\frac{1}{\sqrt{2n+1}} < \frac{2}{3} \times \frac{4}{5} \times \frac{6}{7} \times \cdots \times \frac{2n}{2n+1} < \frac{1}{\sqrt{n+1}}.$$

14. Let F_n be the nth term of the Fibonacci sequence

$$1, 1, 2, 3, 5, 8, \ldots$$

Prove that

$$\frac{1}{3} + \frac{1}{3^2} + \frac{2}{3^3} + \frac{3}{3^4} + \frac{5}{3^5} + \cdots + \frac{F_n}{3^n} < \frac{3}{5}.$$

5.5   Gathering the threads

You now have a very powerful arsenal of techniques which can be used, either singly or in combination, to solve inequalities. First of all, there are the standard results:

A. The fact that a perfect square can never be negative.

B. The inequality of the means: HM $\leq$ GM $\leq$ AM $\leq$ RMS.

C. The Cauchy-Schwarz inequality.

In practice, you will often find that you have a choice and can use more than one of these in a particular problem. This is hardly surprising since they really all stem from the same basic principle.

You also have recourse to several 'technical tricks':

1. Replace the inequality $P \geq Q$ by $P - Q \geq 0$.

2. Replace the inequality $P \geq Q > 0$ by $\frac{P}{Q} \geq 1$.

3. Replace the inequality $P \geq Q > 0$ by $\frac{1}{Q} \geq \frac{1}{P}$.

4. Add the two inequalities $P \geq Q$ and $R \geq S$ to produce $P + R \geq Q + S$.

5. Multiply the two inequalities $P \geq Q > 0$ and $R \geq S > 0$ to produce $PR \geq QS > 0$.

6. To simplify an inequality, try a substitution such as $u = \frac{1}{x}$ or $u = x - a$.

7. If you intend to find an upper or lower bound by using AM-GM, decide whether you need to regard the expression as a sum of terms or a product of terms.

8. If you intend to find an upper or lower bound by using Cauchy-Schwarz, decide whether you need to regard the expression as a sum of products or a product of two sums of squares.

9. If an inequality involves symmetrical expressions in positive x, y, z, consider the effect of assuming, without loss of generality, that $x \geq y \geq z$.

10. If an inequality is non-homogeneous, and there is a condition, try to involve the condition in some way so as to make the inequality homogeneous.

11. Use a trigonometrical substitution if there is a condition which reminds you of a trigonometrical identity.

12. Fix all but one of the variables and explore the effect of changing the remaining variable.

In the final exercise in this chapter, you will need to select appropriate techniques for solving the problems without being told in advance which ones are likely to work.

Exercise 5c

1. Prove that, if $a, b, c > 0$ and $a + b + c = 3$, then
$$4(ab + bc + ca) \leq 3abc + 9.$$

2. For $a, b, c > 0$, prove that $a^2b^2 + b^2c^2 + c^2a^2 \geq abc(a + b + c)$.

3. For $a, b, c > 0$, prove that
$$\frac{a^2}{b^2} + \frac{b^2}{c^2} + \frac{c^2}{a^2} \geq \frac{a}{c} + \frac{c}{b} + \frac{b}{a}.$$

4. For $a, b, c > 0$, prove that
$$\left(\frac{a}{b} + \frac{b}{c} + \frac{c}{a} \right)^2 \geq (a + b + c)\left(\frac{1}{a} + \frac{1}{b} + \frac{1}{c} \right).$$

[BMO2 Feb 2005]

5. For $x, y, z \geq 0$ such that $xyz = 32$, find the minimum value of
$$x^2 + 4xy + 4y^2 + 2z^2.$$

[BMO2 Feb 2000]

6. Find the minimum value of $x^2 + y^2 + z^2$ where
$$x^3 + y^3 + z^3 - 3xyz = 1.$$

[BMO2 Jan 2008]

7. For $p, q, r \geq 0$, which satisfy $p + q + r = 1$, prove that
$$7(pq + qr + rp) \leq 2 + 9pqr.$$

[BMO2 Feb 1999]

8. Suppose that $0 < x_j < 1$, for $j = 1$ to n, and that $\sum x_j = 1$. Prove that
$$\sum x_j^2 \geq n^{2n-1} x_1^2 x_2^2 \cdots x_n^2.$$

9. Let x, y, z be positive real numbers such that $x^2 + y^2 + z^2 = 1$. Prove that
$$x^2yz + xy^2z + xyz^2 \leq \tfrac{1}{3}.$$

[BMO1 Dec 2002]

Chapter 6

Ordered sequences and power means

6.1 Chebyshev's inequality

We start with a very simple idea, which you may have encountered before.

Lemma 6.1 *Suppose $a_1 \geq a_2$ and $b_1 \geq b_2$ then $a_1 b_1 + a_2 b_2 \geq a_1 b_2 + a_2 b_1$.*

PROOF The left-hand side minus the right-hand side is equal to

$$(a_1 - a_2)(b_1 - b_2) \geq 0. \qquad \square$$

Exercise 6a

1. Show how to deduce the fact that $\frac{1}{2}(a + b) \geq \sqrt{ab}$ if $a, b > 0$ from lemma 6.1.

2. Prove that if $a, b > 0$ then $a^5 + b^5 \geq a^4 b + b^4 a \geq a^3 b^2 + b^3 a^2$.

3. Prove that if $a_1 \geq a_2 \geq a_3$ and $b_1 \geq b_2 \geq b_3$, then

$$a_1 b_1 + a_2 b_2 + a_3 b_3 \geq a_1 b_2 + a_2 b_3 + a_3 b_1.$$

4. Give a geometrical interpretation of lemma 6.1 in the case where $a_1 \geq a_2 > 0$ and $b_1 \geq b_2 > 0$, by considering scalar (dot) products.

Before proceeding, it is convenient to make some definitions. A sequence $a_1, a_2, \ldots, a_n$ of real numbers is *decreasing* if $a_1 \geq a_2 \geq \cdots \geq a_n$ and *increasing* if $a_1 \leq a_2 \leq \cdots \leq a_n$. Two sequences $a_1, a_2, \ldots, a_n$ and $b_1, b_2, \ldots, b_n$ (of the same length) are said to be *ordered in the same way* if either both are increasing or both are decreasing. They are *ordered in the opposite way* if one is increasing and the other decreasing.

Theorem 6.1 (The rearrangement lemma) *Suppose* (a_k) *and* (b_k) *are two finite sequences of n real numbers. Let* (B_k) *be a sequence which is a permutation of* (b_k).

(i) *If* (a_k) *and* (b_k) *are ordered in the same way, then*

$$a_1 b_1 + a_2 b_2 + \cdots + a_n b_n \geq a_1 B_1 + a_2 B_2 + \cdots + a_n B_n.$$

(ii) *If* (a_k) *and* (b_k) *are ordered in the opposite way, then*

$$a_1 b_1 + a_2 b_2 + \cdots + a_n b_n \leq a_1 B_1 + a_2 B_2 + \cdots + a_n B_n.$$

Observe that this theorem is a generalisation of exercise 6a question 3 and that its proof uses the same idea as that used for the proof of lemma 6.1.

PROOF We give the proof for the case in which the sequences are ordered in the same way and both decreasing; the both increasing and oppositely ordered cases are very similar.

If $B_k = b_k$ for all $k = 1$ to n, there is nothing to prove. Otherwise there must be two subscripts, say p and q, such that $p < q$ and $B_p \leq B_q$, then, swapping B_p and B_q in the first bracket,

$$(a_1 B_1 + a_2 B_2 + \cdots + a_p B_q + \cdots + a_q B_p + \cdots + a_n B_n)$$
$$- (a_1 B_1 + a_2 B_2 + \cdots + a_p B_p + \cdots + a_q B_q + \cdots + a_n B_n)$$
$$= a_p B_q + a_q B_p - a_p B_p - a_q B_q$$
$$= (a_p - a_q)(B_q - B_p)$$
$$\geq 0$$

since (a_k) is decreasing and $B_p \le B_q$. In other words, any step towards restoring the correct order amongst the B_k, that is, permuting them back towards the b_k, increases the product.

It is intuitively clear and true, but slightly tricky to prove, that we do indeed reach the correct order amongst the B_k after a finite number of such steps. ❑

The proof of theorem 6.1 depends heavily on the fact that the two sequences involved are ordered either in the same or opposite way. This is actually less restrictive in practice than it appears. Often, even if we do not know the precise ordering of the terms of (a_k), we may know that the *same* permutation of (a_k) to put the terms in order either makes a *related* sequence (b_k) sorted in the same way or sorted in the opposite way. Since applying this permutation to the sum $a_1b_1 + a_2b_2 + \cdots + a_nb_n$ does not affect the value of the sum we can deduce from theorem 6.1:

Corollary 6.1 *Under these circumstances, suppose (B_k) is any permutation of (b_k).*

(i) If (a_k) and (b_k) are sorted in the same way, then

$$a_1b_1 + a_2b_2 + \cdots + a_nb_n \ge a_1B_1 + a_2B_2 + \cdots + a_nB_n.$$

(ii) If (a_k) and (b_k) are sorted in the opposite way, then

$$a_1b_1 + a_2b_2 + \cdots + a_nb_n \le a_1B_1 + a_2B_2 + \cdots + a_nB_n.$$

For example, if $a_1 = 4$, $a_2 = 2$, $a_3 = 5$ and $b_k = \frac{1}{a_k}$, so that $b_1 = \frac{1}{4}$, $b_2 = \frac{1}{2}$, $b_3 = \frac{1}{5}$, then the same reordering that sorts (a_k) as an increasing sequence

$$a_2 = 2, \ a_1 = 4, \ a_3 = 5$$

sorts (b_k) in the opposite way

$$b_2 = \tfrac{1}{2}, \ b_1 = \tfrac{1}{4}, \ b_3 = \tfrac{1}{5}.$$

We can then apply theorem 6.1 to these reordered sequences, for which $a_1b_1 + a_2b_2 + a_3b_3 = a_2b_2 + a_1b_1 + a_3b_3$. The key point is that the mapping from (a_k) to (b_k) is order-inverting; other mappings, such as $b_k = a_k^3$, would be order-preserving.

Example 6.1   If $a, b, c > 0$ prove that $a^3 + b^3 + c^3 \geq a^2 c + b^2 a + c^2 b$.

Suppose that without loss of generality $a \geq b \geq c$. Consider the sequences (a^2, b^2, c^2) and (a, b, c). These are ordered in the same way. But (c, a, b) is a permutation of (a, b, c). The result now follows immediately from theorem 6.1.

Example 6.2   If $a, b > 0$ prove that

$$\left(a^4 + b^4\right)(a + b)^2 \geq \left(a^2 + b^2\right)^3.$$

The left-hand side minus the right-hand side comes to

$$2\left(a^5 b + ab^5\right) - 2\left(a^4 b^2 + a^2 b^4\right).$$

Now consider the sequences $(a^4 b, ab^4)$ and (a, b), which are ordered in the same way, and apply theorem 6.1.

Example 6.3   If $a, b, c > 0$ prove that

$$\frac{a}{b + c} + \frac{b}{c + a} + \frac{c}{a + b} \geq \frac{3}{2}.$$

This inequality has already been established using the Cauchy-Schwarz inequality, but it can also be established by rearrangement. If we assume, without loss of generality, that $a \geq b \geq c$, then (a, b, c) and

$$\left(\frac{1}{b + c}, \frac{1}{c + a}, \frac{1}{a + b}\right)$$

are ordered in the same way. Hence we have

$$\frac{a}{b + c} + \frac{b}{c + a} + \frac{c}{a + b} \geq \frac{a}{c + a} + \frac{b}{a + b} + \frac{c}{b + c}$$

and

$$\frac{a}{b + c} + \frac{b}{c + a} + \frac{c}{a + b} \geq \frac{a}{a + b} + \frac{b}{b + c} + \frac{c}{c + a}.$$

Now add.

Example 6.4   We show how to prove AM-GM using corollary 6.1.

Let $a_k > 0$. Define $g = (a_1 a_2 \cdots a_n)^{\frac{1}{n}}$ to be their geometric mean. Define

$$c_1 = \frac{a_1}{g}, \; c_2 = \frac{a_1 a_2}{g^2}, \; c_3 = \frac{a_1 a_2 a_3}{g^3}, \; \ldots, \; c_n = \frac{a_1 a_2 \cdots a_n}{g^n} = 1$$

and $d_k = \dfrac{1}{c_k}$, $k = 1$ to n. Clearly the sequences (c_k) and (d_k) are oppositely sorted, and on using corollary 6.1 in the form

$$c_1 d_1 + c_2 d_2 + \cdots + c_n d_n \le c_1 d_n + c_2 d_1 + \cdots + c_n d_{n-1}$$

we obtain

$$1 + 1 + \cdots + 1 \le \frac{a_1}{g} + \frac{a_2}{g} + \cdots + \frac{a_n}{g},$$

that is, $m \ge g$, where m is the arithmetic mean.

Theorem 6.2 (Chebyshev's inequality) *Let (a_k) and (b_k) be two finite sequences of n real numbers.*

(i) *If the sequences are ordered in the same way, then*

$$n \sum a_k b_k \ge \sum a_k \times \sum b_k.$$

(ii) *If the sequences are ordered in the opposite way, then*

$$n \sum a_k b_k \le \sum a_k \times \sum b_k.$$

The proofs below consider the case where the sequences are ordered in the same way: the other case is very similar.

PROOF 1   The result follows by repeated application of theorem 6.1. The proof for $n = 3$ gives the idea of the general case. The right-hand side may be rewritten with a circulating pattern of terms as $(a_1 b_1 + a_2 b_2 + a_3 b_3) + (a_1 b_2 + a_2 b_3 + a_3 b_1) + (a_1 b_3 + a_2 b_1 + a_3 b_2)$. Now apply theorem 6.1 to each term.   ❑

We provide a proof independent of theorem 6.1, but which uses the same idea, that of lemma 6.1.

PROOF 2 For any pair of suffices p and q, because the sequences are ordered in the same way, we have

$$(a_p - a_q)(b_p - b_q) \geq 0.$$

It follows that

$$a_p b_p + a_q b_q \geq a_p b_q + a_q b_p.$$

Summing over p we get

$$\sum a_p b_p + n a_q b_q \geq b_q \sum a_p + a_q \sum b_p.$$

Summing over q we get

$$2n \sum a_k b_k \geq 2 \sum a_k \sum b_k.$$ ❏

If you have studied correlation in statistics, you may recognise theorem 6.2 as saying that sequences ordered in the same way have non-negative covariance while those ordered in the opposite way have non-positive covariance.

6.2   Inequalities involving sums of powers

Positive powers

As an immediate consequence of theorem 6.2 we have

Theorem 6.3 *If $s, t \geq 0$ are integers and $a_1, a_2, \ldots, a_n > 0$, then*

$$\frac{\sum a_k^{s+t}}{n} \geq \frac{\sum a_k^s}{n} \times \frac{\sum a_k^t}{n}.$$

For example, if $a, b, c > 0$, then

$$3\left(a^5 + b^5 + c^5\right) \geq \left(a^2 + b^2 + c^2\right)\left(a^3 + b^3 + c^3\right).$$

PROOF Since the sums involved do not depend on the order of the terms we may assume that (a_k) is increasing. Then (a_k^s) and (a_k^t) are ordered in the same way and the result follows from theorem 6.2.   ❏

One positive power and one negative power

Theorem 6.4 *If $s > 0$, $t < 0$ are integers and $a_1, a_2, \ldots, a_n > 0$, then*

$$\frac{\sum a_k^{s+t}}{n} \leq \frac{\sum a_k^s}{n} \times \frac{\sum a_k^t}{n}.$$

For example, if $a, b, c > 0$, then

$$3\left(a^2 + b^2 + c^2\right) \leq \left(a^3 + b^3 + c^3\right)\left(\frac{1}{a} + \frac{1}{b} + \frac{1}{c}\right).$$

PROOF As in the proof of theorem 6.3, we may suppose that (a_k) is increasing. Then (a_k^s) and (a_k^t) are ordered in the opposite way and the result follows from theorem 6.2. $\qquad\square$

Negative powers

Theorem 6.5 *If $s, t \leq 0$ are integers and $a_1, a_2, \ldots, a_n > 0$, then*

$$\frac{\sum a_k^{s+t}}{n} \geq \frac{\sum a_k^s}{n} \times \frac{\sum a_k^t}{n}.$$

For example, if $a, b, c > 0$, then

$$3\left(\frac{1}{a^4} + \frac{1}{b^4} + \frac{1}{c^4}\right) \geq \left(\frac{1}{a^3} + \frac{1}{b^3} + \frac{1}{c^3}\right)\left(\frac{1}{a} + \frac{1}{b} + \frac{1}{c}\right).$$

PROOF The proof follows the same lines as that of theorem 6.3. $\qquad\square$

We are now in a position to give a result which compares the mean of integral powers of n positive quantities with their arithmetic mean.

Theorem 6.6 *If s is a positive integer and $a_1, a_2, \ldots, a_n > 0$, then*

(i)
$$\frac{a_1^s + a_2^s + \cdots + a_n^s}{n} \geq \left(\frac{a_1 + a_2 + \cdots + a_n}{n}\right)^s;$$

(ii)
$$\frac{a_1^{-s} + a_2^{-s} + \cdots + a_n^{-s}}{n} \geq \left(\frac{a_1 + a_2 + \cdots + a_n}{n}\right)^{-s}.$$

PROOF The proof of (i) is by induction. It is clearly true for $s = 1$. If now, as an inductive hypothesis, it is true for some integer $s \geq 1$, then theorem 6.3 with $t = 1$ shows that it is true for $s + 1$.

For (ii), we have from (i), with $\frac{1}{a_1}, \frac{1}{a_2}, \ldots, \frac{1}{a_n} > 0$, that

$$\frac{a_1^{-s} + a_2^{-s} + \cdots + a_n^{-s}}{n} \geq \left(\frac{\frac{1}{a_1} + \frac{1}{a_2} + \cdots + \frac{1}{a_n}}{n} \right)^s.$$

Now, from theorem 6.4 with $s = 1$, $t = -1$ (or from theorem 3.2 on page 28), we have

$$1 \leq \frac{\sum a_k}{n} \times \frac{\sum \frac{1}{a_k}}{n}$$

and so (ii) follows. ❑

Notes

1. Putting $s = 2$ into theorem 6.6(i), we have the AM-RMS inequality for n variables, as already proved in example 4.2 on page 39.

2. Putting $s = 1$ into theorem 6.6(ii), we have the HM-AM inequality for n variables, as already established in theorem 3.2 on page 28.

3. In corollary 7.1 on page 99 we consider the case of fractional powers such as $s = \frac{1}{2}$.

The reader should review the above theorems and should check that equality holds in each case if, and only if, certain obvious conditions hold, such as $a_1 = a_2 = \cdots = a_n$.

Example 6.5   Let (a_k), (b_k), (c_k), ... be a collection of sequences of positive numbers all ordered in the same way, and let p, q, r, ... be positive integers. Prove that

$$\frac{\sum a_k^p b_k^q c_k^r \cdots}{n} \geq \left(\sum \frac{a_k}{n} \right)^p \left(\sum \frac{b_k}{n} \right)^q \left(\sum \frac{c_k}{n} \right)^r \cdots.$$

This is proved by a repeated application of theorem 6.2 (Chebyshev).

Example 6.6 Let (a_k), (b_k) be two sequences of positive numbers ordered in the same way. Prove that

$$\left(\sum a_k\right)^2 \left(\sum b_k\right)^2 \left(\sum a_k b_k\right)^2 \leq n^4 \sum a_k^4 \sum b_k^4.$$

From Chebyshev we have $\sum a_k \sum b_k \leq n \sum a_k b_k$. Multiplying by the positive quantity $\sum a_k b_k$ we get

$$\sum a_k \sum b_k \sum a_k b_k \leq n \sum a_k b_k \sum a_k b_k \leq n^2 \sum a_k^2 b_k^2$$

using Chebyshev again. Squaring provides the required result since, by Cauchy-Schwarz,

$$\left(\sum a_k^2 b_k^2\right)^2 \leq \sum a_k^4 \sum b_k^4.$$

Example 6.7 Let $a, b, c, d > 0$ and $\dfrac{1}{a} + \dfrac{1}{b} + \dfrac{1}{c} + \dfrac{1}{d} = 1$. Minimize $a^2 + b^2 + c^2 + d^2$.

Put $\frac{1}{a} = u, \frac{1}{b} = v, \frac{1}{c} = w, \frac{1}{d} = x$ then $u + v + w + x = 1$ and we are required to minimize $\dfrac{1}{u^2} + \dfrac{1}{v^2} + \dfrac{1}{w^2} + \dfrac{1}{x^2}$. Now by theorem 6.6 we have

$$\frac{1}{4}\left(\frac{1}{u^2} + \frac{1}{v^2} + \frac{1}{w^2} + \frac{1}{x^2}\right) \geq \left(\frac{u + v + w + x}{4}\right)^{-2} = 16.$$

Thus the minimum is 64 with equality if, and only if, $a = b = c = d = 4$.

Example 6.8 Let $a, b, c > 0$ and $abc = 2$. Prove that

$$(1 + a^4)(1 + b^4)(1 + c^4) \geq (1 + 2a)(1 + 2b)(1 + 2c).$$

Is it true that if $a, b, c, d > 0$ and $abcd = 2$ that

$$(1 + a^4)(1 + b^4)(1 + c^4)(1 + d^4) \geq (1 + 2a)(1 + 2b)(1 + 2c)(1 + 2d)?$$

[David Monk]

The answer to the second part is 'No' and can be seen by taking $a = \sqrt{2}$, $b = \sqrt{2}$, $c = 1$, $d = 1$.

For the first part the key is to see how to use the condition $abc = 2$, and the trick is to prove the equivalent inequality

$$(1 + a^4)(1 + b^4)(1 + c^4) \geq (1 + a^2bc)(1 + ab^2c)(1 + abc^2).$$

We expand both sides and prove first that $a^4 + b^4 + c^4 \geq abc(a + b + c)$. In fact, by theorem 6.6(i), we have

$$\tfrac{1}{3}(a^4 + b^4 + c^4) \geq \left(\frac{a+b+c}{3}\right)^4$$

so that

$$a^4 + b^4 + c^4 \geq (a + b + c)\left(\frac{a+b+c}{3}\right)^3 \geq (a + b + c)abc,$$

by AM-GM. It remains to prove that

$$a^4b^4 + b^4c^4 + c^4a^4 \geq a^2b^2c^2(ab + bc + ca).$$

But this is the same inequality with bc replacing a etc.

Example 6.9

(a) Prove that if $t > 0$, $t \neq 1$, $x > y > 0$ then

$$t^x + \frac{1}{t^x} > t^y + \frac{1}{t^y}.$$

(b) Deduce that, if $t > 0$, $t \neq 1$, $t^p + t^q > t^r + t^s$ when $p, q, r, s \geq 0$, $p + q = r + s$ and $p - q > r - s \geq 0$.

(c) Prove that when $p, q, r, s \geq 0$ and $p + q = r + s$, $p - q > r - s \geq 0$ and $a_k > 0$ for $k = 1$ to n then

$$\sum a_k^p \sum a_k^q \geq \sum a_k^r \sum a_k^s.$$

For part (a) apply theorem 6.1 to the sequences (t^x, t^y), $(t^{x+y}, 1)$, which are ordered in the same way.

For part (b) use $t^{k+x} + t^{k-x} > t^{k+y} + t^{k-y}$ with $k + x = p$, $k - x = q$, $k + y = r$, $k - y = s$.

For part (c) put $t = \frac{a}{b}$, multiply up by $b^{p+q} = b^{r+s}$ to get

$$a^p b^q + a^q b^p \geq a^r b^s + a^s b^r.$$

Then put $a = a_j$, $b = a_k$ and perform a summation over all pairs (j, k).

Exercise 6b

1. Prove that, if $a, b > 0$, then $16(a^5 + b^5) \geq (a + b)^5$.

2. Prove that if $a, b, c, d > 0$ then
$$(a^3 + b^3 + c^3 + d^3)(a + b + c + d) \geq (a^2 + b^2 + c^2 + d^2)^2.$$

3. Prove that if $a, b, c, d > 0$ then
$$4(a^4 + b^4 + c^4 + d^4) \geq (a^3 + b^3 + c^3 + d^3)(a + b + c + d).$$

4. Prove that, if $a, b, c > 0$ then $9(a^6 + b^6 + c^6) \geq (a^2 + b^2 + c^2)^3$.

5. If $a_1, a_2, \ldots, a_n > 0$ and $a_1 + a_2 + \cdots + a_n = 1$ find the minimum of
$$\sum \left(a_k + \frac{1}{a_k} \right)^2.$$

6. Let (x_k), (y_k) be sequences of n terms that are ordered in the same way, and let (z_k) be a sequence that is a permutation of (y_k). Prove that
$$\sum (x_k - y_k)^2 \leq \sum (x_k - z_k)^2.$$

[IMO 1975]

7. Prove that if (a_k), (b_k), (c_k) are sequences of positive terms ordered in the same way, then

$$\sum a_k \sum b_k \sum c_k \sum a_k b_k c_k \leq n^3 \sum a_k^2 b_k^2 c_k^2.$$

8. Prove that if a, b, c are positive real numbers and $a + b + c \geq 3abc$ then $a^2 + b^2 + c^2 \geq 3abc$.

9. Let $x, y, z > 0$. Prove that

(a) $\dfrac{x^2}{y^2} + \dfrac{y^2}{z^2} + \dfrac{z^2}{x^2} \geq \dfrac{y}{x} + \dfrac{z}{y} + \dfrac{x}{z}$;

(b) $\dfrac{x^2}{y^2} + \dfrac{y^2}{z^2} + \dfrac{z^2}{x^2} \geq \dfrac{x}{y} + \dfrac{y}{z} + \dfrac{z}{x}$.

10. Establish the following homogeneous inequalities when $a, b, c > 0$:

(a) $a^4 + b^4 + c^4 \geq b^2 c^2 + c^2 a^2 + a^2 b^2$;

(b) $2(a^4 + b^4 + c^4) \geq a^3(b + c) + b^3(c + a) + c^3(a + b)$;

(c) $a^4 + b^4 + c^4 \geq abc(a + b + c)$;

(d) $\dfrac{a^2}{b + c} + \dfrac{b^2}{c + a} + \dfrac{c^2}{a + b} \geq \dfrac{a + b + c}{2}$.

11. Prove that, if $a, b, c, d > 0$, then

$$(a^4 + b^4 + c^4 + d^4)(a + b + c + d)^2 \geq (a^2 + b^2 + c^2 + d^2)^3.$$

6.3   Power means inequality

Power mean *For any non-zero integer t, the* power mean *or* mean of order t *of $a_1, a_2, \ldots, a_n > 0$ is*

$$\left(\frac{a_1^t + a_2^t + \cdots + a_n^t}{n} \right)^{\frac{1}{t}}.$$

It will be useful to introduce the notation M_t for the power mean and also $m_t = \frac{a_1^t + a_2^t + \cdots + a_n^t}{n}$, so that $M_t = m_t^{\frac{1}{t}}$. Note that M_1 is the arithmetic mean, M_2 is the root mean square, and M_{-1} is the harmonic mean.

Now if t is allowed to be any non-zero real number then it can be shown that $M_t \to g$ as $t \to 0$, where g is the geometric mean (see result 7.1 on page 102). Hence we define $M_0 = g$.

We now summarise the results so far, using the new notation.

Theorem 6.7 *Using the notation on this page,*

(i) $M_{-1} \leq M_0 \leq M_1 \leq M_2$;

(ii) *if s, t are non-negative integers, then* $m_{s+t} \geq m_s m_t$;

(iii) *if s is a positive integer, then* $m_s \geq m_1^s$, *or equivalently* $M_s \geq M_1$;

(iv) *if s, t are positive integers, then* $m_{s-t} \leq m_s m_{-t}$;

(v) *if s is a non-zero integer,* $m_s m_{-s} \geq 1$;

(vi) *if s, t are non-negative integers, then* $m_{-s-t} \geq m_{-s} m_{-t}$;

(vii) *if s is a positive integer, then* $m_{-s} \geq m_1^{-s}$, *or equivalently* $M_{-s} \leq M_1$.

PROOF These are all previous results rewritten in the new notation:

(i) the HM-GM-AM-RMS inequality;

(ii) theorem 6.3;

(iii) theorem 6.6(i);

(iv) theorem 6.4;

(v) theorem 6.4 with $s = -t$;

(vi) theorem 6.5;

(vii) theorem 6.6(ii). ❑

Now theorem 6.7(i) suggests the following result, stronger than (vii).

Theorem 6.8 *If s is a positive integer, then $M_{-s} \leq M_0 = g$.*

PROOF By AM-GM

$$m_{-s} = \frac{1}{n}\left(\frac{1}{a_1^s} + \frac{1}{a_2^s} + \cdots + \frac{1}{a_n^s}\right) \geq (a_1 a_2 \cdots a_n)^{-\frac{s}{n}} = M_0^{-s}.$$

Hence $M_{-s} = m_{-s}^{-\frac{1}{s}} \leq M_0$. ❑

We now review example 6.9 on page 76 and note that part (a) is true not only if $x > y > 0$, but more generally if $|x| > |y|$. This means that part (b) is true for all p, q, r, s satisfying $p + q = r + s$ and $p - q > r - s \geq 0$. Thus, for example, if $t > 0$,

$$t^3 + t^{-5} \geq t^2 + t^{-4},$$

with equality if, and only if, $t = 1$.

As a second example, if $t > 0$,

$$t^{-3} + t^{-8} \geq t^{-4} + t^{-7},$$

with equality if, and only if, $t = 1$.

The upshot of this is, as in part (c) of example 6.9,

Lemma 6.2 *If p, q, r, s are integers such that $p + q = r + s$ and $p - q > r - s \geq 0$ then*

$$m_p m_q \geq m_r m_s.$$

Now observe that theorem 6.7(i) looks as if it should generalize as

Theorem 6.9 (Power means inequality) *Let $a_1, a_2, \ldots, a_n$ be positive real numbers. Then*

$$\cdots \leq M_{-5} \leq M_{-4} \leq M_{-3} \leq M_{-2} \leq M_{-1} \leq M_0 = g$$
$$\leq M_1 \leq M_2 \leq M_3 \leq M_4 \leq M_5 \leq \cdots$$

PROOF We first give an example on which the proof of the general result is based. We prove $M_5 \geq M_4$ or, what is the same thing, that $m_5^4 \geq m_4^5$. It follows by repeated use of lemma 6.2.

We have $m_5^4 \geq m_5^3 m_4 m_1 \geq m_5^2 m_4^2 m_2 \geq m_5 m_4^3 m_3 \geq m_4^5$.

In general we prove $M_{s+1} \geq M_s$, or, what is the same thing, that $m_{s+1}^s \geq m_s^{s+1}$. We have, for positive $s \geq 2$,

$$m_{s+1}^s \geq m_{s+1}^{s-1} m_s m_1 \geq m_{s+1}^{s-2} m_s^2 m_2 \geq m_{s+1}^{s-3} m_s^3 m_3 \geq \cdots$$
$$\geq m_{s+1} m_s^{s-1} m_{s-1} \geq m_s^{s+1},$$

where some steps have to be omitted if $s = 2$ or 3.

Note that theorem 6.7(i) takes care of $s = 0, 1$.

For negative values of s care has to be taken at the initial stage; for example, to prove $M_{-2} \geq M_{-3}$ the equivalent statement is $m_{-3}^2 \geq m_{-2}^3$

and the proof then goes as follows: $m_{-3}^2 \geq m_{-1}m_{-2}m_{-3} \geq m_2^3$. The general proof for $s \leq -2$ follows the same pattern.

Theorem 6.7(i) takes care of $s = -1$. ❏

As you may imagine, the general power means inequality

$$M_s \leq M_t \text{ for all real numbers } s, t \text{ with } s \leq t$$

is true. A proof of this is given in theorem 7.5 on page 100.

6.4 Hölder's inequality

Example 6.10   Prove that, if s, t are positive integers and $x, y > 0$, then

$$x^s y^t \leq \left(\frac{sx + ty}{s + t} \right)^{s+t}.$$

This is just AM-GM with x appearing s times and y appearing t times.

Example 6.11   Prove that, if α, β are positive rational numbers with $\alpha + \beta = 1$, then

$$x^\alpha y^\beta \leq \alpha x + \beta y.$$

Use the result of example 6.10 with $\alpha = \dfrac{s}{s+t}$ and $\beta = \dfrac{t}{s+t}$.

Theorem 6.10 (Hölder's inequality) *Let p and q be positive rational numbers such that $\frac{1}{p} + \frac{1}{q} = 1$, and let (x_k) and (y_k) be two finite sequences of n positive real numbers. Then*

$$x_1 y_1 + x_2 y_2 + \cdots + x_n y_n \leq \left(x_1^p + x_2^p + \cdots + x_n^p \right)^{\frac{1}{p}} \left(y_1^q + y_2^q + \cdots + y_n^q \right)^{\frac{1}{q}}.$$

PROOF Let (a_k) and (b_k) be two sequences of n positive terms. In example 6.11 put

$$x = \frac{a_k}{\sum a_k} \text{ and } y = \frac{b_k}{\sum b_k}$$

to get

$$\frac{a_k^{\alpha}}{(\sum a_k)^{\alpha}} \times \frac{b_k^{\beta}}{(\sum b_k)^{\beta}} \leq \alpha \frac{a_k}{\sum a_k} + \beta \frac{b_k}{\sum b_k}.$$

Summing over k from 1 to n gives

$$\frac{\sum a_k^{\alpha} b_k^{\beta}}{(\sum a_k)^{\alpha} (\sum b_k)^{\beta}} \leq \alpha + \beta = 1$$

or

$$a_1^{\alpha} b_1^{\beta} + a_2^{\alpha} b_2^{\beta} + \cdots + a_n^{\alpha} b_n^{\beta} \leq (a_1 + a_2 + \cdots + a_n)^{\alpha} (b_1 + b_2 + \cdots + b_n)^{\beta}.$$

Now put $\alpha = \frac{1}{p}$ and $\beta = \frac{1}{q}$ so that $\frac{1}{p} + \frac{1}{q} = 1$. Also put $a_k = x_k^p$ and $b_k = y_k^q$ and we get

$$x_1 y_1 + x_2 y_2 + \cdots + x_n y_n \leq \left(x_1^p + x_2^p + \cdots + x_n^p \right)^{\frac{1}{p}} \left(y_1^q + y_2^q + \cdots + y_n^q \right)^{\frac{1}{q}},$$

as required.   ❏

If $p = q = 2$, then Hölder's inequality is the same as the Cauchy-Schwarz inequality and is therefore a generalization of it.

If you write $\mathbf{x} = (x_1, x_2, \ldots, x_n)$ and $\mathbf{y} = (y_1, y_2, \ldots, y_n)$ and divide both sides by $n = n^{\left(\frac{1}{p} + \frac{1}{q} \right)}$ we may think of the inequality as saying that $\frac{1}{n}(\mathbf{x} \cdot \mathbf{y}) \leq M_p(x) M_q(y)$. If $\mathbf{x} = \mathbf{y}$ this reduces to $M_2^2 \leq M_p M_q$, which one might have anticipated from lemma 6.2 and theorem 6.9.

Exercise 6c

1. Prove in detail, without quoting theorem 6.9, that $M_{-5} \leq M_{-4}$.

2. Prove that for all integers n

$$\cosh^n \{ (n+1)\theta \} \geq \cosh^{n+1}(n\theta).$$

3. Generalize example 6.10, example 6.11 and theorem 6.10 to cover more than two sequences.

4. Prove that if $a_1, a_2, \ldots, a_n > 0$, then

$$(1 + a_1)(1 + a_2) \cdots (1 + a_n) \geq (1 + g)^n,$$

where $g = (a_1 a_2 \cdots a_n)^{\frac{1}{n}}$.

5. Prove that if x, y, z, w are positive real numbers such that $x + y + z + w = 1$, then

$$\left(1 + \frac{1}{x}\right)\left(1 + \frac{1}{y}\right)\left(1 + \frac{1}{z}\right)\left(1 + \frac{1}{w}\right) \geq 625.$$

6. (A particular case of *Minkowski's inequality*.)

Let $(a_k), (b_k), \ldots, (t_k)$ be sequences of n terms of positive real numbers. Prove that

$$\left(a_1^2 + a_2^2 + \cdots + a_n^2\right)^{\frac{1}{2}} + \left(b_1^2 + b_2^2 + \cdots + b_n^2\right)^{\frac{1}{2}} + \cdots$$
$$+ \left(t_1^2 + t_2^2 + \cdots + t_n^2\right)^{\frac{1}{2}}$$
$$\geq \left\{(a_1 + b_1 + \cdots + t_1)^2 + (a_2 + b_2 + \cdots + t_2)^2 + \cdots \right.$$
$$\left. + (a_n + b_n + \cdots + t_n)^2\right\}^{\frac{1}{2}}.$$

The inequalities of Hölder and Minkowski are important in advanced analysis and are included in this book for that reason.

6.5 Muirhead's inequality

Muirhead's theorem is a very powerful general theorem which can be used to solve a large number of symmetric inequalities with little thought (although proficiency with algebra is definitely required). You may find this rather a heavy section which you may want to omit on a first reading of the book.

First, some notation. Let

$$\sum_{\text{sym}} x_1^{a_1} x_2^{a_2} \cdots x_n^{a_n} = \sum_{\sigma} x_{\sigma(1)}^{a_1} x_{\sigma(2)}^{a_2} \cdots x_{\sigma(n)}^{a_n}$$

where the sum on the right is taken over all $n!$ permutations of

$$\{1, 2, \ldots, n\}.$$

Note that in the symmetric sum, every permutation is taken, even if the product is unchanged (which will happen if some of the a_i are the same). For example, if our variables are a, b, c, then:

$$\sum_{\text{sym}} a = a + a + b + b + c + c$$
$$= 2(a + b + c)$$

$$\sum_{\text{sym}} abc = abc + acb + bac + bca + cab + cba$$
$$= 6abc$$

$$\sum_{\text{sym}} a^2 b = a^2 b + b^2 a + b^2 c + c^2 b + a^2 c + c^2 a$$

$$\sum_{\text{sym}} a^3 b^2 c^2 = a^3 b^2 c^2 + a^3 c^2 b^2 + b^3 a^2 c^2 + b^3 c^2 a^2 + c^3 a^2 b^2 + c^3 b^2 a^2$$
$$= 2(a^3 b^2 c^2 + a^2 b^3 c^2 + a^2 b^2 c^3).$$

We often write $[a_1, a_2, \ldots, a_n]$ for $\sum_{\text{sym}} x_1^{a_1} x_2^{a_2} \cdots x_n^{a_n}$; this is called *bracket notation*.

Insisting on using all $n!$ permutations in each symmetrical sum is essential to the statement of Muirhead's theorem. An alternative notation for $\sum_{\text{sym}}$ is $\sum!$ and an alternative common usage (which you will meet in chapter 8) refers to expressions such as $a^2 + b^2 + c^2$ and abc as *symmetric polynomials* (because they are unaltered by any permutation of their variables).

Muirhead's theorem is a way of showing that one symmetric sum is always greater than or equal to another, subject to a condition on the exponents known as *majorization*. It is defined as follows. Let $(a_1, a_2, \ldots, a_n)$ and $(b_1, b_2, \ldots, b_n)$ be sequences of real numbers with the same number of terms. Then $(a_1, a_2, \ldots, a_n)$ is said to *majorize* $(b_1, b_2, \ldots, b_n)$ if:

(i) (a_i) and (b_i) are decreasing sequences, that is, $a_1 \geq a_2 \geq \cdots$ and $b_1 \geq b_2 \geq \cdots$

(ii) $a_1 + \cdots + a_n = b_1 + \cdots + b_n$,

(iii) $a_1 + \cdots + a_i \geq b_1 + \cdots + b_i$ for $1 \leq i < n$.

This is written $(a_1, a_2, \ldots, a_n) \succ (b_1, b_2, \ldots, b_n)$.

For example, with $n = 5$,

$$(5,0,0,0,0) \succ (4,1,0,0,0) \succ (3,2,0,0,0)$$
$$\succ (2,2,1,0,0) \succ (2,1,1,1,0) \succ (1,1,1,1,0).$$

Now suppose $A = (a_1, \ldots, a_n)$ and $B = (b_1, \ldots, b_n)$ are two sequences with $A \succ B$. If A and B are not the same, then since

$$a_1 + \cdots + a_n = b_1 + \cdots + b_n$$

we must have $a_i < b_i$ for some i. Choose the smallest such i, and let that be k. Since $a_1 \geq b_1$ we know $k > 1$. We have $a_{k-1} \geq b_{k-1} \geq b_k > a_k$. Consider the sequence $A' = (a'_1, \ldots, a'_n)$ defined as follows:

(i) $a'_i = a_i$ if $i \neq k-1, k$.

(ii) If $a_{k-1} - b_{k-1} \geq b_k - a_k$ then $a'_k = b_k$ and $a'_{k-1} = a_{k-1} + a_k - b_k$.

(iii) Otherwise, set $a'_{k-1} = b_{k-1}$ and $a'_k = a_k + a_{k-1} - b_{k-1}$.

In other words, we slide a_k and a_{k-1} closer together, keeping their sum the same, until one of them is equal to the corresponding member of B.

For an illustration, both of the construction of A' and lemma 6.3 below, consider $(8,7,4,3,0) \succ (8,5,5,2,2)$. We have $(8,7,4,3,0)' = (8,6,5,3,0)$, by case (ii) with $k = 3$ and, from $(8,6,5,3,0) \succ (8,5,5,2,2)$, we have $(8,6,5,3,0)' = (8,6,5,2,1)$, by case (iii) with $k = 5$ and $(8,6,5,2,1) \succ (8,5,5,2,2)$. But $(8,6,5,2,1)' = (8,6,5,2,1)$: it is possible for $A' = A$ or $A' = B$ to occur.

Lemma 6.3 *With A, B and A' defined as above,*

$$A \succ A' \succ B.$$

PROOF Since $a_k + a_{k-1} = a'_k + a'_{k-1}$ and, apart from these two terms, A and A' are identical we only need show that

(i) the sequence A' is still decreasing and,

(ii) $a_1 + \cdots + a_{k-1} \geq a'_1 + \cdots + a'_{k-1} \geq b_1 + \cdots + b_{k-1}$.

Since, when we formed A', we decreased a_{k-1} and increased a_k the only way the sequence cannot be decreasing is if $a'_{k-1} < a'_k$. We consider the case $a_{k-1} - b_{k-1} \geq b_k - a_k$; the other case is similar. If $a'_{k-1} < a'_k$, then $a_{k-1} + a_k - b_k < b_k$, so

$$a_{k-1} - b_{k-1} \leq a_{k-1} - b_k < b_k - a_k$$

which is a contradiction. So we have shown (i).

For (ii), we note that $a_{k-1} \geq a'_{k-1} \geq b_{k-1}$ (check all cases) and also

$$a_1 + \cdots + a_{k-2} = a'_1 + \cdots + a'_{k-2} \geq b_1 + \cdots + b_{k-2}. \qquad \square$$

We can now prove

Theorem 6.11 (Muirhead) *Let $x_1, x_2, \ldots, x_n$ be positive real numbers, and let (a_k) and (b_k) be two finite sequences of n real numbers. If $(a_1, \ldots, a_n) \succ (b_1, \ldots, b_n)$, then*

$$\sum_{\text{sym}} x_1^{a_1} x_2^{a_2} \cdots x_n^{a_n} \geq \sum_{\text{sym}} x_1^{b_1} x_2^{b_2} \cdots x_n^{b_n}.$$

PROOF We use induction on n.

BASE STEP In the case $n = 2$ we have

$$x_1^{b_1} x_2^{b_1} \left(x_1^{a_1 - b_1} - x_2^{b_2 - a_2} \right) \left(x_2^{b_2 - a_1} - x_1^{a_2 - b_1} \right)$$
$$= x_1^{a_1} x_2^{a_2} + x_1^{a_2} x_2^{a_1} - x_1^{b_1} x_2^{b_2} - x_1^{b_2} x_2^{b_1}.$$

This is easily confirmed by expanding the left-hand side, remembering that $a_1 + a_2 = b_1 + b_2$. Now since the left-hand side is symmetric in x_1 and x_2 we may assume $x_1 \geq x_2$. Then $\left(x_1^{a_1 - b_1} - x_2^{b_2 - a_2} \right) \geq 0$ since $a_1 - b_1 = b_2 - a_2 \geq 0$ and $\left(x_2^{b_2 - a_1} - x_1^{a_2 - b_1} \right) \geq 0$ as $b_2 - a_1 = a_2 - b_1 \leq 0$.

INDUCTION STEP Suppose that the result is true for $n = k - 1$. If A is a sequence of length n, then let $[A]$ denote the symmetric sum formed by the elements of A. If A and B are the same, there is nothing to prove. Otherwise, let A' be the sequence formed from A and B in lemma 6.3. Let a_i and a_{i+1} be the places where the sequence has been changed. Suppose

$j \in \{i, i+1\}$ such that $a'_j = b_j$. Now

$$[A'] = \sum_{\text{sym}} \left(x_1^{a_1} \cdots x_{i-1}^{a_{i-1}} x_{i+2}^{a_{i+2}} \cdots x_k^{a_k} \sum_{\text{sym}} x_i^{a'_i} x_{i+1}^{a'_{i+1}} \right)$$

$$\leq \sum_{\text{sym}} \left(x_1^{a_1} \cdots x_{i-1}^{a_{i-1}} x_{i+2}^{a_{i+2}} \cdots x_k^{a_k} \sum_{\text{sym}} x_i^{a_i} x_{i+1}^{a_{i+1}} \right)$$

$$= [A]$$

by the case $n = 2$ since $(a_i, a_{i+1}) \succ (a'_i, a'_{i+1})$.

Also,

$$[A'] = \sum_{\text{sym}} \left(x_j^{b_j} \sum_{\text{sym}} x_1^{a'_1} \cdots x_{j-1}^{a'_{j-1}} x_{j+1}^{a'_{j+1}} \cdots x_k^{a'_k} \right)$$

$$\geq \sum_{\text{sym}} \left(x_j^{b_j} \sum_{\text{sym}} x_1^{b_1} \cdots x_{j-1}^{b_{j-1}} x_{j+1}^{b_{j+1}} \cdots x_k^{b_k} \right)$$

$$= [B]$$

by the induction hypothesis since the sequence $A' \setminus a'_j$ majorizes $B \setminus b_j$.

So

$$[A] \geq [A'] \geq [B]. \qquad \square$$

Note that, although in most applications, $a_i, b_i \geq 0$, this is not essential for Muirhead's theorem.

Example 6.12　　If $x, y, z > 0$, prove that

$$\left(x^2 + y^2 + z^2 \right)^2 \geq 3xyz(x + y + z).$$

Expanding brackets, this is equivalent to

$$x^4 + y^4 + z^4 + 2\left(x^2 y^2 + y^2 z^2 + z^2 x^2 \right) \geq 3\left(x^2 yz + xy^2 z + xyz^2 \right).$$

But $(4, 0, 0) \succ (2, 1, 1)$ since $4 + 0 + 0 = 2 + 1 + 1$, $4 \geq 2$, $4 + 0 \geq 2 + 1$ and $(2, 2, 0) \succ (2, 1, 1)$ since $2 + 2 + 0 = 2 + 1 + 1$, $2 \geq 2$, $2 + 2 \geq 2 + 1$, so by Muirhead's theorem

$$x^4 + y^4 + z^4 \geq x^2yz + xy^2z + xyz^2$$
$$\text{and} \quad x^2y^2 + y^2z^2 + z^2x^2 \geq x^2yz + xy^2z + xyz^2,$$

from which the required inequality follows immediately.

Example 6.13   If $a, b, c \geq 0$ prove that

$$\frac{a}{b+c} + \frac{b}{c+a} + \frac{c}{a+b} \geq \frac{3}{2}.$$

Multiplying both sides by $(a+b)(b+c)(c+a)$ and expanding brackets we find that the inequality is equivalent to

$$2(a^3 + b^3 + c^3) \geq (a^2b + b^2a + b^2c + c^2b + c^2a + a^2c).$$

In bracket notation, this is $[3,0,0] \geq [2,1,0]$; since $(3,0,0) \succ (2,1,0)$ this is true by Muirhead's theorem.

Example 6.14   Given that $abc = 1$ and $a, b, c > 0$, show that

$$\frac{b+c}{1+a} + \frac{c+a}{1+b} + \frac{a+b}{1+c} \geq 3.$$

Multiplying both sides by $(1+a)(1+b)(1+c)$ and expanding brackets, we see that we want

$$2([2,1,0] + [2,0,0] + [1,1,0] + [1,0,0])$$
$$\geq [0,0,0] + 3[1,0,0] + 3[1,1,0] + [1,1,1].$$

Now we use the condition $abc = 1$ to homogenize this. We make all the terms degree three by multiplying by $(abc)^k = 1$ for an appropriate k. This is the same as adding k to each term inside the square brackets.

For example, the degree two term $[2,0,0] = a^2 + b^2 + c^2$ homogenizes using $(abc)^{\frac{1}{3}} = 1$ to the degree three term

$$(abc)^{\frac{1}{3}}\left(a^2 + b^2 + c^2\right) = a^{\frac{7}{3}}b^{\frac{1}{3}}c^{\frac{1}{3}} + a^{\frac{1}{3}}b^{\frac{7}{3}}c^{\frac{1}{3}} + a^{\frac{1}{3}}b^{\frac{1}{3}}c^{\frac{7}{3}}$$
$$= \left[\tfrac{7}{3}, \tfrac{1}{3}, \tfrac{1}{3}\right]$$
$$= \left[2 + \tfrac{1}{3}, 0 + \tfrac{1}{3}, 0 + \tfrac{1}{3}\right].$$

So we have reduced the problem to:

$$2\left(\left[2,1,0\right] + \left[\tfrac{7}{3}, \tfrac{1}{3}, \tfrac{1}{3}\right] + \left[\tfrac{4}{3}, \tfrac{4}{3}, \tfrac{1}{3}\right] + \left[\tfrac{5}{3}, \tfrac{2}{3}, \tfrac{2}{3}\right]\right)$$
$$\geq \left[1,1,1\right] + 3\left[\tfrac{5}{3}, \tfrac{2}{3}, \tfrac{2}{3}\right] + 3\left[\tfrac{4}{3}, \tfrac{4}{3}, \tfrac{1}{3}\right] + \left[1,1,1\right],$$

that is,

$$\left[2,1,0\right] + \left[2,1,0\right] + \left[\tfrac{7}{3}, \tfrac{1}{3}, \tfrac{1}{3}\right] + \left[\tfrac{7}{3}, \tfrac{1}{3}, \tfrac{1}{3}\right]$$
$$\geq \left[1,1,1\right] + \left[\tfrac{5}{3}, \tfrac{2}{3}, \tfrac{2}{3}\right] + \left[\tfrac{4}{3}, \tfrac{4}{3}, \tfrac{1}{3}\right] + \left[1,1,1\right].$$

This is true by Muirhead's theorem since each term on the left majorizes each term on the right.

Note that in the last example we multiplied out first and then homogenized; this is generally wise, as it simplifies the algebra.

Exercise 6d

Unless otherwise stated, all variables are positive real numbers. It is worth looking back through earlier exercises and examples to see whether Muirhead's theorem could have been used there.

1. Use Muirhead's theorem to prove

(a) the AM-GM inequality in the form

$$x_1^n + x_2^n + \cdots + x_n^n \geq n x_1 x_2 \cdots x_n;$$

(b) the RMS-AM inequality

$$n\left(x_1^2 + x_2^2 + \cdots + x_n^2\right) \geq (x_1 + x_2 + \cdots + x_n)^2$$

in the expanded form

$$(n-1)\left(x_1^2 + x_2^2 + \cdots + x_n^2\right) \geq \sum_{i \neq j} x_i x_j.$$

2. (a) Prove the converse of Muirhead's theorem: if

$$\sum_{\text{sym}} x_1^{a_1} x_2^{a_2} \cdots x_n^{a_n} \geq \sum_{\text{sym}} x_1^{b_1} x_2^{b_2} \cdots x_n^{b_n}$$

for positive real numbers $x_1, x_2, \ldots, x_n$, then

$$(a_1, a_2, \ldots, a_n) \succ (b_1, b_2, \ldots, b_n).$$

(b) Show that there is equality in Muirhead's theorem only if

$$(a_1, a_2, \ldots, a_n) = (b_1, b_2, \ldots, b_n) \quad \text{or} \quad x_1 = x_2 = \cdots = x_n.$$

3. Prove that

$$27(x+y)^2(y+z)^2(z+x)^2 \geq 64xyz(x+y+z)^3.$$

4. Show:

$$\left(\frac{a}{b} + \frac{b}{a}\right)\left(\frac{b}{c} + \frac{c}{b}\right)\left(\frac{c}{a} + \frac{a}{c}\right) \geq 2\left(1 + \frac{a+b+c}{\sqrt[3]{abc}}\right).$$

5. If a, b, c are the sides of a triangle, and $s = \frac{1}{2}(a+b+c)$, show that

$$16s(s-a)(s-b)(s-c)\sum \frac{1}{a^2} \leq 3\sum a^2.$$

6. Let $xyz = 1$. Prove that

$$\frac{x^3}{(1+y)(1+z)} + \frac{y^3}{(1+z)(1+x)} + \frac{z^3}{(1+x)(1+y)} \geq \frac{3}{4}.$$

7. Let $xyz \geq 1$. Show that

$$\frac{x^5 - x^2}{x^5 + y^2 + z^2} + \frac{y^5 - y^2}{x^2 + y^5 + z^2} + \frac{z^5 - z^2}{x^2 + y^2 + z^5} \geq 0.$$

[*IMO 2005*]

Chapter 7

The use of calculus

7.1 Introduction

Calculus is not necessary for national or international competitions such as the Olympiads, in the sense that no problem is set that specifically requires its use. It is even the case that no problem would wittingly be set for which the use of calculus would make it rather easier than if solved by other methods. However, calculus is a useful tool in dealing with inequalities, and for that reason it seems desirable to include a short account of the methods available at an elementary level. On the other hand we quote a number of theorems, rather than prove them, and the reader will either have met the ideas involved already or will do so as an undergraduate, when the study of inequalities becomes much more analytic. For the above reasons only a few illustrative examples and exercises are given. For the purposes of competitions the student is advised to learn Jensen's inequality, as knowledge of convex and concave functions should be known. I also recommend that, as an alternative resource, Lagrange's method of undetermined multipliers should be known for problems with constraints.

7.2 Stationary points

If $f(x)$ is differentiable then $f(x)$ is said to have a *stationary point* at $x = a$ if $f'(a) = 0$.

Theorem 7.1 *Suppose $f(x)$ is twice differentiable and has a stationary value at* $x = a$.

(i) *If $f''(a) > 0$, then the stationary value is a minimum.*

(ii) *If $f''(a) < 0$, then the stationary value is a maximum.*

Note the conditions are not necessary. The obvious counterexample is $f(x) = x^4$, which has a minimum of zero at $x = 0$, but $f''(0) = 0$.

Note also that such a minimum or maximum is local. For example, if there is a calculus minimum at $x = a$, then $f(a \pm \varepsilon) > f(a)$ for all sufficiently small values of $\varepsilon > 0$, but $f(x)$ may take values lower than $f(a)$ elsewhere.

Example 7.1

Prove that $f(x) \equiv x^4 + 4x^3 - 26x^2 - 60x + 225 \geq 0$.

We have

$$f'(x) = 4x^3 + 12x^2 - 52x - 60 = 0$$

where $x = -5$, $x = -1$, $x = 3$.

Now $f(-5) = f(3) = 0$ and $f(-1) = 256$.

Also

$$f''(x) = 12x^2 + 24x - 52$$

and $f''(-5) = f''(3) = 128$ and $f''(-1) = -64$. Hence the points $(-5, 0)$ and $(3, 0)$ are local minima and $(-1, 256)$ is a local maximum. Since $x^4 \to \infty$ as $x \to \pm\infty$ it follows that $f(x) \geq 0$ for all values of x.

This problem may also be solved by purely algebraic methods. If we put $x = y - 1$ then we have

$$f(y - 1) = y^4 - 32y^2 + 256 = (y^2 - 16)^2 \geq 0,$$

with equality if, and only if, $y = \pm 4$. It is also clear that for very small values of y the function is approximately equal to $256 - 32y^2$, showing $y = 0$ is a local maximum.

Example 7.2 Prove that $f(x) \equiv 5 \cosh x + 3 \sinh x \geq 4$, with equality if, and only if, $x = -\ln 2$.

$f(x) = 4e^x + e^{-x}$, so $f'(x) = 4e^x - e^{-x}$. Hence $f'(x) = 0$ when $e^{2x} = \frac{1}{4}$, that is, when $x = -\ln 2$.

Now $f''(-\ln 2) = f(-\ln 2) = 4$, so this is a minimum value.

An algebraic method exists. We have

$$f(x) - 4 = 4e^x - 4 + e^{-x} = (2e^{\frac{x}{2}} - e^{-\frac{x}{2}})^2 \geq 0,$$

with equality if, and only if, $x = -\ln 2$.

Exercise 7a

1. Prove that $3x^4 + 8x^3 - 66x^2 - 144x + 567 \geq 0$.

2. Let $f(x) = \dfrac{6x - 10}{x^2 - 1}$ for $x \neq -1, 1$.

   Prove that $f(x) \geq 9$ when $-1 < x < 1$ and $f(x) \leq 1$ when $x > 1$.

3. Prove that
$$0 \leq \frac{x^4}{(x^2 + 1)^3} \leq \frac{4}{27}.$$

4. Prove that
$$-1 \leq \frac{6x + 8}{x^2 + 1} \leq 9.$$

5. Prove that, for $0 \leq x \leq 1$,
$$\frac{x^2(1 - x)}{1 + x} \leq \left(\frac{\sqrt{5} - 1}{2}\right)^5.$$

6. Prove that
$$-\sqrt{3} \leq \frac{3 \sin x}{2 + \cos x} \leq \sqrt{3}.$$

7. For $a, b, c > 0$, prove that $a^5 + b^5 + c^5 \geq 5abc(b^2 - ac)$. When does equality hold?   *[David Monk]*

7.3 The meaning of the derivative

If $f'(x) > 0$ then the function $f(x)$ is increasing. This leads to a very simple theorem, which is nonetheless useful for managing some types of inequality.

Theorem 7.2 *If $f(x)$ is differentiable, $f(0) = 0$ and $f'(x) > 0$ for $0 < x < a$, then $f(x) > 0$ for $0 < x < a$.*

The interval can, of course, begin at a point different from $x = 0$.

Similarly, from $f(0) = 0$ and $f'(x) \geq 0$ for $0 < x < a$ we can deduce that $f(x) \geq 0$ for $0 < x < a$.

Example 7.3 Prove that, for $0 < x < \frac{\pi}{2}$,

$$x - \frac{x^3}{6} < \sin x < x.$$

Consider first the function $f(x) = x - \sin x$. We have

$$f'(x) = 1 - \cos x > 0$$

on $0 < x < \frac{\pi}{2}$. But $f(0) = 0$, so by theorem 7.2, we have $x - \sin x > 0$ on $0 < x < \frac{\pi}{2}$.

Now consider the function

$$g(x) = \sin x - x + \frac{x^3}{6}.$$

We have

$$g'(x) = h(x) = \cos x - 1 + \tfrac{1}{2}x^2$$

and

$$h'(x) = -\sin x + x = f(x).$$

Now $h(0) = 0$, and we have proved $h'(x) = f(x) > 0$ on $0 < x < \frac{\pi}{2}$ and hence $h(x) > 0$ on the same interval. Next $g(0) = 0$ and we have shown $g'(x) = h(x) > 0$ on the interval and so $g(x) > 0$ on $0 < x < \frac{\pi}{2}$.

Example 7.4   Prove *Huygen's inequality* that, for $0 < x < \frac{\pi}{2}$,

$$2 \sin x + \tan x \geq 3x.$$

Consider $f(x) = 2 \sin x + \tan x - 3x$. We have $f(0) = 0$, and

$$f'(x) = 2 \cos x + \sec^2 x - 3.$$

But by AM-GM

$$\cos x + \cos x + \frac{1}{\cos^2 x} \geq 3,$$

so that $f'(x) \geq 0$. The result now follows from the comment following theorem 7.2.

Exercise 7b

1. Prove that $\sin x > x \cos x$, for $0 < x < \pi$.

2. Prove that, for all $x > 0$ and all positive integers n,

$$e^x > 1 + x + \frac{x^2}{2!} + \cdots + \frac{x^n}{n!}.$$

3. Prove that, for $0 < u \leq x \leq \frac{\pi}{2}$,

$$\frac{\tan x}{x} \geq \frac{\tan u}{u}.$$

4. Prove that, for $0 < u \leq x \leq \frac{\pi}{2}$,

$$\frac{\sin x}{x} \leq \frac{\sin u}{u}.$$

5. Prove that, for $x > 0$, $x \neq 1$,

$$\frac{x \ln x}{x^2 - 1} \leq \frac{1}{2}.$$

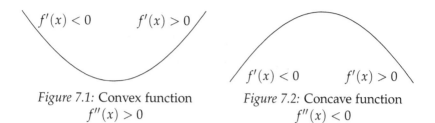

Figure 7.1: Convex function
$f''(x) > 0$

Figure 7.2: Concave function
$f''(x) < 0$

7.4   Concave and convex functions

Figure 7.1 and figure 7.2 illustrate convex and concave functions (when the functions concerned are twice differentiable) and are self-explanatory.

The simplest example of a convex function is $f(x) = x^2$, and the simplest example of a concave function is $f(x) = -x^2$. Sometimes the interval over which a function is convex or concave must be specified. For example, if $f(x) = \sin x$, we have $f''(x) = -\sin x < 0$ for $0 < x < \pi$, so $\sin x$ is concave on the interval $0 < x < \pi$.

A function may pass from being a convex function to being a concave function, and if it does then at the point $x = a$ where its character changes it must satisfy $f''(a) = 0$. A point where the second derivative vanishes is called a *point of inflexion*. Thus $\sin x$ has a point of inflexion at $x = \pi$ and on the interval $\pi < x < 2\pi$ it is convex.

It is also useful to think about how the tangent to the curve behaves. When a function is convex, as in figure 7.1, the tangent is below the curve, and when a function is concave, as in figure 7.2, the tangent is above the curve. At a point of inflexion, the tangent crosses the curve.

7.5   Jensen's inequality

Figure 7.3 shows a convex function $f(t)$ and illustrates Jensen's inequality for three points labelled $t = x, y, z$, where A is the centroid of the shaded triangle. The fact that $AP \geq BP$, shows that

$$\frac{f(x) + f(y) + f(z)}{3} \geq f\left(\frac{x+y+z}{3}\right)$$

with equality if, and only if, $x = y = z$.

More generally we have:

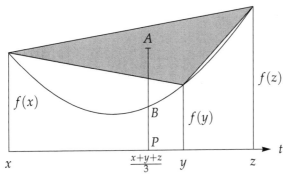

Figure 7.3: Convex function $f(t)$, $AP = \frac{f(x)+f(y)+f(z)}{3}$, $BP = f\left(\frac{x+y+z}{3}\right)$.

Theorem 7.3 (Jensen's inequality) *Let $f(x)$ be a convex function on (a,b) and suppose $a < x_1 \leq x_2 \leq \cdots \leq x_n < b$. Then*

$$\frac{f(x_1) + f(x_2) + \cdots + f(x_n)}{n} \geq f\left(\frac{x_1 + x_2 + \cdots + x_n}{n}\right).$$

If $f(x)$ is concave the direction of the inequality is reversed.
Equality holds if, and only if, $x_1 = x_2 = \cdots = x_n$.

Jensen's inequality opens up a whole new set of possibilities, as well as providing new proofs of known results. This is partly because of the ease of handling fractional indices. Amongst the examples we first give yet another proof of the AM-GM inequality.

Example 7.5 Let $f(x) = \ln x$. We have

$$f'(x) = \frac{1}{x} \quad \text{and} \quad f''(x) = -\frac{1}{x^2}.$$

It follows that $f(x)$ is concave for $x > 0$. Hence from the second part of theorem 7.3, for $x_1, x_2, \ldots, x_n > 0$,

$$\ln\left(\frac{x_1 + x_2 + \cdots + x_n}{n}\right) \geq \frac{\ln x_1 + \ln x_2 + \cdots + \ln x_n}{n}$$

and hence

$$\frac{x_1 + x_2 + \cdots + x_n}{n} \geq (x_1 x_2 \cdots x_n)^{\frac{1}{n}}.$$

Exercise 7c

1. Prove that

    (a) $1 - 2x \leq \cos \pi x$ for $0 \leq x \leq \frac{1}{2}$;

    (b) $\sin \pi x > \pi(x - x^2)$ for $0 < x < 1$.

2. Prove that $1 - 4x^2 \geq \cos \pi x$ for $-\frac{1}{2} \leq x \leq \frac{1}{2}$.
   Deduce that $4x(1 - x) \geq \sin \pi x$ for $0 \leq x \leq 1$.

3. Prove that, if $x, y, z > 0$ and $x + y + z = 24$, then $x^{\frac{1}{3}} + y^{\frac{1}{3}} + z^{\frac{1}{3}} \leq 6$.

4. Prove that, if $l, m, n > 0$, then

$$l^3(m + n) + m^3(n + l) + n^3(l + m) \geq 2lmn(l + m + n).$$

5. Prove that amongst all triangles with inradius 1 the equilateral triangle has the shortest perimeter.

7.6 Bernoulli's inequality

Theorem 7.4 (Bernoulli's inequality) *Let x be a positive real number, not equal to 1. Then*

$$x^p - 1 > p(x - 1) \quad \text{if} \quad p < 0 \text{ or } p > 1;$$
$$x^p - 1 < p(x - 1) \quad \text{if} \quad 0 < p < 1.$$

PROOF Let $f(x) = x^p - 1 - p(x - 1)$. We have $f(1) = 0$. Now

$$f'(x) = p(x^{p-1} - 1).$$

Now if $p > 1$ or $p < 0$, $f'(x)$ is negative for $0 < x < 1$, is zero when $x = 1$ and is positive when $x > 1$. Thus $f(x)$ has a minimum at $x = 1$. But if $0 < p < 1$, then $p - 1 < 0$, and so $x^{p-1} > 1$ for $0 < x < 1$. Hence $f'(x)$ is positive for $0 < x < 1$, is zero when $x = 1$ and is negative for $x > 1$. Accordingly $f(x)$ now has a maximum at $x = 1$. ❑

Corollary 7.1 (Power means) *Let $a_1, a_2, \ldots, a_n > 0$. Then*

(i) *for $t > 1$ or $t < 0$,*

$$\frac{1}{n}\sum a_k^t \geq \left(\frac{1}{n}\sum a_k\right)^t,$$

(ii) *for $0 < t < 1$,*

$$\frac{1}{n}\sum a_k^t \leq \left(\frac{1}{n}\sum a_k\right)^t.$$

PROOF Let $\frac{1}{n}\sum a_k = \mu$. Put $x = \dfrac{a_k}{\mu}$ then, by theorem 7.4 with $p = t$ we have, on multiplying by μ^t,

$$a_k^t - \mu^t \geq t\mu^{t-1}(a_k - \mu).$$

Summing over k gives $\sum a_k^t \geq n\mu^t$, as required. When $0 < t < 1$, the direction of the inequality is reversed, as in theorem 7.4. ❑

For example, if $a, b, c > 0$, then

$$\sqrt{a} + \sqrt{b} + \sqrt{c} \leq \sqrt{3(a + b + c)}.$$

Corollary 7.2 (Weighted power means) *Let $a_1, a_2, \ldots, a_n > 0$ and let $w_1, w_2, \ldots, w_n > 0$, $w_1 + w_2 + \ldots + w_n = 1$. Then*

(i) *for $t > 1$ or $t < 0$,*

$$\sum w_k a_k^t \geq \left(\sum_k w_k a_k\right)^t,$$

(ii) *for $0 < t < 1$,*

$$\sum w_k a_k^t \leq \left(\sum_k w_k a_k\right)^t.$$

PROOF Define

$$x_k = \frac{a_k}{\sum w_k a_k},$$

so that $\sum w_k x_k = 1$. Now from theorem 7.4, for $t < 0$ or $t > 1$, we have

$$w_k x_k^t - w_k \geq t(w_k x_k - w_k).$$

Summing over k gives $\sum w_k x_k^t \geq 1$, from which the result follows. If $0 < t < 1$ the direction of the inequality is reversed, as in theorem 7.4. ❑

In the following theorem, the definition of power mean in section 6.3 on page 78 is extended to allow t to be any non-zero real number:

General power mean *For any non-zero real number t, the* general power mean *of $a_1, a_2, \ldots, a_n > 0$ is*

$$M_t = \left(\frac{a_1^t + a_2^t + \cdots + a_n^t}{n} \right)^{\frac{1}{t}}.$$

Theorem 7.5 (General power means inequality) *Let r, s be real numbers with $r < s$. Then $M_r \leq M_s$.*

PROOF We look at the various cases.

(a) If $0 < r < s$, then apply corollary 7.1 to $a_1^r, a_2^r, \ldots, a_n^r$ with $t = \frac{s}{r} > 1$. This gives

$$\frac{1}{n} \sum (a_i^r)^{\frac{s}{r}} \geq \left(\frac{1}{n} \sum a_i^r \right)^{\frac{s}{r}},$$

and so

$$M_r = \left(\frac{1}{n} \sum a_i^r \right)^{\frac{1}{r}} \leq \left(\frac{1}{n} \sum a_i^s \right)^{\frac{1}{s}} = M_s.$$

(b) If $r < s < 0$, then $0 < -s < -r$ and so, by (a), $M_{-s} \leq M_{-r}$. Applying this to $a_1^{-1}, a_2^{-1}, \ldots, a_n^{-1}$, we have

$$\left(\frac{1}{n} \sum a_i^s \right)^{-\frac{1}{s}} \leq \left(\frac{1}{n} \sum a_i^r \right)^{-\frac{1}{r}},$$

and so

$$M_r = \left(\frac{1}{n} \sum a_i^r \right)^{\frac{1}{r}} \leq \left(\frac{1}{n} \sum a_i^s \right)^{\frac{1}{s}} = M_s.$$

(c) If $r < 0 < s$, then by AM-GM on $a_1^s, a_2^s, \ldots, a_n^s$

$$g = \sqrt[n]{a_1 a_2 \cdots a_n} \leq \left(\frac{1}{n} \sum a_i^s \right)^{\frac{1}{s}} = M_s.$$

Using the same result, but with $a_1^{-1}, a_2^{-1}, \ldots, a_n^{-1}$, we have

$$M_{-r} = \left(\frac{1}{n} \sum (a_i^{-1})^{-r} \right)^{-\frac{1}{r}} \geq \frac{1}{\sqrt[n]{a_1 a_2 \cdots a_n}} = \frac{1}{g}$$

and so

$$M_r = \left(\frac{1}{n}\sum a_i^r\right)^{\frac{1}{r}} \le g.$$

Hence again $M_r \le M_s$ since $M_r \le g \le M_s$.

(d) Finally, if one of r or s is equal to zero, we use the fact that $M_0 = g$ and the result proved in (c). $\square$

7.7 Taylor series

Infinite series expansions may be used to prove certain inequalities. We quote, without proof, the following theorem:

Theorem 7.6 (Taylor's theorem) *If f, f', f'', ..., $f^{(n-1)}$ are continuous in the interval $a \le x \le a+h$, and $f^{(n)}$ exists for $a < x < a+h$, then*

$$f(a+h) = f(a) + hf'(a) + \frac{h^2}{2!}f''(a) + \cdots + \frac{h^{n-1}}{(n-1)!}f^{(n-1)}(a) + R_n,$$

where $R_n = \dfrac{h^n}{n!}f^{(n)}(a+\theta h)$ with $0 < \theta < 1$.

The term R_n is a remainder, which may be thought of as a truncation error if omitted. The form of the remainder term given here is due to Lagrange. In school mathematics the limit of Taylor's theorem as $n \to \infty$ is quoted without much attention being given to the convergence of the resulting Taylor series expansion.

Example 7.6   Prove that

$$x < \tfrac{1}{2}\ln\frac{1+x}{1-x}$$

for $0 < x < 1$.

The Taylor series for the function on the right, valid for $0 < x < 1$ is

$$x + \frac{x^3}{3} + \frac{x^5}{5} + \cdots + \frac{x^{2n+1}}{2n+1} + \cdots > x.$$

Two more important examples of Taylor series expansions are the following:

$$e^x = 1 + x + \frac{x^2}{2!} + \frac{x^3}{3!} + \cdots + \frac{x^n}{n!} + \cdots$$

$$\ln(1+x) = x - \frac{x^2}{2} + \frac{x^3}{3} - \cdots + (-1)^{n+1}\frac{x^n}{n} + \cdots$$

The first of these converges for all x and the second for $-1 < x \leq 1$.

We now use these series to prove the result quoted in section 6.3 about M_t, the mean of order t, and g, the geometric mean, of $a_1, a_2, \ldots, a_n$:

Result 7.1 $M_t \to g$ as $t \to 0$.

PROOF First we write

$$a_i^t = e^{t \ln a_i} = 1 + t \ln a_i + \mathcal{O}(t^2)$$

where the notation $\mathcal{O}(t^2)$ means that all subsequent terms involve a power of t which is at least 2. It follows that

$$\sum a_i^t = n + t \sum \ln a_i + \mathcal{O}(t^2)$$
$$= n + t \ln(a_1 a_2 \cdots a_n) + \mathcal{O}(t^2),$$

so that

$$\frac{\sum a_i^t}{n} = 1 + t \ln g + \mathcal{O}(t^2)$$

and hence

$$\ln\left(\frac{\sum a_i^t}{n}\right) = t \ln g + \mathcal{O}(t^2),$$

using the logarithmic series. Hence $\ln M_t = \ln g + \mathcal{O}(t)$ and $M_t \to g$ as $t \to 0$. ❑

7.8   Functions of two real variables

Let $f(x,y)$ be a function of two real variables with continuous partial derivatives of all orders, then the Taylor series expansion about the point

(a, b) is

$$f(a + h, b + k) =$$

$$f(a, b) + h\frac{\partial f}{\partial x} + k\frac{\partial f}{\partial y} + \frac{1}{2}\left(h^2\frac{\partial^2 f}{\partial x^2} + 2hk\frac{\partial^2 f}{\partial x \partial y} + k^2\frac{\partial^2 f}{\partial y^2}\right) + \cdots$$

where the partial derivatives are calculated at (a, b). The point (a, b) is said to be a *stationary point* if the first-order terms vanish for all h, k. This happens if, and only if,

$$\frac{\partial f}{\partial x} = 0 \quad \text{and} \quad \frac{\partial f}{\partial y} = 0.$$

The stationary point (a, b) is a *minimum* if the second-order terms are positive definite. This is so if

$$\frac{\partial^2 f}{\partial x^2} > 0 \quad \text{and} \quad \frac{\partial^2 f}{\partial x^2} \times \frac{\partial^2 f}{\partial y^2} > \left(\frac{\partial^2 f}{\partial x \partial y}\right)^2.$$

Similarly, the stationary point (a, b) is a *maximum* if the second-order terms are negative definite. This is so if

$$\frac{\partial^2 f}{\partial x^2} < 0 \quad \text{and} \quad \frac{\partial^2 f}{\partial x^2} \times \frac{\partial^2 f}{\partial y^2} > \left(\frac{\partial^2 f}{\partial x \partial y}\right)^2.$$

If the stationary point is neither a maximum or a minimum, it is known as a *saddle point*. This is like a pass between two mountains. It is a minimum as one follows the path from one peak to the other, but it is a maximum as one crosses from one valley to the other via the pass.

Example 7.7   Find all the stationary points of the function

$$f(x, y) = x^3 + 2xy - 3y^2 + 1$$

and determine whether any of them are maxima or minima.

We have

$$\frac{\partial f}{\partial x} = 0 = 3x^2 + 2y$$

$$\text{and} \quad \frac{\partial f}{\partial y} = 0 = 2x - 6y$$

so $x = 3y$ and $27y^2 + 2y = 0$. Hence $y = 0, x = 0$ and $y = -\frac{2}{27}, x = -\frac{2}{9}$ are the two stationary points.

Now

$$\frac{\partial^2 f}{\partial x^2} = 6x, \quad \frac{\partial^2 f}{\partial y^2} = -6, \quad \text{and} \quad \frac{\partial^2 f}{\partial x\, \partial y} = 2.$$

Hence the point $(0,0)$ is neither a maximum nor a minimum. But at the point $\left(-\frac{2}{9}, -\frac{2}{27}\right)$ the second-order terms are negative definite and there is a maximum.

Exercise 7d

1. Show that the function $f(x,y) = x^2 + xy + y^2 - 3x$ has one stationary point, which is a minimum.

2. Find the maxima, minima or saddle points of the function $f(x,y) = 2x^2 - 4xy + y^4 - 9y$.

3. Find the maxima, minima or saddle points of the function $f(x,y) = x^3 - 12x + y^3 + 3y^2 - 9y$.

4. Find the maxima, minima or saddle points of the function $f(x,y) = e^{-x^3+3x-3y^2}$.

5. Find the maxima, minima or saddle points of the function

$$f(x,y) = \frac{x + y - 1}{2x^2 + y^2 + 2}.$$

Sometimes when there are two or more variables and the stationary point is known it is more effective to use purely algebraic methods, rather than calculus methods, to determine whether a maximum or a minimum is involved.

Example 7.8   Suppose $x, y, z > 0$ and let

$$f(x,y,z) \equiv 2(xy^2 + yz^2 + zx^2) - 3xyz - (x^2y + y^2z + z^2x).$$

Prove that there exists a neighbourhood of $x = y = z = m > 0$ for which $f(x,y,z) \geq 0$.

Note first that $f(m,m,m) = 0$. We investigate the value of $f(x,y,z)$ close to the point (m,m,m). Make the substitutions $x = m + u$, $y = m + v$, $z = m + w$ where u, v, w are small quantities, to give

$$f(m+u, m+v, m+w) = 2((m+u)(m+v)^2 + \cdots)$$
$$- 3(m+u)(m+v)(m+w) - ((m+u)^2(m+v) + \cdots). \quad (7.1)$$

This expression might seem to be a cubic in m, but the term in m^3 is $f(m,m,m)$, which is zero. The coefficient of m^2 is

$$2\left(\sum u + 2\sum u\right) - 3\sum u - \left(\sum u + 2\sum u\right),$$

which is also zero. So actually the expression (7.1) is linear in m. The coefficient of m is

$$2\left(\sum u^2 + 2\sum uv\right) - 3\sum uv - \left(\sum u^2 + 2\sum uv\right) = \sum u^2 - \sum uv.$$

Finally, the constant term is clearly $f(u,v,w)$. Hence we have shown, without too much explicit algebra, but simply by a consideration of symmetric functions of u, v and w, that

$$f(m+u, m+v, m+w) = f(u,v,w) + m(u^2 + v^2 + w^2 - vw - wu - uv).$$

By equation (2.1), and because $m > 0$, the final term in this expression is non-negative. The expression $f(u,v,w)$ is a cubic, and hence is much smaller in magnitude than the quadratic expression $m(u^2 + v^2 + w^2 - vw - wu - uv)$ for small values of u, v and w. This means that, even if $f(u,v,w) < 0$, its negative effect will be cancelled out by the positive contribution of $m(u^2 + v^2 + w^2 - vw - wu - uv)$. As a result we know that, for all sufficiently small values of u, v and w,

$$f(m+u, m+v, m+w) \geq 0$$

with equality if, and only if, $u = v = w$.

This style of argument turns out to be very important in the next section, in order to establish that particular points in three (or more) dimensions which we believe to be maxima or minima really are maxima or minima.

7.9 Lagrange's method of undetermined multipliers

This is a method for determining the stationary values of a function of several variables subject to a number of *constraints* (or *side conditions*, as they are sometimes called). We describe the method by giving some examples.

Example 7.9   Find the minimum value of

$$f(x,y,z) = x^2 + 2y^2 + 3z^2$$

subject to $x + y + z = 11$.

We consider the function $F(x,y,z) = f(x,y,z) - \lambda(x + y + z - 11)$ where λ is known as the multiplier. Any minimum of f will give a minimum of F. So now we simply solve the equations

$$\frac{\partial F}{\partial x} = \frac{\partial F}{\partial y} = \frac{\partial F}{\partial z} = 0.$$

This gives $2x - \lambda = 4y - \lambda = 6 - \lambda = 0$ and so $\lambda = 2x = 4y = 6z$. Since $x + y + z = 11$ we therefore have four equations for the four unknowns λ, x, y, z. It follows that

$$\frac{\lambda}{2} + \frac{\lambda}{4} + \frac{\lambda}{6} = 11$$

and hence $\lambda = 12$ and $x = 6, y = 3, z = 2$. Then $f(x,y,z) = 66$.

To show this is a minimum put $x = 6 + u, y = 3 + v, z = 2 + w$. Since $x + y + z = 11$ we have $u + v + w = 0$. Also

$$x^2 + 2y^2 + 3z^2 = 66 + 12(u + v + w) + u^2 + 2v^2 + 3w^2$$
$$= 66 + (u^2 + 2v^2 + 3w^2)$$
$$\geq 66.$$

Example 7.10 What is the minimum distance from the origin to the plane with equation $2x + 3y + 6z = 49$?

In a similar fashion to example 7.9 we construct the function

$$F(x,y,z) = x^2 + y^2 + z^2 - \lambda(2x + 3y + 6z - 49)$$

and set its three partial derivatives to zero, giving

$$2x - 2\lambda = 2y - 3\lambda = 2z - 6\lambda = 0,$$

from which $\lambda = 2$, $x = 2$, $y = 3$, $z = 6$ and $\sqrt{x^2 + y^2 + z^2} = 7$. The fact that this is a minimum is evident from geometrical considerations. Alternatively, precisely the same method as in example 7.9 will show it is a minimum.

Both this and the previous example may be solved using the Cauchy-Schwarz inequality.

In general if there is a function of n variables $x_1, x_2, \ldots, x_n$ subject to m constraints, we have to use m multipliers $\lambda_1, \lambda_2, \ldots, \lambda_m$. The m constraints together with n partial derivatives put equal to zero produce $m + n$ equations for the $m + n$ unknowns $x_1, x_2, \ldots, x_n, \lambda_1, \lambda_2, \ldots, \lambda_m$.

The problem with using the method of Lagrange multipliers in inequality problems in two variables is that it only demonstrates the existence of (local) maxima or minima in the x and y directions. It may well be that a particular point turns out to be a saddle point and with more than three variables this becomes more complicated still. Moreover, like any calculus method, it does not guarantee that a point is a global maximum or minimum.

The strength of the Lagrange multiplier method is that is provides a relatively easy way to identify 'critical points', which may turn out to be maxima or minima. Having found these points, it can be very tedious to specify their exact nature. If we are lucky, this might be evident from geometrical or other considerations. Failing that, the usual approach is the one illustrated in example 7.9, and it involves the following steps, described for the two variable case.

(a) We consider a point in the neighbourhood of the critical point (a, b). This point is represented as $(a + u, b + v)$, where u and v are small quantities.

(b) The fact that the side condition still holds will give us a constraint involving u and v.

(c) Denoting by $f(x,y)$ the expression which is to be maximised or minimised, we calculate its value $f(a + u, b + v)$ at a neighbouring point and we aim to show that $f(a + u, b + v) - f(a,b) \geq 0$ for a minimum or that $f(a + u, b + v) - f(a,b) \leq 0$ for a maximum. This must be true whatever (small) values of u and v are taken.

(d) This is usually done by incorporating the constraint into $f(a + u, b + v) - f(a,b)$ and showing that it is always positive or negative.

However, if this technique uses the fact that u and v are small, then it still only establishes the existence of a local maximum or minimum. Note that the argument in example 7.9 involves the expression $u^2 + 2v^2 + 3w^2$, guaranteeing that the minimum is a global one.

In fact, it seems as though we have simply replaced one constrained maximisation problem by another one! Our hope is, of course, that it is a much simpler problem and that we can solve it. However, there is nearly always a better approach than Lagrange multipliers for the types of problems which are set in Olympiad competitions. Remember, above all, that if you identify the critical point but fail to demonstrate that it is a maximum or minimum you will not be judged to have solved the problem.

Example 7.11   Find the lengths of the axes of the conic in which the ellipsoid

$$x^2 + \frac{y^2}{2} + \frac{z^2}{5} = 1$$

meets the plane with equation $x + y + z = 0$.

The ellipsoid is symmetrical about the origin, which lies in the plane, so the ellipse—the central conic which is formed by their intersection—is also symmetrical about the origin. The distance of the point (x, y, z) from the origin is $\sqrt{x^2 + y^2 + z^2}$ and the ellipse's major and minor axis are given by the points which are farthest from and closest to the centre. Hence we need to find the stationary values of $x^2 + y^2 + z^2$ subject to the above side conditions.

We therefore form the function

$$F(x, y, z) = x^2 + y^2 + z^2 + \lambda\left(x^2 + \frac{y^2}{2} + \frac{z^2}{5} - 1\right) + 2\mu(x + y + z),$$

where λ and 2μ are the multipliers. The solution to the problem arises therefore from the five equations

$$x^2 + \frac{y^2}{2} + \frac{z^2}{5} = 1,$$

$$x + y + z = 0,$$

$$x + \lambda x + \mu = 0,$$

$$y + \frac{\lambda y}{2} + \mu = 0,$$

$$z + \frac{\lambda z}{5} + \mu = 0.$$

Multiplying the last three equations by x, y, z respectively and adding gives

$$f = x^2 + y^2 + z^2 = -\lambda\left(x^2 + \frac{y^2}{2} + \frac{z^2}{5}\right) - \mu(x + y + z) = -\lambda.$$

Hence the stationary values of f are given by

$$(f - 1)x - \mu = 0,$$
$$(f - 2)y - 2\mu = 0,$$
$$(f - 5)z - 5\mu = 0,$$
$$x + y + z = 0.$$

Hence

$$\frac{1}{f - 1} + \frac{2}{f - 2} + \frac{5}{f - 5} = \frac{x + y + z}{\mu} = 0$$

from which $f = 3$ or $\frac{5}{4}$, which are the squares of the lengths of the axes.

The reason for the adjective 'undetermined' can be seen from this example, as μ does not need to be evaluated.

Exercise 7e

1. Let $x, y, z > 0$ and $x + 4y + 9z = 3$. Find the stationary value of

$$\frac{1}{x} + \frac{1}{y} + \frac{1}{z},$$

deciding whether it is a maximum or a minimum.

2. Let $a, b, c, x, y, z > 0$. Find the stationary value of

$$\frac{a}{x} + \frac{b}{y} + \frac{c}{z}$$

given $ax + by + cz = 1$, deciding whether it is a maximum or a minimum.

3. If $x, y, z \geq 0$ and $xy + yz + zx = 9$ find the stationary value of $x + y + z$, deciding whether it is a maximum or a minimum.

4. Find the minimum value of $x^2 + 5y^2 + 8z^2$ given $xy + yz + zx = -1$.

5. Find the maximum and minimum values of xy subject to

$$3x^2 + 4xy + 3y^2 = 10.$$

Chapter 8

Polynomial equations

8.1 Symmetric polynomials

The inequalities we have been studying often contain expressions like these:

$$a + b + c$$
$$ab + ac + ad + bc + bd + cd$$
$$a^3 + b^3$$
$$abcde$$

Such expressions are called *symmetric polynomials*. These are polynomials in n variables which have the property that, if the variables are permuted amongst themselves, the value of the expression remains the same. Formally, we have the following definition.

Definition *A polynomial $P(x_1, x_2, \ldots, x_n)$ in n variables is symmetric if, for any permutation $(\sigma(1), \sigma(2), \ldots, \sigma(n))$ of the subscripts $(1, 2, \ldots, n)$,*

$$P(x_{\sigma(1)}, x_{\sigma(2)}, \ldots, x_{\sigma(n)}) \equiv P(x_1, x_2, \ldots, x_n).$$

Suppose, for example, that we rearrange the subscripts $(1, 2, 3, 4)$ in the order $(2, 3, 1, 4)$. Then the expression $x_1^2 + x_2^2 + x_3^2 + x_4^2$ becomes $x_2^2 + x_3^2 + x_1^2 + x_4^2$, which is identical, and since this happens for any such permutation of $(1, 2, 3, 4)$ the expression is symmetric. In contrast, the expression $x_1 x_2^2 + x_2 x_3^2 + x_3 x_4^2 + x_4 x_1^2$ becomes $x_2 x_3^2 + x_3 x_1^2 + x_1 x_4^2 + x_4 x_2^2$, which is different, so this expression is not symmetric.

In what follows, we will use a and b for the variables in a symmetric polynomial with two variables; similarly a, b, c will denote three variables and a, b, c, d will denote four.

A particular group of symmetric polynomials is especially important. For four variables, these are:

$$a + b + c + d$$
$$ab + ac + ad + bc + bd + cd$$
$$abc + abd + acd + bcd$$
$$abcd$$

These are known as the *elementary symmetric polynomials*. They comprise sums of all products formed by taking the four variables one at a time, two at a time, three at a time and four at a time. Notice, for example, that the second of these consists of six terms since there are $\binom{4}{2} = 6$ ways of choosing two objects out of four. An important result, which we will quote but not prove, assures us that every symmetric polynomial P can be written in terms of elementary symmetric polynomials. For example,

$$a^2 + b^2 + c^2 + d^2 = (a + b + c + d)^2 - 2(ab + ac + ad + bc + bd + cd)$$

It will be helpful to express this using sigma notation:

$$\sum a^2 = \left(\sum a\right)^2 - 2\sum ab.$$

8.2   Roots of polynomial equations

Suppose that a quadratic equation $x^2 - px + q = 0$ has roots a and b. Then the quadratic can be factorised as $(x - a)(x - b) = 0$ and it follows that $p = a + b$ and $q = ab$. This generalises to any number of roots. For instance, the quartic $x^4 - px^3 + qx^2 - rx + s = 0$ has roots a, b, c, d if, and only if,

$$p = \sum a, \quad q = \sum ab, \quad r = \sum abc, \quad s = abcd.$$

It is possible to use this fact to discover relationships between symmetric polynomials. For instance, since a, b, c, d are roots it follows that we have four equations of the form

$$a^4 - pa^3 + qa^2 - ra + s = 0.$$

Adding these together, we conclude that

$$\sum a^4 - p \sum a^3 + q \sum a^2 - r \sum a + 4s = 0$$

and, in turn, we have

$$\sum a^4 - \sum a \sum a^3 + \sum ab \sum a^2 - \sum abc \sum a + 4abcd = 0.$$

Example 8.1   Prove that, if $a + b + c \geq 0$, then $a^3 + b^3 + c^3 \geq 3abc$.

Consider the cubic $x^3 - px^2 + qx - r = 0$ with roots a, b, c. Then $p = \sum a$, $q = \sum ab$ and $r = abc$. By adding together three equations of the form $a^3 - pa^2 + qa - s = 0$, we obtain $\sum a^3 = p \sum a^2 - q \sum a + 3r$, and so

$$\sum a^3 - 3abc = \sum a^3 - 3r = p(p^2 - 2q) - pq = p(p^2 - 3q).$$

Since $p \geq 0$ it suffices to show that $p^2 - 3q \geq 0$. This is just $\sum a^2 \geq \sum ab$, which is inequality (2.1) on page 10.

This is the same problem as example 2.2 on page 12, but the method here avoids using the factorisation and might be considered to be more natural.

8.3   Cubic equations with real roots

A cubic equation $y^3 - 3ry^2 + sy - t = 0$ can always be reduced, by means of the substitution $y = x + r$, to one of the form $x^3 - 3px + q = 0$. It turns out that there is a condition, sufficiently simple to remember and therefore useful for problem-solving, for such a cubic to have three real roots.

Theorem 8.1 *The cubic* $P(x) \equiv x^3 - 3px + q = 0$ *has three real roots if, and only if,*

$$4p^3 \geq q^2. \tag{8.1}$$

PROOF The simplest proof of this fact uses calculus. It is possible to avoid this, but the resulting argument is somewhat tortuous.

If $p = 0$ and $q \neq 0$, there is one real and two complex roots and (8.1) does not hold.

If $q = 0$, then the roots are $0, \pm\sqrt{3p}$, so we need $p \geq 0$ for real roots, and (8.1) is again trivial.

So we assume that neither p nor q is zero.

We have $P'(x) \equiv 3x^2 - 3p$. If there are three real roots, there must be two turning points, so we need $p \geq 0$. The coordinates of the turning points are $(-\sqrt{p}, q + 2p\sqrt{p})$, which is a maximum, and $(\sqrt{p}, q - 2p\sqrt{p})$ which is a minimum. The maximum must have positive y-coordinate and the minimum a negative y-coordinate, so we obtain (8.1).

Conversely, if (8.1) holds, we have $p \geq 0$, a positive maximum and a negative minimum, so there are three real roots. $\square$

Exercise 8a

1. If $a, b, c > 0$, find all solutions of the equations $abc = 2 + a + b + c$ and $ab + bc + ca = 12$.

2. If $a + b + c + d = 0$, prove that $a^3 + b^3 + c^3 + d^3 > 0$ if, and only if, $a^5 + b^5 + c^5 + d^5 > 0$.   *[BMO2 Feb 2004, adapted]*

3. Show that the cubic equation $2x^3 + 3x^2 - 12x + k = 0$ (where k is real) has three real roots if, and only if, $-20 \leq k \leq 7$.

4. Let a, b, c be distinct integers satisfying
$$\frac{a}{b} + \frac{b}{c} + \frac{c}{a} = 3.$$
Find the maximum value of $\dfrac{b}{a} + \dfrac{c}{b} + \dfrac{a}{c}$.

5. Let a, b, c, d be distinct real numbers such that
$$\frac{a}{b} + \frac{b}{c} + \frac{c}{d} + \frac{d}{a} = 4$$
and $ac = bd$. Find the maximum value of $\dfrac{a}{c} + \dfrac{b}{d} + \dfrac{c}{a} + \dfrac{d}{b}$.

6. Let a, b, c be real numbers satisfying $a \leq b \leq c$, $a + b + c = 6$ and $ab + bc + ca = 9$. Prove that $0 \leq a \leq 1 \leq b \leq 3 \leq c \leq 4$.

8.4 Polynomials with positive roots

From the point of view of creating inequalities, it is particularly useful to consider polynomial equations for which all the roots are positive. It follows that the coefficients of the polynomial are also positive, given that we write them, as above, with alternating signs.

First, we consider a quadratic $P(x) \equiv x^2 - px + q$ with positive roots a and b. Since the roots are real we have $p^2 \geq 4q$ and so $\frac{p}{2} \geq \sqrt{q}$. This is, of course, the AM-GM inequality for a and b.

Next, take the cubic polynomial $P(x) \equiv x^3 - px^2 + qx - r$. As it has three positive roots, the x-coordinates of the two turning points in between are also positive. We can therefore differentiate $P(x)$ and apply the quadratic analysis to $P'(x) \equiv 3x^2 - 2px + q$, resulting in the inequality $p^2 \geq 3q$. Now consider the cubic $Q(x) \equiv rx^3 - qx^2 + px - 1$, whose roots are the reciprocals of a, b and c. Differentiating, we obtain $Q'(x) \equiv 3rx^2 - 2qx + p$ and another inequality $q^2 \geq 3pr$. Combining these, we immediately obtain $p^3 \geq 27r$, which is the AM-GM inequality for a, b and c.

We can now continue in this vein, differentiating enough times to produce a quadratic with non-negative discriminant, and remembering also to consider related polynomials with coefficients 'reversed'. Thus for the quartic $P(x) \equiv x^4 - px^3 + qx^2 - rx + s$ we obtain inequalities

$$3p^2 \geq 8q, \quad 4q^2 \geq 9pr, \quad 3r^2 \geq 8qs.$$

These, as might by now be expected, can be combined to produce the AM-GM inequality for a, b, c and d. However, it is worthwhile looking at this process a little more systematically, and deriving a whole sequence of inequalities as a result.

8.5 Inequalities for symmetric functions

Define the following p_i, for $1 \leq i \leq n$, which are symmetric functions of the n positive real numbers $a_1, a_2, \ldots, a_n$:

$$np_1 = \sum a_i$$

$$\binom{n}{2} p_2^2 = \sum a_i a_j$$

$$\binom{n}{3} p_3^3 = \sum a_i a_j a_k$$

$$\vdots$$

$$p_n^n = a_1 a_2 \cdots a_n.$$

It is also convenient to define p_0 as 1. If the polynomial with positive roots $a_1, a_2, \ldots, a_n$ is written

$$P(x) \equiv x^n - q_1 x^{n-1} + q_2 x^{n-2} - \cdots + (-1)^i q_i x^{n-i} + \cdots + (-1)^n q_n$$

then $p_i^i = q_i \binom{n}{i}^{-1}$, so we can also write

$$P(x) \equiv x^n - \binom{n}{1} p_1 x^{n-1} + \binom{n}{2} p_2^2 x^{n-2} - \cdots$$
$$+ (-1)^i \binom{n}{i} p_i^i x^{n-i} + \cdots + (-1)^n p_n^n$$

$$\equiv \sum_{r=0}^{n} (-1)^{n-r} \binom{n}{n-r} p_{n-r}^{n-r} x^r.$$

Lemma 8.1 *With $P(x)$ defined as above,*

$$p_{i+1}^{2(i+1)} \geq p_i^i \, p_{i+2}^{i+2}$$

for $n \geq 2$ and $0 \leq i \leq n-2$.

PROOF We use induction on n.

For $n = 2$, the result translates as $\left(\frac{q_1}{2}\right)^2 \geq q_2$, which has been derived above.

Assume that the result is true for $n = k$ and consider

$$P(x) \equiv \sum_{r=0}^{k+1} (-1)^{k+1-r} \binom{k+1}{k+1-r} p_{k+1-r}^{k+1-r} x^r.$$

Differentiating, we obtain

$$P'(x) \equiv \sum_{r=1}^{k+1} (-1)^{k+1-r} \binom{k+1}{k+1-r} r \, p_{k+1-r}^{k+1-r} x^{r-1}$$

$$\equiv \sum_{r=0}^{k} (-1)^{k-r} \binom{k+1}{k-r} (r+1) p_{k-r}^{k-r} x^r,$$

where we have reindexed the summation. Now, if we write

$$P'(x) \equiv (k+1) \sum_{r=0}^{k} (-1)^{k-r} \binom{k}{k-r} p_{k-r}^{k-r} x^r$$

$$\equiv (k+1)Q(x),$$

(after a little work on the binomial coefficient) we see that $Q(x)$ is a polynomial of degree k, to which we can apply the induction hypothesis to obtain

$$p_{i+1}^{2(i+1)} \geq p_i^i \, p_{i+2}^{i+2}$$

for $0 \leq i \leq k-2$. However, there is one more inequality to derive, namely

$$p_k^{2k} \geq p_{k-1}^{k-1} p_{k+1}^{k+1}.$$

This is obtained by 'reversing' the polynomial $P(x)$ and applying the same treatment. ❑

Note also that, in the preceding analysis, unless the roots $a_1, a_2, \ldots, a_n$ of $P(x)$ are all equal, the roots of the derived polynomials will be distinct and these inequalities become strict.

It is also worth pointing out that these relations are necessary for $P(x)$ to have n positive real roots, but they are not sufficient. Incidentally, the argument which has been made can be rephrased in terms of a homogeneous polynomial $P(x) \equiv x^n - q_1 x^{n-1} y + q_2 x^{n-2} y^2 - \cdots + (-1)^n q_n y^n$ and applying partial differentiation.

Theorem 8.2 *With p_i defined as on page 115,*

$$p_1 \geq p_2 \geq \cdots \geq p_n$$

with equality if, and only if, $a_1 = a_2 = \cdots = a_n$.

PROOF This can be rephrased as $p_i \geq p_{i+1}$ for $1 \leq i \leq n-1$. We use induction on i.

When $i = 1$ we obtain from lemma 8.1 that $p_1^1 \geq p_2^2$ (since $p_0 = 1$) and take square roots.

Suppose now that the result is true for $i = k$, so we have $p_{k-1} \geq p_k$. Using lemma 8.1, we have $p_k^{2k} \geq p_{k-1}^{k-1} p_{k+1}^{k+1}$, and by the induction hypothesis $p_{k-1}^{k-1} p_{k+1}^{k+1} \geq p_k^k p_{k+1}^{k+1}$, so we obtain $p_k^k \geq p_{k+1}^{k+1}$ and, after taking roots, the induction step is proved. The statement about equality follows from the observation following lemma 8.1. ❑

To make this clearer we write out these inequalities in full in the case of four positive variables a, b, c, d.

We have

$$\frac{a+b+c+d}{4} \geq \left(\frac{ab+ac+ad+bc+bd+cd}{6}\right)^{\frac{1}{2}}$$

$$\geq \left(\frac{abc+abd+acd+bcd}{4}\right)^{\frac{1}{3}}$$

$$\geq (abcd)^{\frac{1}{4}}.$$

Observe that $p_1 \geq p_4$ is the AM-GM inequality for four variables.

Exercise 8b

1. If $a, b, c, d > 0$ and $ab + bc + ca + ad + bd + cd = 54$, find the least value of $a + b + c + d$ and the greatest value of $abcd$.

2. Given the same data as in question 1 prove that
$$(a+b+c+d)(bcd+acd+abd+abc) \leq 1296.$$

3. If $a, b > 0$ are the roots of the equation $x^2 - 2p_1x + p_2^2 = 0$, find the equation whose roots are $\sqrt{a}$ and $\sqrt{b}$.

   Deduce that
   $$\left(\frac{\sqrt{a}+\sqrt{b}}{2}\right)^2 \leq \frac{a+b}{2}$$
   or, in the terminology of section 6.3, that $M_{\frac{1}{2}} \leq M_1$.

4. Prove that for the quadratic equation $x^2 - 2p_1x + p_2^2 = 0$ where $p_2 > 0$, the condition $p_1 \geq p_2$ is both necessary and sufficient for it to have two positive real roots, with equality if, and only if, the roots are coincident.

Chapter 9

Geometrical inequalities

9.1 Pre-requisites

In this chapter, we will use the standard labelling of the triangle. It will have angles A, B and C and the sides opposite A, B and C have lengths a, b and c respectively.

For any triangle, we will use the following without proof:

Cosine rule: $a^2 = b^2 + c^2 - 2bc \cos A$.

Sine rule: $\dfrac{a}{\sin A} = \dfrac{b}{\sin B} = \dfrac{c}{\sin C} = 2R$,

where R is the circumradius of the triangle ABC.

Area of a triangle: $[ABC] = \frac{1}{2}ab \sin C$.

We will also find useful the following trigonometric identities:

(a) $\sin^2 A + \cos^2 A = 1$;

(b) $\sin(A \pm B) = \sin A \cos B \pm \sin B \cos A$;

(c) $\cos(A \pm B) = \cos A \cos B \mp \sin A \sin B$;

(d) $\sin 2A = 2 \sin A \cos A$;

(e) $\cos 2A = \cos^2 A - \sin^2 A = 1 - 2\sin^2 A = 2\cos^2 A - 1$.

Proofs of the above can be found in any standard A level textbook.

We will also find particularly useful the following factor formulae:

(f) $\sin A + \sin B = 2 \sin \frac{A+B}{2} \cos \frac{A-B}{2}$;

(g) $\sin A - \sin B = 2\cos\frac{A+B}{2}\sin\frac{A-B}{2}$;

(h) $\cos A + \cos B = 2\cos\frac{A+B}{2}\cos\frac{A-B}{2}$;

(i) $\cos A - \cos B = -2\sin\frac{A+B}{2}\sin\frac{A-B}{2}$.

In terms of geometry, we also assume the reader has met the *centroid*, *circumcentre*, *orthocentre*, *incentre* and *excentres* of a triangle as well as the basic properties of the Euler line and the nine-point circle. Definitions can either be found in *Crossing the Bridge* [4] or *Plane Euclidean Geometry* [1], both published by the UKMT.

9.2   The triangle inequality

The simplest geometric inequality is the triangle inequality (see result 4.1 on page 42):

Triangle inequality *Let* **x** *and* **y** *be two vectors. Then*

$$|\mathbf{x}+\mathbf{y}| \le |\mathbf{x}| + |\mathbf{y}| \quad and \quad |\mathbf{x}-\mathbf{y}| \le |\mathbf{x}| + |\mathbf{y}|.$$

This states simply that no triangle side can be longer than the sum of the lengths of the other two sides. In other words,

$$a \le b + c$$
$$c \le a + b$$
$$b \le c + a$$

with equality if, and only if, the triangle is degenerate, that is, the three vertices all lie on a straight line.

This can also be proved easily using the cosine rule: indeed, since $-1 \le \cos A \le 1$ we have

$$b^2 + c^2 - 2bc \le b^2 + c^2 - 2bc\cos A \le b^2 + c^2 + 2bc,$$

that is,

$$(b-c)^2 \le a^2 \le (b+c)^2$$

and so $|b - c| \le a \le b + c$. We have equality if, and only if, A is a multiple of $180°$, hence the straight line condition.

Many applications of the triangle inequality require some use of basic properties of parallelograms, similar triangles and other simple geometric facts.

Example 9.1   In triangle ABC, let D be the midpoint of BC. Prove that $AD < \frac{1}{2}(AB + AC)$.

The fact that this inequality can be rewritten as $2AD < AB + BC$ suggests that we produce AD to E so that $AE = 2AD$. This is done in figure 9.1.

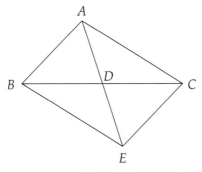

Figure 9.1

It then follows by congruent triangles that $ACEB$ is a parallelogram, and so $BE = AC$ and $CE = AB$. Hence the triangle inequality for triangle ABE gives $AE < AB + BE$, which then gives the result by substitution.

Example 9.2   Prove that if AL, BM, CN are the medians of triangle ABC and $AL + BM + CN = k$ and $AB + BC + CA = p$, then

$$\frac{3p}{2} > k > \frac{3p}{4}.$$

Let $\ell = AL$, $m = BM$ and $n = CN$ and let G be the centroid of triangle ABC. From triangle LAC we have $LC + CA > AL$ from which $a + 2b > 2l$. Adding in two similar inequalities $3(a + b + c) > 2(\ell + m + n)$ and hence $\frac{3p}{2} > k$. From triangle GAC we have $AG + GC > CA$ from which $2(n + \ell) > 3b$. Adding in two similar inequalities we get $4(\ell + m + n) > 3(a + b + c)$ and hence $k > \frac{3p}{4}$.

Exercise 9a

1. Let P be any point inside a triangle ABC. Prove that $PA + PB + PC > \frac{1}{2}(AB + BC + CA)$.

2. Prove that the sum of the lengths of a diagonal of a convex quadrilateral lies between its semi-perimeter and its perimeter.

3. Let $ABCD$ be an isosceles trapezium with AD parallel to BC and $AB = CD$. Points X and Y lie on AB and CD respectively such that $AX = CY$. Show that $XY > \frac{1}{2}(AD + BC)$.

4. In a triangle ABC, let D be the point on AB such that CD bisects the angle C. Prove that CD is smaller than the geometric mean of BC and CA.

5. Let $\mathcal{L}$ be a line and A, B be points, not on $\mathcal{L}$, such that AB is not parallel to $\mathcal{L}$. Locate the point X on $\mathcal{L}$ which maximises $|XA - XB|$.

6. (a) Show that if M is inside the triangle ABC, then $AM + BM < AC + BC$.

   (b) Prove also that $AM + BM + CM$ is smaller than the perimeter of ABC.

9.3 Equivalent forms

We now consider more general geometric inequalities and how they can be rewritten.

It is often the case that a geometrical inequality may appear in three different forms, which at first sight bear no obvious relationship to one another, but which are, in fact, equivalent. These forms are

(i) a relationship concerning a geometrical figure,

(ii) a relationship involving angles, and

(iii) a relationship involving side lengths.

We refer to these three presentations as the *geometrical, trigonometrical* and *algebraic* versions of the inequality, respectively.

To illustrate this, consider what is perhaps the best known geometrical inequality of all. This, in its geometrical form, is $R \geq 2r$, where R is the circumradius and r is the inradius of a triangle.

We can recast this in a trigonometric form as follows.

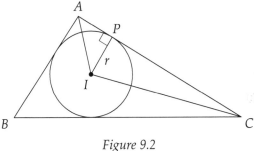

Figure 9.2

Figure 9.2 shows the incentre I of a triangle ABC. Using the sine rule on AIC, we obtain

$$\begin{aligned}
\frac{AI}{\sin \frac{1}{2}C} &= \frac{AC}{\sin(180° - \frac{1}{2}A - \frac{1}{2}C)} \\
&= \frac{2R \sin B}{\sin(\frac{1}{2}A + \frac{1}{2}C)} \\
&= \frac{2R \sin B}{\cos \frac{1}{2}B} \\
&= 4R \sin \frac{1}{2}B.
\end{aligned}$$

So $r = AI \sin \frac{1}{2}A = 4R \sin \frac{1}{2}B \sin \frac{1}{2}C \sin \frac{1}{2}A$. This turns $R \geq 2r$ into

$$8 \sin \frac{1}{2}A \sin \frac{1}{2}B \sin \frac{1}{2}C \leq 1. \tag{9.1}$$

We could also have recast this into an algebraic inequality using the formulae for the area of a triangle. On the one hand,

$$[ABC] = \tfrac{1}{2}(a + b + c)r,$$

which comes from joining the incentre to the three vertices. Alternatively,

$$[ABC] = \tfrac{1}{2}ab \sin C$$
$$= \tfrac{1}{2}ab\frac{c}{2R}$$
$$= \frac{abc}{4R} \qquad (9.2)$$

and, using the area of a triangle and cosine formulae,

$$[ABC]^2 = \tfrac{1}{4}a^2b^2 \sin^2 C$$
$$= \tfrac{1}{4}a^2b^2(1 - \cos^2 C)$$
$$= \tfrac{1}{16}\left(4a^2b^2 - (a^2 + b^2 - c^2)^2\right)$$
$$= \tfrac{1}{16}(2ab + a^2 + b^2 - c^2)(2ab - a^2 - b^2 + c^2)$$
$$= \tfrac{1}{16}((a+b)^2 - c^2)(c^2 - (a-b)^2)$$
$$= \tfrac{1}{16}(a+b+c)(a+b-c)(b+c-a)(c+a-b). \qquad (9.3)$$

Hence $R \geq 2r$ becomes

$$\frac{abc}{4[ABC]} \geq \frac{4[ABC]}{a+b+c}$$

and so

$$abc(a + b + c) \geq 16[ABC]^2$$
$$= (a+b+c)(a+b-c)(b+c-a)(c+a-b).$$

Therefore

$$abc \geq (a+b-c)(b+c-a)(c+a-b), \qquad (9.4)$$

which is our third version of the inequality.

It may not always be feasible to transfer a problem from one form to another but when this is possible, it is worth considering which is the best framework to work in. In practice, in the rest of the chapter we shall solve the trigonometric and algebraic inequalities and rewrite geometric inequalities into one of these forms.

Before we go further, it is worth pointing out that the following many trigonometric inequalities can be transformed into algebraic ones using the sine and cosine rules.

In fact, for the inequality considered in this section, there is a geometric proof, using the following result.

Result 9.1 *Let O and I are the circumcentre and incentre, respectively, of triangle ABC. Then $OI^2 = R^2 - 2Rr$.*

PROOF Let AI meet the circumcircle at P and let POQ be a diameter of the circumcircle. We have $(AI)(IP) = R^2 - OI^2$, by the intersecting chord theorem. Now extend AIP to I_A, the excentre opposite A. Since triangle ABC is the nine-point circle of the triangle of excentres and I is its orthocentre we have $IP = PI_A$. But $\angle IBI_A = 90°$ and so II_A is a diameter of circle IBI_A and hence $IP = PB = 2R \sin \frac{1}{2}A$ since $\angle BAP = \frac{1}{2}A$. Also $AI = r \operatorname{cosec} \frac{1}{2}A$ and it follows that $(AI)(IP) = 2Rr$ and hence $OI^2 = R^2 - 2Rr$. ❏

Corollary 9.1 (Euler's inequality) $R \geq 2r$ *with equality if, and only if, triangle ABC is equilateral.*

PROOF Since a square is non-negative it follows at once from result 9.1 that $R \geq 2r$.

Also, if ABC is equilateral we have $\frac{r}{R} = \sin 30° = \frac{1}{2}$ so $R = 2r$.

Finally, if $R = 2r$, then I and O coincide, so $AI = r \operatorname{cosec} \frac{1}{2}A = R = 2r$ so $\angle A = 60°$ or $120°$. Similarly for $\angle B$ and $\angle C$ and hence triangle ABC is equilateral. ❏

9.4 Side length inequalities

For the inequalities we are going to prove in the rest of this chapter, we will largely be using the tools that have been developed so far:

- the AM-GM inequality;
- the Cauchy-Schwarz inequality;
- the rearrangement inequality;
- Chebyshev's inequality;
- Jensen's inequality.

There is a further standard technique for handling inequalities involving the lengths of the sides of a triangle. If we set $a = m + n$, $b = n + \ell$, $c = \ell + m$, the triangle inequalities become $\ell, m, n > 0$. Geometrically this is the equivalent of introducing the distances between the vertices and the points of contact of the incircle, as shown in figure 9.3 on the next page.

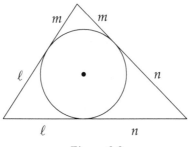

Figure 9.3

Example 9.3   We prove the algebraic inequality, (9.4) on page 124:

$$abc \geq (a+b-c)(b+c-a)(c+a-b)$$

Introducing ℓ, m and n as above replaces this inequality with

$$(m+n)(n+\ell)(\ell+m) \geq 8\ell mn,$$

which follows at once from multiplying three inequalities of the form $m+n \geq 2\sqrt{mn}$. Equality holds if, and only if, $\ell = m = n$, which is equivalent to $a = b = c$.

Example 9.4   Prove that if a, b, c are the side lengths of a triangle, then

$$\tfrac{3}{2} \leq \frac{a}{b+c} + \frac{b}{c+a} + \frac{c}{a+b} < 2.$$

It is less tempting to insert $a = m+n$, and so on, here, as that just makes the inequality messier. Instead for the left-hand inequality multiply up and one is left to prove

$$2(a^3 + b^3 + c^3) \geq b^2c + c^2b + c^2a + a^2c + a^2b + b^2a.$$

This follows from adding together three inequalities of the form

$$(b-c)(b^2 - c^2) \geq 0.$$

Note that this side of the inequality does not in fact require a, b and c to be lengths of a triangle: indeed all we need here is that $a + b$, $b + c$ and $c + a$ are all positive. It is best possible, as can be seen by letting $a = b = c$.

For the right-hand inequality, since $a < b + c$ it follows that

$$\frac{a}{b+c} < \frac{2a}{a+b+c}.$$

Adding three similar inequalities completes the proof. This inequality is best possible, as can be seen by letting $a \to b$ and $c \to 0$.

The right-hand inequality is the same as exercise 5b question 10.

Example 9.5 Prove that if triangle ABC is acute-angled with sides a, b, c then

$$\left(b^2 + c^2 - a^2\right)^{\frac{1}{2}} + \left(c^2 + a^2 - b^2\right)^{\frac{1}{2}} + \left(a^2 + b^2 - c^2\right)^{\frac{1}{2}} \leq a + b + c.$$

Since the angles of triangle ABC are acute the cosine rule implies that $a^2 < b^2 + c^2$, $b^2 < c^2 + a^2$ and $c^2 < a^2 + b^2$, so a^2, b^2, c^2 are the sides of another triangle. Hence, setting $a^2 = m + n$, $b^2 = n + \ell$, $c^2 = \ell + m$, the inequality reduces to

$$\sqrt{\ell} + \sqrt{m} + \sqrt{n} \leq \sqrt{\frac{\ell + m}{2}} + \sqrt{\frac{m + n}{2}} + \sqrt{\frac{n + \ell}{2}}.$$

Now by the AM-RMS inequality we have

$$\frac{\sqrt{\ell} + \sqrt{m}}{2} \leq \sqrt{\frac{\ell + m}{2}}.$$

Adding three such inequalities, we obtain the desired result.

In questions which involve either the circumradius or the area of the triangle, the following results can also be useful. Let $s = \frac{a+b+c}{2}$.

Result 9.2 (Area-circumradius-inradius formula) *For a triangle ABC,*

$$[ABC] = \frac{abc}{4R} = rs.$$

PROOF This was proved in equation (9.2) on page 124.   ❑

Result 9.3 (Heron's formula) *For a triangle ABC,*

$$[ABC] = \sqrt{s(s-a)(s-b)(s-c)}.$$

PROOF This was essentially proved in equation (9.3) on page 124 since $s - a = \frac{1}{2}(b + c - a)$, and so on.   ❑

Example 9.6   Prove that if a, b, c are the sides of the triangle and $[ABC]$ its area then $a^2 + b^2 + c^2 \geq 4\sqrt{3}[ABC]$.

Let $s = \frac{1}{2}(a + b + c)$ then by the AM-GM inequality, we have

$$\{(s-a) + (s-b) + (s-c)\} \geq 3\{(s-a)(s-b)(s-c)\}^{\frac{1}{3}}.$$

Cubing, multiplying by s and using Heron's formula we get

$$\tfrac{1}{2}(a + b + c)^2 \geq 6\sqrt{3}[ABC].$$

Hence, using the AM-RMS inequality,

$$a^2 + b^2 + c^2 \geq \tfrac{1}{3}(a + b + c)^2 \geq 4\sqrt{3}[ABC].$$

Example 9.7   Show that, if a triangle has a fixed perimeter, then its area is maximised when it is equilateral.

We have for the area $[ABC]^2 = s(s-a)(s-b)(s-c)$, where a, b, c are the lengths of the sides and s is the fixed semi-perimeter. Now by AM-GM we have

$$\frac{s}{3} = \frac{(s-a) + (s-b) + (s-c)}{3} \geq \{(s-a)(s-b)(s-c)\}^{\frac{1}{3}}.$$

From these two relations we have

$$[ABC]^2 \leq \frac{s^4}{27}$$

with equality if, and only if, $s - a = s - b = s - c$, that is if, and only if, the triangle is equilateral.

Exercise 9b

1. If a, b, c are the sides of a triangle prove that

$$\frac{1}{b+c-a} + \frac{1}{c+a-b} + \frac{1}{a+b-c} \geq \frac{1}{a} + \frac{1}{b} + \frac{1}{c} \geq \frac{9}{a+b+c}.$$

2. If a, b, c are the sides of a triangle, prove that

$$\frac{1}{2} < \frac{bc + ca + ab}{a^2 + b^2 + c^2} \leq 1.$$

3. Let a, b, c be the sides of a triangle. Find the smallest number k such that

$$k(ab + bc + ca) > a^2 + b^2 + c^2.$$

4. If a, b, c are the sides of a triangle, prove that

$$2(a^2b + b^2c + c^2a + ab^2 + bc^2 + ca^2) \geq a^3 + b^3 + c^3 + 9abc.$$

5. If a, b, c are the sides of a triangle prove that $abc(a+b+c)$ is at least

$$bc(c+a-b)(a+b-c) + ca(a+b-c)(b+c-a)$$
$$+ ab(b+c-a)(c+a-b).$$

6. Let a, b, c be the sides of a triangle. Prove that

$$a^3 + b^3 + c^3 + 6abc \geq (ab + bc + ca)(a+b+c) > a^3 + b^3 + c^3 + 5abc.$$

7. In triangle ABC let the radii of the circumcircle and incircle be R and r respectively. Prove that

(a) $(abc)^{\frac{2}{3}} \geq 6Rr$,

(b) $[ABC]^2 \geq \frac{27}{2} Rr^3$,

(c) $(a+b+c)^2 \geq 54Rr$.

8. A triangle has inradius 1 and semi-perimeter s. Prove that $s > 5$.

9. Prove that if x, y, z are real numbers satisfying $x + y + z = 0$, and a, b, c are the sides of a triangle, then

$$x^2(b^2 + c^2 - a^2) + y^2(c^2 + a^2 - b^2) + z^2(a^2 + b^2 - c^2) \geq 0$$

with equality if, and only if, $x = y = z = 0$.

9.5 Trigonometric inequalities

In dealing with the trigonometric forms of inequalities, in addition to our standard list of inequalities, the following results can be useful.

Result 9.4 *If A and B are both acute, then*

(i) $\cos A + \cos B \le 2 \cos \frac{1}{2}(A + B)$;

(ii) $\sin A + \sin B \le 2 \sin \frac{1}{2}(A + B)$.

PROOF (i) follows from $\cos A + \cos B = 2 \cos \frac{1}{2}(A + B) \cos \frac{1}{2}(A - B)$. (ii) is similar. ❑

Result 9.5 *If A, B and C are the angles of a triangle, then*

(i) $\tan A + \tan B + \tan C = \tan A \tan B \tan C$;

(ii) $\tan A + \tan B + \tan C \ge 3\sqrt{3}$;

(iii) $\tan A \tan B \tan C \ge 3\sqrt{3}$.

PROOF (i) follows from $\tan(A + B) = -\tan C$. The other parts follow from (i) together with the AM-GM inequality. ❑

Result 9.6 *If A, B, C are the angles of a triangle, then*

$$\cos^2 A + \cos^2 B + \cos^2 C + 2 \cos A \cos B \cos C = 1.$$

PROOF The result follows from the trigonometric formulae given in section 9.1 on page 119. Indeed it is equivalent to

$$1 + \cos 2A + \cos 2B + \cos 2C + 4 \cos A \cos B \cos C = 0.$$

But the left-hand side is

$$
\begin{aligned}
1 &+ 2\cos(A + B)\cos(A - B) - 4 \cos A \cos B \cos(A + B) + \cos 2C \\
&= 1 + 2\cos(A + B)(\sin A \sin B - \cos A \cos B) + \cos 2C \\
&= 1 - 2\cos^2(A + B) + \cos 2C \\
&= 1 - 2\cos^2 C + \cos 2C \\
&= 0,
\end{aligned}
$$

as required. ❑

Result 9.7 *If $A + B + C = 360°$, then*

$$\cos^2 A + \cos^2 B + \cos^2 C = 1 + 2\cos A \cos B \cos C.$$

PROOF This follows in the same way as result 9.6. In fact if $VABC$ is a tetrahedron and the angles of the plane faces at V are A, B, C and $VA = d$, $VB = e$, $VC = f$, then the volume of the tetrahedron is given by

$$[VABC] = \tfrac{1}{36} d^2 e^2 f^2 (1 + 2\cos A \cos B \cos C - \cos^2 A - \cos^2 B - \cos^2 C)$$

which is positive unless the tetrahedron flattens out into a plane with zero volume. ❑

Result 9.8 *If $A + B + C = 180°$, then*

(i) $\sin A + \sin B + \sin C \le \tfrac{3}{2}\sqrt{3}$;

(ii) $\sin A \sin B \sin C \le \tfrac{3}{8}\sqrt{3}.$

PROOF Part (i) is established using Jensen's inequality (theorem 7.3 on page 97). For angles in the given range, the sine function is concave, and so

$$\frac{\sin A + \sin B + \sin C}{3} \le \sin\left(\frac{A + B + C}{3}\right) = \sin 60° = \tfrac{1}{2}\sqrt{3}.$$

For part (ii), use AM-GM to show that

$$(\sin A \sin B \sin C)^{\frac{1}{3}} \le \frac{\sin A + \sin B + \sin C}{3},$$

and now part (i) gives the desired result. ❑

Example 9.8   Find the maximum value of

$$f(x, y) = \cos x \cos y \sin(x + y)$$

for positive x, y and $x + y < 90°$.
By a factor formula,

$$f(x, y) = \tfrac{1}{2}\{\cos(x - y) + \cos(x + y)\} \sin(x + y)$$
$$= \tfrac{1}{4}\{2\sin(x + y)\cos(x - y) + \sin 2(x + y)\}.$$

For fixed $(x + y)$, since $\sin(x + y) > 0$ we know that $f(x, y)$ has its maximum when $\cos(x - y) = 1$, that is, when $x = y$. Then

$$f(x, x) = F(x) = \tfrac{1}{2}\sin 2x(1 + \cos 2x), \quad 0 < 2x < 90°.$$

Hence $F(x) = \tfrac{1}{2}(1 - c)^{\frac{1}{2}}(1 + c)^{\frac{3}{2}}$, where $c = \cos 2x$, so $0 < c < 1$. Now by AM-GM

$$\frac{3}{2} = \tfrac{1}{4}\{3(1 - c) + (1 + c) + (1 + c) + (1 + c)\}$$
$$\geq \{3(1 - c)(1 + c)^3\}^{\frac{1}{4}}$$

with equality when $3(1 - c) = (1 + c)$, that is $c = \tfrac{1}{2}$ or $x = 30°$. Squaring gives a maximum value of $f(x, y)$ as $\tfrac{3}{8}\sqrt{3}$ when $x = y = 30°$.

Example 9.9   To prove $\sin \tfrac{1}{2}A \sin \tfrac{1}{2}B \sin \tfrac{1}{2}C \leq \tfrac{1}{8}$, the trigonometric version of $R > 2r$ from page 123.

There are two standard ways of proceeding. The more elementary way uses the approach of section 5.3 on page 57. Fix the angle C, then maximize $\sin \tfrac{1}{2}A \sin \tfrac{1}{2}B$ and finally vary angle C to obtain the overall maximum. We have

$$2\sin \tfrac{1}{2}A \sin \tfrac{1}{2}B = \cos \tfrac{1}{2}(A - B) - \cos \tfrac{1}{2}(A + B) \leq 1 - \sin \tfrac{1}{2}C$$

since $A + B + C = 180°$. Hence $\sin \tfrac{1}{2}A \sin \tfrac{1}{2}B \sin \tfrac{1}{2}C \leq \tfrac{1}{2}s(1 - s)$, where $s = \sin \tfrac{1}{2}C$. Now by the AM-GM inequality $1 = s + 1 - s \geq 2\sqrt{s(1 - s)}$ from which $s(1 - s) \leq \tfrac{1}{4}$, and the result follows. Furthermore equality holds if, and only if, $A = B$ and $s = \tfrac{1}{2}$, that is, if, and only if, $A = B = C = 60°$.

The second way uses Jensen's inequality (theorem 7.3 on page 97). As in the proof of result 9.8(i), we have

$$\frac{\sin x + \sin y + \sin z}{3} \leq \sin\left(\frac{x + y + z}{3}\right).$$

Now put $x = \tfrac{1}{2}A$, $y = \tfrac{1}{2}B$, $z = \tfrac{1}{2}C$, where $x + y + z = 90°$, to obtain

$$\tfrac{1}{3}(\sin \tfrac{1}{2}A + \sin \tfrac{1}{2}B + \sin \tfrac{1}{2}C) \leq \tfrac{1}{2},$$

with equality if, and only if, $A = B = C = 60°$. But by the AM-GM inequality

$$\tfrac{1}{3}(\sin \tfrac{1}{2}A + \sin \tfrac{1}{2}B + \sin \tfrac{1}{2}C) \geq (\sin \tfrac{1}{2}A \sin \tfrac{1}{2}B \sin \tfrac{1}{2}C)^{\frac{1}{3}}$$

from which the inequality follows, with equality if, and only if, $A = B = C = 60°$.

Note that the second way has actually given us more than we needed, and has yielded a second result that $\sin \tfrac{1}{2}A + \sin \tfrac{1}{2}B + \sin \tfrac{1}{2}C \leq \tfrac{3}{2}$, a sharper result than the one involving their product. It is not always immediately obvious what the geometrical significance of a trigonometrical inequality is.

Example 9.10   Prove that

$$\cos A \cos B \cos C \leq \tfrac{1}{8} \quad \text{and} \quad \cos^2 A + \cos^2 B + \cos^2 C \geq \tfrac{3}{4}.$$

The first can be proved with the cosine rule. It amounts to proving

$$a^2b^2c^2 \geq (b^2 + c^2 - a^2)(c^2 + a^2 - b^2)(a^2 + b^2 - c^2).$$

Since the inequality is trivial for obtuse or right-angled triangles we may suppose the triangle is acute, and then setting $b^2 + c^2 - a^2 = x^2$, $c^2 + a^2 - b^2 = y^2$ and $a^2 + b^2 - c^2 = z^2$ the inequality reduces to the product of three inequalities of the form $2a^2 = y^2 + z^2 \geq 2yz$.

Result 9.6 may now be used to establish the second inequality.

Example 9.11   Prove that if x, y, z are real numbers and A, B, C are the angles of a triangle, then

$$x^2 + y^2 + z^2 \geq 2yz \cos A + 2zx \cos B + 2xy \cos C.$$

The difference between the left-hand side and right-hand side is equal to

$$(x - z \cos B - y \cos C)^2 + (y \sin C - z \sin B)^2 \geq 0$$

with equality if, and only if, $x \operatorname{cosec} A = y \operatorname{cosec} B = z \operatorname{cosec} C$.

Example 9.12   Prove that if A, B, C are the angles of a triangle,

$$\sin 2A + \sin 2B + \sin 2C \leq \sin A + \sin B + \sin C$$
$$\leq \cos \tfrac{1}{2}A + \cos \tfrac{1}{2}B + \cos \tfrac{1}{2}C.$$

Using result 9.2 on page 127 and Euler's inequality (corollary 9.1 on page 125), we have

$$\frac{abc}{4R} = \tfrac{1}{2}r(a+b+c) \leq \tfrac{1}{4}R(a+b+c).$$

Hence, by the sine rule, $4\sin A \sin B \sin C \leq \sin A + \sin B + \sin C$. An identity, for $A + B + C = 180°$, which is easily proved, tells us that $\sin 2A + \sin 2B + \sin 2C = 4\sin A \sin B \sin C$, and this gives the left-hand side of the desired result.

For the right-hand inequality, use the identity

$$\sin A + \sin B + \sin C = 4\cos \tfrac{1}{2}A \cos \tfrac{1}{2}B \cos \tfrac{1}{2}C.$$

Now since the three cosines are all positive we can use the AM-GM inequality to show that

$$27 \cos \tfrac{1}{2}A \cos \tfrac{1}{2}B \cos \tfrac{1}{2}C \leq \left(\cos \tfrac{1}{2}A + \cos \tfrac{1}{2}B + \cos \tfrac{1}{2}C\right)^3.$$

The cosine function is concave for acute angles, so by Jensen's inequality (theorem 7.3 on page 97), we have

$$\tfrac{1}{3}\left(\cos \tfrac{1}{2}A + \cos \tfrac{1}{2}B + \cos \tfrac{1}{2}C\right) \leq \cos\left(\frac{A+B+C}{6}\right) = \cos 30° = \tfrac{1}{2}\sqrt{3}.$$

Putting these last three results together, we obtain

$$\sin A + \sin B + \sin C = 4\cos \tfrac{1}{2}A \cos \tfrac{1}{2}B \cos \tfrac{1}{2}C$$
$$\leq \tfrac{4}{27}\left(\cos \tfrac{1}{2}A + \cos \tfrac{1}{2}B + \cos \tfrac{1}{2}C\right)^3$$
$$\leq \tfrac{4}{3}\left(\tfrac{1}{2}\sqrt{3}\right)^2\left(\cos \tfrac{1}{2}A + \cos \tfrac{1}{2}B + \cos \tfrac{1}{2}C\right)$$
$$= \cos \tfrac{1}{2}A + \cos \tfrac{1}{2}B + \cos \tfrac{1}{2}C.$$

Example 9.13   Prove that if A, B, C are the angles of a triangle then

$$\sin 2A \sin^2 A + \sin 2B \sin^2 B + \sin 2C \sin^2 C$$
$$- \sin 2A \sin 2B \sin 2C \le \tfrac{3}{4}\sqrt{3}.$$

Use the sine rule and double angle formula to reduce the inequality to

$$a^3 \cos A + b^3 \cos B + c^3 \cos C - 4abc \cos A \cos B \cos C \le 3R^3 \sqrt{3}.$$

Using the cosine rule, after some massive cancellation, this reduces to $abc \le 3\sqrt{3}R^3$, or equivalently

$$\sin A \sin B \sin C \le \tfrac{3}{8}\sqrt{3},$$

and this is result 9.8(ii).

Exercise 9c

1. If A, B, C are the angles of a triangle, prove that

$$\cos^2 A + \cos^2 B + \cos^2 C$$

is greater than, equal to, or less than 1 according as to whether triangle ABC is obtuse, right-angled or acute.

2. If R is the circumradius of the triangle ABC, show that

$$a^2 + b^2 + c^2 \le 9R^2.$$

3. If A, B, C are the angles of a triangle prove that

$$(1 - \cos A)(1 - \cos B)(1 - \cos C) \ge \cos A \cos B \cos C.$$

4. H is the orthocentre of triangle ABC. Prove that

$$\frac{BC}{AH} + \frac{CA}{BH} + \frac{AB}{CH} \ge 3\sqrt{3}.$$

5. In triangle ABC, $AB = 2AC$. Find the minimum value of $\cot B - \cot C$. [David Monk]

6. If A, B, C are the angles of an acute-angled triangle prove that

$$\frac{\cos A}{\cos B \cos C} + \frac{\cos B}{\cos C \cos A} + \frac{\cos C}{\cos A \cos B} \geq 6.$$

7. Let x, y, z be angles each lying strictly between $0°$ and $45°$ with $x + y + z = 90°$. Prove that

$$1 \leq \tan^2 x + \tan^2 y + \tan^2 z < 2.$$

8. Prove that if A, B, C are the angles of an acute-angled triangle then

$$\sin A + \sin B + \sin C > \cos A + \cos B + \cos C.$$

[David Monk]

9. Prove that

$$\frac{s}{2R} \leq \cos A \cos \tfrac{1}{2}A + \cos B \cos \tfrac{1}{2}B + \cos C \cos \tfrac{1}{2}C,$$

where s is the semi-perimeter and R the circumradius of an acute-angled triangle ABC.

10. For $0 < a, b, c < 1$ and $a + b + c = 2$, prove that

$$8(a + b - c)(b + c - a)(c + a - b) \leq 27a^2b^2c^2.$$

9.6 More inequalities involving triangles

We now consider inequalities involving properties of triangles, and their associated circles, other than those stated in terms of a, b, c, A, B, C, R, s and r. You will find it helpful to draw your own diagrams as you read through the examples.

Example 9.14 In triangle ABC, the length of the median through A is ℓ and the length of the internal bisector of angle BAC is u. Prove that

$$\frac{\ell^2}{u^2} \geq \frac{(b+c)^2}{4bc}.$$

This can be done by finding expressions for ℓ and u in terms of the side lengths of ABC. Indeed if the median through A meets BC at D, the cosine rule applied to ABD and ADC gives

$$\ell^2 = \tfrac{1}{4}\left(2b^2 + 2c^2 - a^2\right),$$

which is known as *Apollonius's theorem*.

Equally, if the angle bisector through A meets BC at E, then the angle bisector theorem says that the lengths BE and EC are in the ratio c to b. Then the cosine rule applied to ABE and AEC gives

$$c^2 = u^2 + BE^2 - 2uBE\cos\theta$$
$$b^2 = u^2 + CE^2 + 2uCE\cos\theta$$

where $\theta = \angle AEB$. Eliminating $\cos\theta$, we obtain, after some manipulation,

$$u^2 = \frac{bc}{(b+c)^2}\left[(b+c)^2 - a^2\right].$$

The desired inequality then reduces to proving that

$$2b^2 + 2c^2 \geq (b+c)^2,$$

which is standard.

For the next example, we need the following definition.

Definition *The pedal triangle of a point P with respect to a triangle ABC is the triangle whose vertices are the feet of the perpendiculars from P to the sides of ABC.*

Example 9.15   For a point P varying inside triangle ABC and LMN its pedal triangle, with L, M, N on BC, CA, AB respectively, show that

(a) $BL^2 + CM^2 + AN^2 \geq \frac{1}{4}(a^2 + b^2 + c^2)$ and

(b) $[ABC]^2 \leq (BL^2 + CM^2 + AN^2)(PL^2 + PM^2 + PN^2)$.

We use the notation $BL = x$, $CM = y$, $AN = z$, $PL = u$, $PM = v$, $PN = w$. Applying Pythagoras' theorem to triangles AMP, MPC, CPL, LPB, BPN and NPA, we get

$$x^2 + y^2 + z^2 = (a - x)^2 + (b - y)^2 + (c - z)^2.$$

This implies

$$ax + by + cz = \frac{1}{2}(a^2 + b^2 + c^2).$$

Now the Cauchy-Schwarz inequality gives

$$(ax + by + cz)^2 \leq (a^2 + b^2 + c^2)(x^2 + y^2 + z^2)$$

from which

$$x^2 + y^2 + z^2 \geq \frac{1}{4}(a^2 + b^2 + c^2),$$

with equality if, and only if, $x = \frac{1}{2}a$, $y = \frac{1}{2}b$, $z = \frac{1}{2}c$ and P is the circumcentre. We also have, by the Cauchy-Schwarz inequality,

$$4[ABC]^2 = (au + bv + cw)^2 \leq (a^2 + b^2 + c^2)(u^2 + v^2 + w^2),$$

with equality if, and only if, $u : v : w = a : b : c$, that is when P is the symmedian point. (If the medians of a triangle are reflected in the internal bisectors of the angles, the resulting lines are concurrent in the *symmedian point*. Properties of this can be found in [2].) Putting the two inequalities together we get

$$[ABC]^2 \leq (x^2 + y^2 + z^2)(u^2 + v^2 + w^2),$$

with equality if, and only if, the triangle is equilateral and P is its circumcentre.

Example 9.16   Show that if ABC is an acute-angled triangle with orthocentre H and AH meets circle BHC again at D', BH meets circle CHA again at E' and CH meets circle AHB again at F', then

$$(HD')(HE')(HF') \le 8R^3.$$

Since $\angle BHC = 180° - \angle A$ it follows that triangles $D'BC$ and ABC are congruent and so have the same circumradius R.

Now $\angle CBH = 90° - C$ so $\angle D'BH = 90° + B - C$ and we have

$$HD' = 2R\sin(90° + B - C) = 2R\cos(C - B) \le 2R,$$

with equality if, and only if, $B = C$. Similar results hold for HE' and HF' and so the inequality holds, with equality if, and only if, ABC is equilateral.

Example 9.17   Prove that, if I is the incentre of triangle ABC, circumradius R, and I_A, I_B, I_C are the excentres opposite A, B, C, respectively, then

$$(II_A)(II_B)(II_C) \le 8R^3 \quad \text{and} \quad \frac{[I_A I_B I_C]}{[ABC]} \ge 4.$$

The quadrilateral IBI_AC is cyclic. Let P be the intersection of the circumcircle of ABC with AI_A. Since PB, PC subtend equal angles at A they are equal, and hence P is the midpoint of II_A and the centre of the circle IBI_AC. Now by the sine rule for triangle PAC we have

$$PC = 2R\sin\tfrac{1}{2}A$$

and so

$$II_A = 4R\sin\tfrac{1}{2}A.$$

Hence

$$(II_A)(II_B)(II_C) = 64R^3\sin\tfrac{1}{2}A\sin\tfrac{1}{2}B\sin\tfrac{1}{2}C$$
$$\le 8R^3,$$

using example 9.9.

From isosceles triangle $I_A CP$,

$$I_A C = 4R \sin \tfrac{1}{2}A \cos \tfrac{1}{2}B.$$

Similarly

$$I_B C = 4R \sin \tfrac{1}{2}B \cos \tfrac{1}{2}A.$$

Adding we get

$$I_A I_B = 4R \cos \tfrac{1}{2}C.$$

Furthermore, since ABC is the nine-point circle of triangle $I_A I_B I_C$ the latter triangle has circumradius $2R$ and so

$$[I_A I_B I_C] = 8R^2 \cos \tfrac{1}{2}A \cos \tfrac{1}{2}B \cos \tfrac{1}{2}C,$$

using result 9.2 on page 127. But

$$[ABC] = 2R^2 \sin A \sin B \sin C$$

and the required result follows since

$$\sin \tfrac{1}{2}A \sin \tfrac{1}{2}B \sin \tfrac{1}{2}C \leq \tfrac{1}{8}.$$

Example 9.18   Suppose that ABC is a triangle with incircle S and inradius r, and that circles S_A, S_B, S_C of radii r_A, r_B, r_C, respectively, are drawn, each touching two sides of ABC and touching S externally, with S_A touching AB, AC and S externally etc. Prove that

$$r \leq r_A + r_B + r_C < 2r.$$

Let J_B be the centre of S_B, and let L_B and L be the feet of the perpendiculars from J_B and I on to BC. $BJ_B I$ is a straight line, the internal bisector of $\angle ABC$. Now $\angle J_B L_B B = \angle ILB = 90°$, so triangles $BJ_B L_B$ and BIL are similar. Let $J_B B = x$, then we have

$$\frac{r_B}{x} = \frac{r}{r + r_B + x}.$$

But $x = r_B \operatorname{cosec} \frac{1}{2}B$. Eliminating x we find

$$r_B = r \frac{1 - \sin\frac{1}{2}B}{1 + \sin\frac{1}{2}B} = r\left(-1 + \frac{2}{1 + \sin\frac{1}{2}B}\right),$$

with similar expressions for r_C, r_A. To prove that $r_A + r_B + r_C \geq r$, it is sufficient to prove that

$$\frac{1}{1 + \sin\frac{1}{2}A} + \frac{1}{1 + \sin\frac{1}{2}B} + \frac{1}{1 + \sin\frac{1}{2}C} \geq 2. \qquad (9.5)$$

By theorem 3.2 on page 28, we have

$$\frac{1}{1 + \sin\frac{1}{2}A} + \frac{1}{1 + \sin\frac{1}{2}B} + \frac{1}{1 + \sin\frac{1}{2}C}$$

$$\geq \frac{9}{3 + \sin\frac{1}{2}A + \sin\frac{1}{2}B + \sin\frac{1}{2}C}.$$

But, by Jensen's inequality, we have $\sin\frac{1}{2}A + \sin\frac{1}{2}B + \sin\frac{1}{2}C \leq \frac{3}{2}$. Combining these results we deduce that inequality (9.5) holds.

To prove that $r_A + r_B + r_C < 2r$ we add three inequalities of the form $r_A < r(1 - \sin\frac{1}{2}A)$. Hence it is sufficient to show that

$$1 < \sin\frac{1}{2}A + \sin\frac{1}{2}B + \sin\frac{1}{2}C. \qquad (9.6)$$

Now

$$\sin\frac{1}{2}A + \sin\frac{1}{2}B + \sin\frac{1}{2}C$$

$$= 2\sin\frac{A + B}{4}\cos\frac{A - B}{4} + 1 - 2\sin^2\frac{A + B}{4}$$

$$= 1 + 2\sin\frac{A + B}{4}\left(\cos\frac{1}{4}A - \sin\frac{1}{4}A\right)\left(\cos\frac{1}{4}B - \sin\frac{1}{4}B\right)$$

$$> 1$$

since $\frac{1}{4}A, \frac{1}{4}B < 45°$.

Example 9.19   In this example, P is an internal point of triangle ABC, and $AP = x$, $BP = y$, $CP = z$. Show how to minimize $F(x, y, z)$ as P varies.

Unless $F(x, y, z)$ has some special form such as $x + y + z$, for which special methods are available, it is best to use calculus. Suppose that the coordinates of the points are $P(p, q)$, $A(a, d)$, $B(b, e)$, $C(c, f)$. We have

$$x^2 = (p - a)^2 + (q - d)^2,$$
$$y^2 = (p - b)^2 + (q - e)^2,$$
$$z^2 = (p - c)^2 + (q - f)^2.$$

Now

$$x\frac{\partial x}{\partial p} = (p - a), \quad y\frac{\partial y}{\partial p} = (p - b), \quad z\frac{\partial z}{\partial p} = (p - c),$$

with similar expressions for derivatives with respect to q. But

$$\frac{\partial F}{\partial p} = \frac{\partial F}{\partial x}\frac{\partial x}{\partial p} + \frac{\partial F}{\partial y}\frac{\partial y}{\partial p} + \frac{\partial F}{\partial z}\frac{\partial z}{\partial p},$$

and at a turning value this must vanish. Hence

$$0 = \frac{\partial F}{\partial x}\frac{p - a}{x} + \frac{\partial F}{\partial y}\frac{p - b}{y} + \frac{\partial F}{\partial z}\frac{p - c}{z}.$$

Similarly

$$0 = \frac{\partial F}{\partial x}\frac{q - d}{x} + \frac{\partial F}{\partial y}\frac{q - e}{y} + \frac{\partial F}{\partial z}\frac{q - f}{z}.$$

Hence

$$\frac{\partial F}{\partial x} : \frac{\partial F}{\partial y} : \frac{\partial F}{\partial z} = \frac{(p - b)(q - f) - (p - c)(q - e)}{yz} : \cdots : \cdots.$$

However, from coordinate geometry, $(p - b)(q - f) - (p - c)(q - e)$ is twice the area of the triangle PBC and so

$$\frac{(p - b)(q - f) - (p - c)(q - e)}{bc} = \frac{2[BPC]}{BP \times CP} = \sin \angle BPC.$$

We therefore have the general result that for a turning value

$$\frac{\partial F}{\partial x} : \frac{\partial F}{\partial y} : \frac{\partial F}{\partial z} = \sin \angle BPC : \sin \angle CPA : \sin \angle APB.$$

For example, if $F(x, y, z) = x + y + z$, then the angles are equal, and provided the triangle has all its angles less that 120°, we deduce $AP + BP + CP$ has a minimum at the Fermat point F, where

$$\angle BFC = \angle CFA = \angle AFB = 120°.$$

Example 9.20 For a point P varying inside an acute-angled triangle ABC and u, v, w the perpendicular distances of P from BC, CA, AB, respectively, find the maximum values of

(a) $avw + bwu + cuv$ and

(b) uvw,

and in each case we determine the position of P that gives the maximum value.

For part (a) we maximize

$$f(u, v, w) = avw + bwu + cuv$$

subject to

$$au + bv + cw = 2[ABC],$$

using a Lagrange multiplier λ and obtain

$$bw + cv = \lambda a,$$
$$cu + aw = \lambda b$$
$$\text{and} \quad av + bu = \lambda c.$$

These equations and the constraint are satisfied by $\lambda = R$, the circumradius, and $u = R\cos A$, $v = R\cos B$, $w = R\cos C$. The point P is therefore the circumcentre and the maximum value is $\frac{1}{4}abc$, where in obtaining this we have used the expansion of $\sin(A + B + C)$.

For part (b) we use the AM-GM inequality to give

$$2[ABC] = au + bv + cw \geq 3(abcuvw)^{\frac{1}{3}}$$

so the maximum value of uvw is

$$\frac{8[ABC]^3}{27abc}.$$

The point P is when $au = bv = cw$, which is when P coincides with the centroid G.

Exercise 9d

1. Prove that the length of the internal bisector of the angle A of triangle ABC does not exceed $\frac{1}{2}(b + c)$.

2. Let AP be the internal bisector of $\angle BAC$ and suppose Q is the point on BC such that $BQ = PC$. Prove that $AQ \geq AP$.

3. ABC is an acute-angled triangle, circumcentre O and circumradius R. AO meets circle BOC again at D. BO meets circle COA again at E. CO meets circle AOB again at F. Prove that

$$(OD)(OE)(OF) \geq 8R^3.$$

4. ABC is a triangle. Its incircle touches the sides BC, CA, AB at X, Y, Z, respectively. The points P, Q, R are the feet of the perpendiculars from X to YZ, from Y to ZX and from Z to XY, respectively. Prove that $[ABC] \geq 16[PQR]$.

5. ABC is a triangle with incentre I. AI, BI, CI meet the circumcircle of ABC at X, Y, Z. Prove that

$$(AI)(BI)(CI) \leq (IX)(IY)(IZ).$$

6. ABC is a triangle with circumradius R. The circle through A touching BC at its midpoint has radius R_1. The radii R_2, R_3 are similarly defined. Prove that

$$R_1^2 + R_2^2 + R_3^2 \geq \frac{27R^2}{16}.$$

7. Use the result of example 9.19 to show that $AP^2 + BP^2 + CP^2$ is a minimum as P varies over the inside of triangle ABC when P lies at the centroid G.

8. Use the result of example 9.19 to show that $a(AP) + b(BP) + c(CP)$ is a minimum as P varies over the inside of the acute-angled triangle ABC when P lies at the orthocentre H.

9.7 Areal coordinates

For some of the following problems the use of *areal* (or *barycentric*) coordinates is required, so a brief account of the properties of such coordinates is now given. Fuller details can be found in *Plane Euclidean Geometry* [1].

If O is an arbitrary point and P a point in the same plane as the triangle ABC, then basic vector algebra gives

$$\begin{aligned}
\mathbf{OP} &= \mathbf{OA} + m\mathbf{AB} + n\mathbf{AC} \\
&= (1 - m - n)\mathbf{OA} + m\mathbf{OB} + n\mathbf{OC} \\
&= \ell\mathbf{OA} + m\mathbf{OB} + n\mathbf{OC}
\end{aligned}$$

where $\ell + m + n = 1$. The following facts may also be shown using vector algebra.

(i) The values of ℓ, m and n are independent of the choice of O.
(ii) The values of ℓ, m and n are given by

$$\ell = \frac{[PBC]}{[ABC]}, \quad m = \frac{[APC]}{[ABC]}, \quad n = \frac{[ABP]}{[ABC]},$$

with the convention that ℓ is negative if P is on the opposite side of BC from A, and so on. Indeed if AP meets BC at L, it is easy to see that $AP = (m + n)AL$, so that $PL = \ell AL$ and hence $[PBC] = \ell[ABC]$.

The values (ℓ, m, n) are called the *areal coordinates* of the point P. Their usefulness lies in the fact that they allow us to turn geometric problems into algebraic ones and the resulting algebra usually exhibits some symmetry in a, b and c, which makes it more manageable than expressions obtained from Cartesian coordinates.

For simplicity, it is usual to give areal coordinates (ℓ, m, n) in an *unnormalised* form, that is, with $l + m + n \neq 1$, and just remember that it is the ratio of the areal coordinates that is being expressed rather than the actual ones. For example, in table 9.1 the actual (normalised) areal coordinates of the midpoint of BC are $(0, \frac{1}{2}, \frac{1}{2})$, though it is simpler to leave them in the (unnormalised) form $(0, 1, 1)$.

Table 9.1 gives the unnormalised areal coordinates of some important points.

Point	Coordinates
A, B, C	$(1,0,0)$, $(0,1,0)$, $(0,0,1)$
midpoints of BC, CA, AB	$(0,1,1)$, $(1,0,1)$, $(1,1,0)$
centroid G	$(1,1,1)$
circumcentre	$(\sin 2A, \sin 2B, \sin 2C)$
orthocentre	$(\tan A, \tan B, \tan C)$
incentre	(a, b, c)

Table 9.1: Unnormalised areal coordinates

If $P_1(\ell_1, m_1, n_1)$ and $P_2(\ell_2, m_2, n_2)$ lie in the plane ABC, then any point P on the line joining them has postion vector

$$\mathbf{OP} = \lambda \mathbf{OP_1} + (1 - \lambda)\mathbf{OP_2}.$$

Thus if P has areal coordinates (x, y, z), then

$$x = \lambda \ell_1 + (1 - \lambda)\ell_2$$
$$y = \lambda m_1 + (1 - \lambda)m_2$$
$$z = \lambda n_1 + (1 - \lambda)n_2$$

Eliminating λ gives

$$(m_1 n_2 - n_1 m_2)x + (n_1 \ell_2 - \ell_1 n_2)y + (\ell_1 m_2 - m_1 \ell_2)z = 0.$$

This works irrespective of whether the areal coordinates are normalised or not. A convenient way of remembering this is to use the determinant form

$$\begin{vmatrix} x & y & z \\ \ell_1 & m_1 & n_1 \\ \ell_2 & m_2 & n_2 \end{vmatrix} = 0.$$

With distances, it is quite another matter. The square of the distance between the points $P_1(\ell_1, m_1, n_1)$ and $P_2(\ell_2, m_2, n_2)$ is

$$-a^2yz - b^2zx - c^2xy,$$

where $(x, y, z) = (\ell_1 - \ell_2, m_1 - m_2, n_1 - n_2)$. However, this is only true if (ℓ_1, m_1, n_1) and (ℓ_2, m_2, n_2) are normalised coordinates. The proof of this follows quite easily using the scalar (dot) product from vector geometry, with the origin O taken as the circumcentre; indeed

$$
\begin{aligned}
(x\mathbf{OA} + &y\mathbf{OB} + z\mathbf{OC}).(x\mathbf{OA} + y\mathbf{OB} + z\mathbf{OC}) \\
&= R^2(x^2 + y^2 + z^2) + 2R^2(yz\cos 2A + zx\cos 2B + xy\cos 2C) \\
&= R^2(x + y + z)^2 - 4R^2(yz\sin^2 A + zx\sin^2 B + xy\sin^2 C) \\
&= -(a^2yz + b^2zx + c^2xy)
\end{aligned}
$$

since $x + y + z = 0$.

There is also a useful formula for the area of the triangle T with vertices (x_1, y_1, z_1), (x_2, y_2, z_2), (x_3, y_3, z_3), which again need to be in normalised form:

$$[T] = [ABC]\begin{vmatrix} x_1 & y_1 & z_1 \\ x_2 & y_2 & z_2 \\ x_3 & y_3 & z_3 \end{vmatrix}.$$

Finally, the following theorem can be used to create geometric inequalities using areal coordinates.

Theorem 9.1 *Let K and P be points in the plane ABC and suppose the normalised areal coordinates of K are (ℓ, m, n). Then*

(i) $\ell AP^2 + mBP^2 + nCP^2 = \ell AK^2 + mBK^2 + nCK^2 + PK^2$

(ii) $\ell AP^2 + mBP^2 + nCP^2 \geq \ell AK^2 + mBK^2 + nCK^2$, *with equality if, and only if, P and K are the same point.*

PROOF For (i), we have

$$AP^2 = \mathbf{AP.AP} = (\mathbf{AK} + \mathbf{KP}).(\mathbf{AK} + \mathbf{KP}) = AK^2 + KP^2 + 2\mathbf{AK.KP}.$$

Using two similar expressions for BP^2 and CP^2 we get

$$
\begin{aligned}
\ell AP^2 + mBP^2 + nCP^2 = \ell AK^2 &+ mBK^2 + nCK^2 + (\ell + m + n)PK^2 \\
&+ 2(\ell\mathbf{AK} + m\mathbf{BK} + n\mathbf{CK}).\mathbf{PK}.
\end{aligned}
$$

The result now follows since $\ell + m + n = 1$ and $\ell \mathbf{AK} + m \mathbf{BK} + n \mathbf{CK} = \mathbf{0}$.
The inequality (ii) is an immediate consequence of (i).   ❑

We now give some worked examples.

Example 9.21   Prove that if a point K is chosen inside triangle ABC
and AK meets BC at L, and M and N are similarly defined, then

$$\frac{[LMN]}{[ABC]} \leq \tfrac{1}{4},$$

with equality if, and only if, K is the centroid.

Let the areal coordinates of K be (ℓ, m, n). Then the equation of the
line AK is $ny = mz$ and that of the side BC is $x = 0$, and so the
areal coordinates of L are $(0, m, n)$. By a similar argument, the areal
coordinates of M and N are $(\ell, 0, n)$ and $(\ell, m, 0)$. In order to use the
area formula, these must be normalised, so the coordinates of L must
be written as $\frac{1}{m+n}(0, m, n)$ and similarly with M and N. We now have

$$\frac{[LMN]}{[ABC]} = \frac{2\ell mn}{(\ell + m)(m + n)(n + \ell)},$$

so the required inequality is $(\ell + m)(m + n)(n + \ell) \geq 8\ell mn$, which
follows from three applications of the AM-GM inequality.

Example 9.22   Let O be any internal point of triangle ABC, and let
AO, BO and CO meet BC, CA and AB at points D, E and F. Prove that,
if $p > q > r$, then

$$p + q > p\frac{AO}{AD} + q\frac{BO}{BE} + r\frac{CO}{CF} > q + r.$$

Let the normalised areal coordinates of O be (ℓ, m, n). Then

$$\frac{AO}{AD} = m + n, \quad \frac{BO}{BE} = n + \ell \quad \text{and} \quad \frac{CO}{CF} = \ell + m.$$

Calling the expression to be bounded S, we have

$$p + q - S = (p+q)(\ell + m + n) - p(m+n) - q(n+\ell) - r(\ell + m),$$
$$= (p-r)\ell + (q-r)m > 0.$$

The right-hand inequality is proved in much the same way.

Example 9.23 Prove that if H is the orthocentre, N the nine-point centre and R the circumradius of triangle ABC, then

$$AN^2 + BN^2 + CN^2 \leq 3R^2 \leq AH^2 + BH^2 + CH^2.$$

From theorem 9.1(i) with $\ell = m = n = \frac{1}{3}$ we have

$$AP^2 + BP^2 + CP^2 = AG^2 + BG^2 + CG^2 + 3PG^2$$

for any point P in the plane ABC. Let $NG = d$, then $OG = 2d$ and $HG = 4d$, where O is the circumcentre, using the ratio property of the Euler line. Taking P to be successively O, N, H and writing $AG^2 + BG^2 + CG^2 = D^2$ we have

$$3R^2 = D^2 + 12d^2,$$
$$AN^2 + BN^2 + CN^2 = D^2 + d^2,$$
$$AH^2 + BH^2 + CH^2 = D^2 + 48d^2,$$

from which the result follows.

Exercise 9e

1. Given a triangle ABC and an arbitrary point P internal to it, let the line through P parallel to BC meet AC at M, and similarly let the lines through P parallel to CA, AB meet AB, BC at N, L respectively. Show that

$$\frac{BL}{LC} \times \frac{CM}{MA} \times \frac{AN}{NB} \leq \frac{1}{8}.$$

[BMO1 Nov 2007]

2. Let P be a point in the plane of the triangle ABC. If the triangle is acute-angled, prove that

$$\tan A(PA)^2 + \tan B(PB)^2 + \tan C(PC)^2$$

is a maximum when P is at the orthocentre, and that the stationary value is

$$8R^2 \sin A \sin B \sin C.$$

If the triangle is obtuse-angled, show that the same expression is minimised, with the same stationary value, at the orthocentre.

3. ABC is an acute-angled triangle. D is the reflection of A in the side BC, with E and F similarly defined. Prove that

$$\frac{[DEF]}{[ABC]} \le 4.$$

4. If G is the centroid of triangle ABC and S is the symmedian point (defined in example 9.15 on page 138), prove that

$$\frac{AS}{AG} + \frac{BS}{BG} + \frac{CS}{CG} \le 3.$$

5. Locate the points P on the circumcircle of the (non-equilateral) triangle ABC such that $PA^2 + PB^2 + PC^2$ is a maximum or a minimum.

Appendices

Appendix A

Types of mean

The *arithmetic mean* of $a_1, a_2, \ldots, a_n > 0$ is

$$\frac{a_1 + a_2 + \cdots + a_n}{n}.$$

The *geometric mean* of $a_1, a_2, \ldots, a_n > 0$ is

$$\sqrt[n]{a_1 a_2 \cdots a_n}.$$

The *harmonic mean* of $a_1, a_2, \ldots, a_n > 0$ is defined by

$$\frac{1}{h} = \frac{1}{n}\left(\frac{1}{a_1} + \frac{1}{a_2} + \cdots + \frac{1}{a_n}\right).$$

The *root mean square* of $a_1, a_2, \ldots, a_n > 0$ is

$$\sqrt{\frac{a_1^2 + a_2^2 + \cdots + a_n^2}{n}}.$$

For any non-zero integer t, the *power mean* or *mean of order t* of $a_1, a_2, \ldots, a_n > 0$ is

$$\left(\frac{a_1^t + a_2^t + \cdots + a_n^t}{n}\right)^{\frac{1}{t}}.$$

Appendix B

Selected inequalities

Inequality of the means

Let $a_1, a_2, \ldots, a_n$ be positive real numbers. Then

$$\text{HM} \leq \text{GM} \leq \text{AM} \leq \text{RMS}.$$

Equality holds if, and only if, $a_1 = a_2 = \cdots = a_n$.

Cauchy-Schwarz inequality

Let $x_1, x_2, \ldots, x_n, y_1, y_2, \ldots, y_n$ be real numbers. Then

$$(x_1 y_1 + x_2 y_2 + \cdots + x_n y_n)^2 \leq \left(x_1^2 + x_2^2 + \cdots + x_n^2\right)\left(y_1^2 + y_2^2 + \cdots + y_n^2\right).$$

Equality holds if, and only if, $x_i y_j = x_j y_i$ for all $1 \leq i < j \leq n$.

Schur's inequality

Let x, y, z be non-negative real numbers and let t be a positive real number. Then

$$x^t(x - y)(x - z) + y^t(y - z)(y - x) + z^t(z - x)(z - y) \geq 0.$$

Equality holds if, and only if, one of the following four conditions holds:

(i) $x = y = z$;
(ii) $x = y$ and $z = 0$;
(iii) $y = z$ and $x = 0$;
(iv) $z = x$ and $y = 0$.

Chebyshev's inequality

Let (a_k) and (b_k) be two finite sequences of n real numbers.

(i) If the sequences are ordered in the same way, then

$$n \sum a_k b_k \geq \sum a_k \times \sum b_k.$$

(ii) If the sequences are ordered in the opposite way, then

$$n \sum a_k b_k \leq \sum a_k \times \sum b_k.$$

Power means inequality

Let $a_1, a_2, \ldots, a_n$ be positive real numbers. Then

$$\cdots \leq M_{-5} \leq M_{-4} \leq M_{-3} \leq M_{-2} \leq M_{-1} \leq M_0 = g$$
$$\leq M_1 \leq M_2 \leq M_3 \leq M_4 \leq M_5 \leq \cdots$$

Muirhead's theorem

Let $x_1, x_2, \ldots, x_n$ be positive real numbers, and let (a_k) and (b_k) be two finite sequences of n real numbers.
If $(a_1, \ldots, a_n) \succ (b_1, \ldots, b_n)$, then

$$\sum_{\text{sym}} x_1^{a_1} x_2^{a_2} \cdots x_n^{a_n} \geq \sum_{\text{sym}} x_1^{b_1} x_2^{b_2} \cdots x_n^{b_n}.$$

Equality holds if, and only if,

$$(a_1, a_2, \ldots, a_n) = (b_1, b_2, \ldots, b_n) \quad \text{or} \quad x_1 = x_2 = \cdots = x_n.$$

Jensen's inequality

Let $f(x)$ be a convex function on (a, b) and suppose $a < x_1 \le x_2 \le \cdots \le x_n < b$. Then

$$\frac{f(x_1) + f(x_2) + \cdots + f(x_n)}{n} \ge f\left(\frac{x_1 + x_2 + \cdots + x_n}{n}\right).$$

If $f(x)$ is concave the direction of the inequality is reversed.
Equality holds if, and only if, $x_1 = x_2 = \cdots = x_n$.

Hölder's inequality

Let p and q be positive rational numbers such that $\frac{1}{p} + \frac{1}{q} = 1$, and let (x_k) and (y_k) be two finite sequences of n positive real numbers. Then

$$x_1 y_1 + x_2 y_2 + \cdots + x_n y_n \le \left(x_1^p + x_2^p + \cdots + x_n^p\right)^{\frac{1}{p}} \left(y_1^q + y_2^q + \cdots + y_n^q\right)^{\frac{1}{q}}.$$

Equality holds if, and only if, the sequence $\left(x_k^p\right)$ is equal to $\left(\lambda y_k^q\right)$ for some constant λ.

Bernoulli's inequality

Let x be a positive real number, not equal to 1. Then

$$x^p - 1 > p(x - 1) \quad \text{if} \quad p < 0 \text{ or } p > 1;$$
$$x^p - 1 < p(x - 1) \quad \text{if} \quad 0 < p < 1.$$

Triangle inequality

Let $\mathbf{x}$ and $\mathbf{y}$ be two vectors. Then

$$|\mathbf{x} + \mathbf{y}| \le |\mathbf{x}| + |\mathbf{y}| \quad \text{and} \quad |\mathbf{x} - \mathbf{y}| \le |\mathbf{x}| + |\mathbf{y}|.$$

Solutions and commentary

Exercise 1a

1. (a) Draw the graph of $y = \frac{1}{x}$ and you will see that you need a and b to be both positive or both negative.

    (b) Draw the graph of $y = x^2$ and you will see that you need a and b to be non-negative.

    (c) Draw the graph of $y = x^3$ and you will see that this is always true.

    (d) Draw the graph of $y = \log_k x$ and you will see that you need $k > 1$. If $0 < k < 1$, then the inequality is reversed.

    (e) As you will have seen by now, this depends on a and b lying in a part of the graph where the function is increasing.

    (f) Here the function must be decreasing on the appropriate part of the graph.

2. $x > 2$.

3. $x \leq -2$ or $x \geq 2$.

4. $0 \leq x \leq 16$

Exercise 1b

1. $-5 < x < -2$.

2. $x < -14$ or $-2 < x < 2$.

3. $x < 1$ or $\frac{7}{3} < x < 3$ or $x > 7$.

4. Use the method of example 1.10 on page 7. The maximum is attained at $x = 4$.

5. The maximum is 0.5 when $x = -1$ and the minimum is -0.1 when $x = -7$.

6. Using the method of example 1.9 on page 6, the maximum value is 15.

7. Use the method of example 1.10 and watch out for the difference of two squares.

Exercise 2a

1. Write as $x^4 + (x+?)^2 + ?$.

2. Write $5x^2 = 4x^2 + x^2$.

3. Use $x^2 - x + \frac{1}{4} = \left(x - \frac{1}{2}\right)^2$.

4. $-2\sqrt{3} < k < 2\sqrt{3}$.

5. $k < -2$.

6. $0 < k < 24$.

7. $k < -1, k \neq 0$. Why is the second condition necessary?

8. Start with $\left(1 - \sqrt{a}\right)^2$. We have equality if, and only if, $a = 1$.

9. Start with $\left(\sqrt{a} - \sqrt{b}\right)^2$. We have equality if, and only if, $a = b$.

10. Write as a sum of three squares. The conditions for equality are that $x = y = -z$. (The result is also immediate from inequality (2.1) on page 10.)

11. Start with $(a - b)^2$. We have equality if, and only if, $a = b$.

12. Rewrite the left-hand side as $2(a^3 + b^3) - (a + b)(a - b)^2$. We have equality if, and only if, $a = b$. Why is the condition $a, b > 0$ necessary?

Exercise 2b

1. $a + b \geq 2\sqrt{ab}$ etc. We have equality if, and only if, $a = b = c$.

2. Put $u = \frac{1}{x}$, $v = \frac{1}{y}$, $w = \frac{1}{z}$ and bring all terms over to the left-hand side. Rearrange the resulting expression as in example 2.3 on page 12, to obtain $u(v - w)^2 + v(w - u)^2 + w(u - v)^2$. We have equality if, and only if, $x = y = z$.

3. Use a rearrangement of example 2.5 on page 14, adding three such inequalities together. Equality holds if, and only if, $a = b = c$.

4. For the left-hand inequality, use the expression

$$\left(a^2 - b^2\right)^2 + \left(b^2 - c^2\right)^2 + \left(c^2 - a^2\right)^2,$$

   or use result (2.1) on page 10, and for the right-hand inequality use

$$a^2(b - c)^2 + b^2(c - a)^2 + c^2(a - b)^2.$$

   In both parts, we have equality if, and only if, $a = b = c$.

5. Use the results of question 4. Again, we have equality if, and only if, $a = b = c$.

6. Use the results of questions 11 and 12 in exercise 2a. We have equality if, and only if, $a = b$.

7. Use the result $x^2 + y^2 \geq 2xy$ twice, first with $x = pv$, $y = qu$ and then with $x = pu$, $y = 3qv$. We have equality if, and only if, $u = \sqrt{3}v$, $p = \sqrt{3}q$ or $u = -\sqrt{3}v$, $p = -\sqrt{3}q$.

8. The given expression is equal to

$$\frac{\left(x - 1 - \sqrt{x+2}\right)^2}{x - 1}.$$

   Equality holds when $x = \frac{1}{2}(3 + \sqrt{13})$.

9. The first result is equivalent to $(z - 1)^2 \geq 0$. If $y > 0$ we have

$$\frac{y(3 - z)}{1 + z} \leq \frac{y}{z}$$

   and two similar inequalities by cyclic change of x, y, z. Put $x = \frac{c}{b}$, $y = \frac{a}{c}$, $z = \frac{b}{a}$ and add the inequalities.

   Equality holds when $a = b = c$.

10. Part (a) follows quickly from subtracting and factorising; the condition for equality is $a = b$. For part (b), one method is to add three versions of (a) to give

$$2(a^3 + b^3 + c^3) \geq a^2b + a^2c + b^2c + b^2a + c^2a + c^2b.$$

   This can then be used to produce the required result; the condition for equality is $a = b = c$.

11. Divide throughout by the positive xyz to change the problem to showing that

$$\frac{x^2}{y} + \frac{y^2}{z} + \cdots + \frac{z^2}{y} \geq 2(x+y+z).$$

This can be obtained by adding together three inequalities of the form

$$\frac{x^2}{y} + \frac{y^2}{x} \geq x+y,$$

which reduces to $(x-y)^2(x+y) \geq 0$.

Exercise 2c

1. Using the side condition we obtain

$$x^4 + y^4 - 2xy = \tfrac{3}{2} - \tfrac{1}{2}(2xy+1)^2,$$

and again using the side condition we find $-\tfrac{1}{2} \leq xy \leq \tfrac{1}{2}$. It follows that the maximum and minimum are $\tfrac{3}{2}$ and $-\tfrac{1}{2}$ respectively.

2. Rewrite the expression to be minimised as $xz + \frac{1}{xz}$ and use the result, equivalent to question 9 of exercise 2a, that $a + \frac{1}{a} \geq 2$ for $a > 0$.

3. Make the inequality homogeneous by multiplying the right-hand side by $ad - bc$. Subtracting, we are now required to prove that

$$a^2 + b^2 + c^2 + d^2 + ac + bd - \sqrt{3}(ad - bc) \geq 0.$$

This suggests that the left-hand side can be written as a sum of squares. This takes a little experiment, but one of them turns out to be $\tfrac{1}{4}(2a + c - \sqrt{3}d)^2$.

4. First note that we need only consider positive values of y since $\frac{x^2+y^2}{y}$ is to be positive. The expression to be minimised is of degree 1, so it would be useful to square it.

Then the inequality to be proved can be made homogeneous by multiplying the right-hand side by the expression $7x^2 + 3xy + 3y^2$. It now remains to show that $y^4 - 3xy^3 + x^2y^2 + 4x^4 \geq 0$. It is useful to realise that this has a factor $(y - 2x)^2$. Equality is achieved when $(x, y) = (\tfrac{1}{5}, \tfrac{2}{5})$.

5. Using the square of the side condition to eliminate both $x^4 + y^4$ and $x^2 + y^2$ we obtain

$$f(x,y) = 10 - \tfrac{2}{9}(xy + 2)^2$$

showing $f(x,y) \leq 10$ with equality when $xy = -2$ and $x^2 + y^2 = 6$, that is when $x^2 = 3 + \sqrt{5}$ and $y^2 = 3 - \sqrt{5}$ (or *vice versa*). Now use the side condition to show that the minimum value of xy is -5, showing that $f(x,y) \geq 8$ with equality when $x = \sqrt{5}$ and $y = -\sqrt{5}$ (or *vice versa*).

Exercise 3a

1. Use AM-GM. There is equality if $xz^2 = y$.

2. Let the three sides of fencing have lengths a, b, a with $2a + b = 30$. AM-GM on $2a$, b gives maximum area 112.5 when $a = 7.5$, $b = 15$. Can you see why this also follows geometrically from example 3.2 on page 22?

3. AM-GM shows that if $xy = 1\,000\,000$, then $x + y \geq 2000$ with equality if $x = y = 1000$.

4. Let d be the distance between the towns. Cyclist A takes time $\frac{d}{2}\left(\frac{1}{x} + \frac{1}{y}\right)$; cyclist B takes time $\frac{2d}{x+y}$. Use HM $\leq$ AM to show that B arrives first, unless $x = y$ when they arrive simultaneously.

5. If the shorter sides have lengths x, y, we need to show that $x + y \leq \sqrt{2}\sqrt{x^2 + y^2}$: square and rearrange. There is equality if $x = y$.

6. Rearrange $(a - b)^2 \geq 0$. Then apply the result to each term on the left-hand side.

7. Use AM-GM.

8. Immediate from $\sin x \cos x \leq \frac{1}{2}(\sin^2 x + \cos^2 x) = \frac{1}{2}$, attained when $x = 45°$.

9. The left-hand side is clear on squaring; the right-hand side comes from AM $\leq$ RMS (or from question 5, which also provides a geometrical interpretation).

10. The left-hand side is

$$\frac{1}{2}\left\{\left(\frac{a+b}{2}\right) + \left(\frac{c+d}{2}\right)\right\}.$$

11. Maximise $2ab$ subject to $4a + 3b = 1200$. The solution is an area of $60\,000\,\text{m}^2$ when $a = 150$ and $b = 200$.

    For k internal fences, the maximum area is $\frac{180\,000}{k+2}\,\text{m}^2$ attained when $a = \frac{300}{k+1}$, $b = \frac{600}{k+2}$.

12. This is equivalent to finding the minimum value of

$$\frac{(x+a)(x+b)}{x} = a+b+x+\frac{ab}{x}.$$

Use the AM-GM inequality. The required maximum value is

$$\frac{1}{\left(\sqrt{a}+\sqrt{b}\right)^2},$$

attained when $x = \sqrt{ab}$.

13. Multiply together $x \geq \sqrt{bc}$ (from AM-GM) with two similar inequalities for y, z.

14. The total surface area is

$$2xy + \frac{648}{xy} \geq 2\sqrt{2 \times 648} = 72,$$

with equality if $xy = 18$, $x+y = 18$ yielding $x, y = 9 \pm 3\sqrt{7}$ and $h = 1$.

Exercise 3b

1. Apply AM-GM to x^2 once, $\frac{1}{2}y^2$ twice and $\frac{1}{3}z^2$ three times. xy^2z^3 has a maximum of $\frac{1}{36}\sqrt{3}$ when $x = \frac{1}{\sqrt{6}}, y = \frac{1}{\sqrt{3}}, z = \frac{1}{\sqrt{2}}$.

2. Maximise $x^3y^9z^{12}$. The maximum of xy^3z^4 is $\dfrac{3}{2^{\frac{16}{3}}}$ when $x^3 = \frac{y^3}{3} = \frac{z^3}{4} = \frac{1}{8}$.

3. Use AM-GM with $\frac{\sin^2\theta}{p}$ used p times and $\frac{\cos^2\theta}{q}$ used q times.

4. AM-GM on $(2x+5)$ five times and $(35-5x)$ twice. The maximum is

$$\frac{5^5 \times 19^7}{7^7}$$

when $x = \frac{30}{7}$.

5. This is AM-GM on $1, x, x^2, \ldots, x^{n-1}$.

6. If the cylinder has base radius r, height h, then its surface area is $2\pi r^2 + \frac{2V}{r}$. Use AM-GM on $2\pi r^2$, $\frac{V}{r}$, $\frac{V}{r}$ to see that the minimum surface area is $3\sqrt[3]{2\pi V^2}$ attained when $r = \frac{1}{2}h = \sqrt[3]{\frac{V}{2\pi}}$.

7. Let h be the distance of the base from the centre of the sphere. Then $V = \frac{1}{3}\pi(r+h)^2(r-h)$. Now apply AM-GM to $\frac{1}{2}(r+h)$ twice and $(r-h)$ once. The maximum is attained when $h = \frac{r}{3}$ and is equal to $\frac{32}{81}\pi r^3$.

8. $\dfrac{N^3}{27abc}$ when $x = \dfrac{N}{3a}$, $y = \dfrac{N}{3b}$, $z = \dfrac{N}{3c}$.

9. $\dfrac{N^3}{27abc}$ when $\dfrac{ax^2}{y} = \dfrac{by^2}{z} = \dfrac{cz^2}{x} = \dfrac{N}{3}$.

10. $\left(\dfrac{N}{p+q+r}\right)^{p+q+r}\dfrac{p^p q^q r^r}{a^p b^q c^r}$ when $ax = \dfrac{pN}{p+q+r}$ etc.

11. An immediate application of AM-GM.

12. At most one of the factors on the right-hand side is less than or equal to zero (by contradiction): the inequality is then trivial. Otherwise, use AM-GM on $y+z-x$, $z+x-y$, $x+y-z$.

13. Since $\frac{a_i}{a_j} + \frac{a_j}{a_i} \geq 2$, by question 7 of exercise 3a, we have

$$(a_1 + a_2 + \cdots + a_n)\left(\frac{1}{a_1} + \frac{1}{a_2} + \cdots + \frac{1}{a_n}\right) = n + \sum_{i<j}\left(\frac{a_i}{a_j} + \frac{a_j}{a_i}\right)$$
$$\geq n + 2 \times \tfrac{1}{2}n(n-1)$$
$$= n^2.$$

Exercise 3c

1. Use AM-GM to show the left-hand side is greater than or equal to $10\sqrt{2} > 14$.

2. Expand the left-hand side and use $a^3 + b^3 + c^3 \geq 3abc$ and $b^3c^3 + c^3a^3 + a^3b^3 \geq 3a^2b^2c^2$.

   Generalisation is $(1+a^4)(1+b^4)(1+c^4)(1+d^4) \geq (1+abcd)^4$, etc.

3. Apply AM-GM to $1, a+1, b+1, c+1$.

4. Apply AM-GM to $x^2, 2xy$ (twice), $4y^2, z^2$ (twice). The minimum is 96 when $x = 4, y = 2, z = 4$ and this can occur since then $x^2 = 2xy = 4y^2 = z^2 = 16$.

5. Start with $n = 2, 3$ and see how it goes. In general, the left-hand side can be written as

$$\frac{1}{n} \sum_j \left(x_0^n + \cdots + \hat{x}_j^n + \cdots + x_n^n \right)$$

where $\hat{x}_j^n$ denotes an omitted term: then use AM-GM on each term.

6. Apply AM-GM either

to n numbers equal to $\frac{1}{n}$ and x numbers equal to $\frac{1}{n+x}$, or

to n numbers equal to $1 + \frac{x}{n}$ and x numbers equal to 1.

7. Apply AM-GM on 1 once and $\frac{n}{n+1}$ $(n+1)$ times.

The sequence $\left(1 + \frac{1}{n}\right)^{n+1}$ decreases monotonically to e.

8. Use $xy + yz + zx \geq 3(xyz)^{\frac{2}{3}}$ and $(x+y+z)^2 \geq 3(xy + yz + zx)$ (prove it!), giving $0 < xyz \leq 1$ and $x + y + z \geq 1$.

9. The final inequality is immediate from AM-GM on a^2, b^2, c^2, d^2. For the central inequality use $ab^3 + ba^3 \geq 2a^2b^2$. For the first one use $(a-b)(a^3 - b^3) \geq 0$.

10. Suppose $x^2 + y^2 + z^2 < \frac{3}{4}$. Then $\frac{3}{4} > x^2 + y^2 + z^2 \geq 3(xyz)^{\frac{2}{3}}$ and so $|xyz| < \frac{1}{8}$. Hence $x^2 + y^2 + z^2 + 2xyz < 1$. Contradiction. Inequality is sharp: consider $x = y = z = \frac{1}{2}$.

11. $a_1^r + a_2^r + \cdots + a_r^r \geq r a_1 a_2 \cdots a_r$. In $\binom{n}{r}$ inequalities of this type a_1^r occurs in $\binom{n-1}{r-1}$ of them. So adding all these inequalities together gives $\binom{n-1}{r-1} S_r \geq r P_r$, from which the result follows.

12. Use $\dfrac{1}{\mathrm{HM}} \geq \dfrac{1}{\mathrm{AM}}$ on $x_1, x_2, \ldots, x_{j-1}, x_{j+1}, \ldots, x_n$ to give

$$\frac{1}{n-1}\left(\frac{1}{x_1} + \frac{1}{x_2} + \cdots + \frac{1}{x_{j-1}} + \frac{1}{x_{j+1}} + \cdots + \frac{1}{x_n} \right) \geq \frac{n-1}{s - x_j}.$$

Now sum over j from 1 to n.

13. Put $u = \frac{r}{p}$, $v = \frac{r}{q}$ as fractions in their lowest terms so that $p + q = r$. Then apply AM-GM with s^u p times and t^v q times.

14. See example 3.12 on page 33.

15. Write the left-hand side as

$$\frac{1}{n}\left(n^{\frac{n+1}{n}} + n^{\frac{n+2}{n+1}} + \cdots + n^{\frac{2n}{2n-1}}\right)$$

and apply AM-GM first to this expression and then to the indices.

16. One way is to apply theorem 3.2 to

$$\frac{x+y+z}{y+z}, \frac{x+y+z}{z+x} \text{ and } \frac{x+y+z}{x+y}.$$

17. (a) One way is to write the left-hand side as

$$\tfrac{1}{3}\left(a^3 + a^3 + b^3\right) + \tfrac{1}{3}\left(b^3 + b^3 + c^3\right) + \tfrac{1}{3}\left(c^3 + c^3 + a^3\right)$$

and use AM-GM on each term. For the first term, for example, AM-GM gives $\tfrac{1}{3}\left(a^3 + a^3 + b^3\right) \geq \sqrt[3]{a^3 \times a^3 \times b^3}$.

(b) One proof was given in example 2.5 on page 14. As there, we may suppose the factors on the right-hand side are all positive. Let $x = a + b - c$, $y = b + c - a$, $z = c + a - b$ so that the required inequality becomes

$$\frac{x+z}{2} \times \frac{x+y}{2} \times \frac{y+z}{2} \geq xyz,$$

which follows from AM-GM on each term of the left-hand side as in exercise 3a question 13 on page 24.

18. Equivalently, minimise

$$(1+x)\left(1 + \frac{y}{x}\right)\left(1 + \frac{z}{y}\right)\left(1 + \frac{16}{z}\right)$$

using the result of question 2 of this exercise. The maximum value is $\frac{1}{81}$ attained when $x = 2$, $y = 4$, $z = 8$.

Exercise 4a

1. Let $(x_1, x_2, x_3) = (a, b, c)$ and $(y_1, y_2, y_3) = (a^2, b^2, c^2)$ in Cauchy-Schwarz. There is equality if, and only if, $a^2b = b^2a$ and so on, which reduces to $a = b = c$.

2. In Cauchy-Schwarz let $(x_1, x_2, x_3) = (a^{\frac{3}{2}}, b^{\frac{3}{2}}, c^{\frac{3}{2}})$ and $(y_1, y_2, y_3) = (\frac{1}{\sqrt{a}}, \frac{1}{\sqrt{b}}, \frac{1}{\sqrt{c}})$. There is equality if, and only if, $\frac{a^{\frac{3}{2}}}{\sqrt{b}} = \frac{b^{\frac{3}{2}}}{\sqrt{a}}$ and so on, which reduces to $a = b = c$.

3. Let $x_i = a_i$ and $y_i = i$ and then use
$$1^2 + 2^2 + \cdots + n^2 = \tfrac{1}{6}n(n+1)(2n+1) < \tfrac{1}{6}n(2n+1)^2.$$

4. (a) The quadratic can have at most one solution, hence its discriminant is greater than or equal to 0.

   (b) $P(t) = (y_1^2 + y_2^2)t^2 - 2(x_1y_1 + x_2y_2)t + (x_1^2 + x_2^2)$. Now write down the inequality for the discriminant.

   (c) Equality occurs when the discriminant is 0, that is, there is one t for which $P(t) = 0$. For this value of t, we therefore have $x_i = ty_i$ for $i = 1, 2$.

Exercise 4b

1. Let $(x_1, x_2, x_3) = (\sqrt{1+x}, \sqrt{1+y}, \sqrt{1+z})$ and $(y_1, y_2, y_3) = (1, 1, 1)$ in Cauchy-Schwarz. There is equality if, and only if, $x = y = z = \frac{1}{3}$.

2. Apply Cauchy-Schwarz to $(x_1, x_2, x_3) = (2, 3, 6)$ and $(y_1, y_2, y_3) = (x, y, z)$. The maximum value is 7.

3. Apply Cauchy-Schwarz to $(x_1, x_2, x_3) = (1, 2, 3)$ and $(y_1, y_2, y_3) = (x, y, z)$. The minimum value is $\frac{8}{7}$.

4. (a) The maximum value is $\sqrt{a_1^2 + a_2^2 + \cdots + a_n^2}$.

   (b) The minimum value is $\dfrac{1}{\sqrt{a_1^2 + a_2^2 + \cdots + a_n^2}}$.

   For both parts, let $x_i = x_i$ and $y_i = a_i$ in Cauchy-Schwarz.

5. The minimum value is 40. Use the same method as example 4.3 on page 45.

6. Let $(x_1, x_2) = (\cos\theta, \sin\theta)$ and $(y_1, y_2) = (\sqrt{a}\cos\theta, \sqrt{b}\sin\theta)$ in Cauchy-Schwarz.

7. In Cauchy-Schwarz let $(x_1, x_2, x_3) = (\sqrt{x}, \sqrt{y}, \sqrt{z})$ and $(y_1, y_2, y_3) = \left(\sqrt{\frac{1}{x}+1}, \sqrt{\frac{1}{y}+1}, \sqrt{\frac{1}{z}+1}\right)$.

8. In Cauchy-Schwarz let $(x_1, x_2, x_3) = (\sqrt{x}, \sqrt{y}, \sqrt{z})$ and $(y_1, y_2, y_3) = \left(\sqrt{1-\frac{1}{x}}, \sqrt{1-\frac{1}{y}}, \sqrt{1-\frac{1}{z}}\right)$.

9. Apply Cauchy-Schwarz to

$$(x_1, x_2, x_3) = (\sqrt{x+y}, \sqrt{y+z}, \sqrt{z+x})$$
$$\text{and} \quad (y_1, y_2, y_3) = \left(\frac{1}{\sqrt{x+y}}, \frac{1}{\sqrt{y+z}}, \frac{1}{\sqrt{z+x}}\right).$$

10. Apply Cauchy-Schwarz to

$$(x_1, x_2, x_3) = (\sqrt{c}, \sqrt{a}, \sqrt{b})$$
$$\text{and} \quad (y_1, y_2, y_3) = \left(\frac{a}{\sqrt{c}}, \frac{b}{\sqrt{a}}, \frac{c}{\sqrt{b}}\right).$$

11. Apply Cauchy-Schwarz with

$$x_1 = \sqrt{\frac{x}{ay+bz}}, \quad y_1 = \sqrt{x(ay+bz)}$$

and so on, and note

$$y_1^2 + y_2^2 + y_3^2 = (a+b)(xy+yz+zx) \leq \tfrac{1}{3}(a+b)(x+y+z)^2.$$

12. Let $p(x) = a_n x^n + a_{n-1}x^{n-1} + \cdots + a_0$. By the condition, $a_n + a_{n-1} + \cdots + a_0 = 1$. Now apply Cauchy-Schwarz with $x_i = \sqrt{a_i x^i}$ and $y_i = \sqrt{\frac{a_i}{x^i}}$ for $i = 0$ to n.

13. Put $a = \frac{1}{x}, b = \frac{1}{y}, c = \frac{1}{z}$ and apply Cauchy-Schwarz with

$$(x_1, x_2, x_3) = \left(\frac{x}{\sqrt{y+z}}, \frac{y}{\sqrt{z+x}}, \frac{z}{\sqrt{x+y}}\right)$$
$$\text{and} \quad (y_1, y_2, y_3) = \left(\sqrt{y+z}, \sqrt{z+x}, \sqrt{x+y}\right).$$

Then make a final application of AM-GM, using $xyz = 1$.

Exercise 4c

1. Take

$$(x_1, x_2, x_3) = \left(\sqrt{\frac{a}{d}}, \sqrt{\frac{b}{e}}, \sqrt{\frac{c}{f}} \right)$$

   and $(y_1, y_2, y_3) = \left(\sqrt{ad}, \sqrt{be}, \sqrt{cf} \right),$

   then Cauchy-Schwarz gives

$$(a + b + c)^2 \le (ad + be + cf) \left(\frac{a}{d} + \frac{b}{e} + \frac{c}{f} \right).$$

   But $ad + be + cf = 2[ABC]$, so

$$\frac{a}{d} + \frac{b}{e} + \frac{c}{f} \ge \frac{(a + b + c)^2}{2[ABC]}$$

   with equality if, and only if, $d = e = f$, that is, P is at the incentre.

2. Use $p^2 = a^2 + b^2 + c^2 + 54$ for the upper and the lower bounds. Adding the triangle inequality in the form $a^2 \le ab + ac$ and so on then shows that $p \le 6\sqrt{3}$. Cauchy-Schwarz with $(x_1, x_2, x_3) = (a, b, c)$ and $(y_1, y_2, y_3) = (b, c, a)$ then gives $p \ge 9$.

   The bounds are attained by triangles with sides 3, 3, 3 and $3\sqrt{3}$, $3\sqrt{3}$, 0.

3. The triangles are similar.

4. Let PM meet AB at T. Then since $TPLB$ is a parallelogram it follows that $[APB] = \frac{BL}{BC}[ABC]$ and hence

$$\frac{BL}{BC} + \frac{CM}{CA} + \frac{AN}{AB} = 1,$$

   that is,

$$\frac{LC}{BC} + \frac{MA}{CA} + \frac{NB}{AB} = 2.$$

   Cauchy-Schwarz then implies

$$\left(\frac{BC}{LC} + \frac{CA}{MA} + \frac{AB}{NB} \right) \left(\frac{LC}{BC} + \frac{MA}{CA} + \frac{NB}{AB} \right) \ge 9$$

and so

$$\left(\frac{BC}{LC} + \frac{CA}{MA} + \frac{AB}{NB}\right) \geq \frac{9}{2}.$$

The inequality now follows from $BC = BL + LC$ and so on.

Exercise 5a

1. (a) This has already been treated in example 5.1 on page 55.

    (b) Substitute $x = a^2$, $y = b^2$, $z = c^2$ in the first, and compare what you have with what you need to prove. It turns out that you need to show that

    $$a^4(b^2 + c^2) + b^4(c^2 + a^2) + c^2(a^2 + b^2)$$
    $$- 2(b^3c^3 + c^3a^3 + a^3b^3) \geq 0.$$

    This is easily written in terms of three perfect squares.

2. Subtract the right-hand side from the left and after some simplification obtain

    $$a^2(a - b)(a - c) + b^2(b - c)(b - a) + c^2(c - a)(c - b) \geq 0,$$

    which is true by Schur's inequality.

    We have equality if, and only if, $a = b = c$.

3. Multiply example 2.2 by 2 and example 5.1 by 3 and add them together.

4. We can use the condition to write $f(x, y, z)$ in terms of two variables $u = xy$ and z. From the condition, $(x^2 + y^2)^2 = (1 - z^2)^2$ and so

    $$x^4 + y^4 + 2x^2y^2 = 1 - 2z^2 + z^4.$$

    Hence

    $$f(x, y, z) = 1 - 2z^2 - z^4 - 2u^2 - 3\sqrt{2}uz.$$

    We first minimise

    $$g(u, z) = 2u^2 + 3\sqrt{2}uz$$

    for fixed z. In fact

    $$g(u, z) = 2\left\{\left(u + \frac{3\sqrt{2}z}{4}\right)^2 - \frac{9z^2}{8}\right\} \geq -\frac{9z^2}{4},$$

    with equality if, and only if, $u = -\frac{3}{4}\sqrt{2}z$.

    Then

    $$f(x, y, z) \leq 1 + \tfrac{1}{4}z^2 - z^4 = \frac{65}{64} - \left(z^2 - \tfrac{1}{8}\right)^2 \leq \frac{65}{64}$$

with equality if, and only if, $z^2 = \frac{1}{8}$. Equality is possible since the simultaneous equations $x^2 + y^2 = \frac{7}{8}$ and $xy = \pm\frac{3}{8}$ permit solutions.

5. Make the substitutions $x = r\cos\theta$ and $y = r\sin\theta$ and it turns out that we have to minimise r^2 given that $r^2 \sin 4\theta = 4$. This clearly happens when $\sin 4\theta = 1$, which gives a minimum value of 4.

6. Make the substitution $x = b\tan\theta$, and the expression becomes

$$\frac{a + b\tan\theta}{b\sec\theta} = \frac{a\cos\theta + b\sin\theta}{b} = \frac{\sqrt{a^2 + b^2}}{b}\cos(\theta - \alpha),$$

where $\alpha = \tan^{-1}\left(\frac{b}{a}\right)$. The expression therefore has a maximum value of $\frac{\sqrt{a^2+b^2}}{b}$, which is achieved when $\theta = \alpha$ and so $x = \frac{b^2}{a}$.

Exercise 5b

1. This is similar to example 5.4 on page 59.

2. You will need to show that $2k^2 > (k+1)^2$ for sufficiently large k.

3. The essential part of the induction step is to show that, for $k \geq 2$,

$$\frac{3(k+1)}{2k+3} - \frac{3k}{2k+1} < \frac{1}{(k+1)^2}.$$

4. This can be rewritten in terms of binomial coefficients as $\binom{n}{i}^2 < n!$ for $n \geq 5$ and $1 \leq i \leq n$. For a fixed n, it is enough to prove this for the largest $\binom{n}{i}$. For $n = 2m$, this will be $\binom{2m}{m}$ and for $n = 2m + 1$, it will be $\binom{2m+1}{m}$. The proof of the induction step now proceeds from even to odd k and from odd to even k.

5. Prove, by considering ratios of successive terms of the sequence, that this reduces to showing that $(k+3)^{k+1} > 3(k+1)^{k+1}$ for $k \geq 2$. This is equivalent to

$$\left(1 + \frac{2}{k+1}\right)^{k+1} > 3,$$

which is easily proved by considering the binomial expansion.

6. This is a straightforward induction on n.

7. For $n = 2$ this reduces to $(a_1 - 1)(a_2 - 1) > 0$. Use a similar argument to prove the induction step.

8. Cross-multiply and check that it works.

9. Show, by repeated squaring, that this is equivalent to $0 < 1$. There is no such integer since $\sqrt{n} + \sqrt{n+1} > \sqrt{4n+1}$.

10. The fact that a, b, c are sides of a triangle shows that in each fraction the numerator is less than the denominator. Now use the method of example 5.5 on page 61.

11. Use the method of theorem 5.2 on page 60 to show that the sum is between 1 and 2.

12. The sum is

$$\frac{1}{31} + \frac{1}{81} + \frac{1}{151} + \cdots$$

$$< \frac{1}{10}\left(\frac{1}{3} + \frac{1}{8} + \frac{1}{15} + \cdots\right)$$

$$= \frac{1}{20}\left[\left(\frac{1}{1} - \frac{1}{3}\right) + \left(\frac{1}{2} - \frac{1}{4}\right) + \left(\frac{1}{3} - \frac{1}{5}\right) + \left(\frac{1}{4} - \frac{1}{6}\right) + \cdots\right]$$

$$= \frac{3}{40}.$$

13. Let $N = \frac{2}{3} \times \frac{4}{5} \times \frac{6}{7} \times \cdots \times \frac{2n}{2n+1}$. Show that

$$\frac{1}{2} \times \frac{3}{4} \times \frac{5}{6} \times \cdots \times \frac{2n-1}{2n} < N < \frac{3}{4} \times \frac{5}{6} \times \frac{7}{8} \times \cdots \times \frac{2n+1}{2n+2}$$

and multiply this inequality through by N. Or use induction as in question 6.

14. Expand the product

$$\left(1 - x - x^2\right)\left(F_1 x + F_2 x^2 + \cdots + F_n x^n + \cdots\right)$$

to obtain an expression for $F_1 x + F_2 x^2 + \cdots + F_n x^n + \cdots$, and then substitute a value for x.

Exercise 5c

1. We use the result of example 5.1 on page 55 that

$$a^3 + b^3 + c^3 + 3abc \geq b^2c + bc^2 + c^2a + ca^2 + a^2b + ab^2.$$

Then

$$\begin{aligned}
9abc + 27 &= 9abc + (a+b+c)^3 \\
&= a^3 + b^3 + c^3 \\
&\quad + 3(b^2c + bc^2 + c^2a + ca^2 + a^2b + ab^2) + 15abc \\
&\geq 4(b^2c + bc^2 + c^2a + ca^2 + a^2b + ab^2) + 12abc \\
&= 4(b^2c + bc^2 + c^2a + ca^2 + a^2b + ab^2 + 3abc) \\
&= 4(a+b+c)(ab+bc+ca) \\
&= 12(ab+bc+ca)
\end{aligned}$$

2. Use Cauchy-Schwarz with (ab, bc, ca) and (ca, ab, bc), or use inequality (2.1) on page 10.

3. Use Cauchy-Schwarz with $\left(\frac{a}{b}, \frac{b}{c}, \frac{c}{a}\right)$ and $\left(\frac{b}{c}, \frac{c}{a}, \frac{a}{b}\right)$, or use inequality (2.1).

4. Many methods will work here. One is to apply Cauchy-Schwarz to $(1,1,1)$ and $\left(\frac{a}{b}, \frac{b}{c}, \frac{c}{a}\right)$, and then use the AM-GM inequality on $\frac{a}{b}, \frac{b}{c}$ and $\frac{c}{a}$ and on $\frac{a}{c}, \frac{b}{a}$ and $\frac{c}{b}$. Some manipulation then yields the desired result.

5. Use the AM-GM inequality on $x^2, 2xy, 2xy, 4y^2, z^2$ and z^2 to show that the minimum is 96, and check that this bound is achievable when $(x, y, z) = (4, 2, 4)$.

6. Factorise the condition as on page 12 and prove that both factors are positive. Now, writing $A = x^2 + y^2 + z^2$ and $B = x + y + z$, show that $A = \frac{1}{3}\left(B^2 + \frac{2}{B}\right)$ and use the AM-GM inequality to show that the minimum value of A is 1, checking that this is achievable when $(x, y, z) = (1, 0, 0)$, for example.

7. Make the inequality homogeneous by inserting expressions $(p + q + r)$ and $(p + q + r)^3$. This produces an inequality which can be proved to be true by adding together three similar inequalities of the form $p^3 + q^3 \geq p^2q + pq^2$ which result from AM-GM.

Full proofs of questions 4, 5, 6 and 7 can be found in the *Yearbooks* published by the UKMT [5].

8. A technique that sometimes works, and does here, is to insert something between the left-hand side and right-hand side and to prove the two resulting inequalities. Here we insert $\frac{1}{n}$. Using the AM-RMS inequality, we have

$$\frac{\sum x_j^2}{n} \geq \left(\frac{\sum x_j}{n}\right)^2 = \frac{1}{n^2},$$

so

$$\sum x_j^2 \geq \frac{1}{n}.$$

But, by the AM-GM inequality, we have

$$\frac{1}{n} = \frac{\sum x_j}{n} \geq (x_1 x_2 \cdots x_n)^{\frac{1}{n}},$$

so that

$$\frac{1}{n} \geq n^{2n-1} x_1^2 x_2^2 \cdots x_n^2.$$

Putting these together, we obtain the desired result.

9. Using the GM-AM-RMS inequality, we have

$$\sqrt[3]{xyz} \leq \frac{x+y+z}{3} \leq \sqrt{\frac{x^2+y^2+z^2}{3}} = \frac{1}{\sqrt{3}}.$$

Hence $xyz \leq \frac{1}{3\sqrt{3}}$ and $x + y + z \leq \sqrt{3}$, and the desired result is obtained by multiplying these together. Note that we have equality if, and only if, $x = y = z = \frac{1}{\sqrt{3}}$.

Exercise 6a

1. Without loss of generality, $a \geq b$. Apply lemma 6.1 on page 67 to $\sqrt{a} \geq \sqrt{b}$ (twice).

2. We may suppose $a \geq b$, so $a^4 \geq b^4$ as well since $a, b > 0$. Then use lemma 6.1 for the left-hand inequality; the other follows from $a \geq b$, $a^2 \geq b^2$ in a similar way.

3. Two applications of lemma 6.1 give

$$a_1 b_1 + a_2 b_2 + a_3 b_3 \geq a_1 b_2 + a_2 b_1 + a_3 b_3 \geq a_1 b_2 + a_2 b_3 + a_3 b_1.$$

4. Consider the points $A(a_1, a_2)$, $B(b_1, b_2)$, $C(b_2, b_1)$ and compare angles $\angle AOB$ and $\angle AOC$, calculated from scalar products on

$$\binom{a_1}{a_2}, \binom{b_1}{b_2} \text{ and } \binom{b_2}{b_1}.$$

Exercise 6b

1. Use theorem 6.6(i) on page 73 with $n = 2$, $s = 5$, $a_1 = a$, $a_2 = b$.

2. Multiply out and use $a^3 b + b^3 a \geq 2a^2 b^2$ etc.

3. This is a direct application of theorem 6.3 with $n = 4$, $s = 3$, $t = 1$.

4. Apply theorem 6.6(i) with $s = 3$ to the sequence (a^2, b^2, c^2).

5. $\sum (a_k + \frac{1}{a_k})^2 = 2n + \sum a_k^2 + \sum a_k^{-2}$. By theorem 6.6

$$\sum a_k^2 \geq n \left(\sum \frac{a_k}{n} \right)^2 = \frac{1}{n}$$

and $\sum a_k^{-2} \geq n(\sum \frac{a_k}{n})^{-2} = n^3$. Hence the minimum is

$$n^3 + \frac{1}{n} + 2n = \frac{(1 + n^2)^2}{n}$$

attained when $a_1 = a_2 = \cdots = a_n = \frac{1}{n}$.

6. The squares cancel and what remains is a statement of the rearrangement lemma. IMOs have got harder since 1975!

7. From Chebyshev we have

$$\sum a_k \sum b_k \sum c_k \sum a_k b_k c_k \le n^2 \left(\sum a_k b_k c_k\right)^2 \le n^3 \sum a_k^2 b_k^2 c_k^2$$

by Cauchy-Schwarz.

8. $\frac{1}{3}(a^2 + b^2 + c^2) \ge \{\frac{1}{3}(a+b+c)\}^2 \ge \frac{1}{3}(a+b+c) \times (abc)^{\frac{1}{3}}$, using RMS $\ge$ AM $\ge$ GM.

Hence $(a^2 + b^2 + c^2)^2 \ge (a+b+c)^2(abc)^{\frac{2}{3}} \ge 3(a+b+c)(abc) \ge 9(abc)^2$, by AM $\ge$ GM and $a+b+c \ge 3abc$.

9. (a) Apply corollary 6.1 on page 69 to the sequence $\left(\frac{x}{y}, \frac{y}{z}, \frac{z}{x}\right)$.

   Note that $\frac{y}{x} = \frac{y}{z} \times \frac{z}{x}$ etc.

   (b) Put $\frac{y}{z} = a$, $\frac{z}{x} = b$, $\frac{x}{y} = c$ then the inequality to be proved is $a^2 + b^2 + c^2 \ge a + b + c$ given $abc = 1$. In fact, using RMS $\ge$ AM $\ge$ GM,

   $$a^2 + b^2 + c^2 \ge (a+b+c) \times \frac{a+b+c}{3} \ge (a+b+c)(abc)^{\frac{1}{3}}.$$

10. (a) $(a^2 - b^2)^2 + (b^2 - c^2)^2 + (c^2 - a^2)^2 \ge 0$.

    (b) By the rearrangement lemma $a^4 + b^4 \ge a^3 b + b^3 a$ etc.

    (c) By theorem 6.3 on page 72 with $s = 3$ and $t = 1$,

    $$a^4 + b^4 + c^4 \ge \frac{a^3 + b^3 + c^3}{3} \times (a+b+c) \ge abc(a+b+c),$$

    by AM-GM.

    Alternatively, see the approach in example 6.8 on page 75.

    (d) Suppose without loss of generality that $a \ge b \ge c$ then

    $$(a^2, b^2, c^2) \quad \text{and} \quad \left(\frac{1}{b+c}, \frac{1}{c+a}, \frac{1}{a+b}\right)$$

    are ordered in the same way. Hence

    $$\frac{a^2}{b+c} + \frac{b^2}{c+a} + \frac{c^2}{a+b} \ge \frac{a^2}{c+a} + \frac{b^2}{a+b} + \frac{c^2}{b+c}$$

and also

$$\frac{a^2}{b+c} + \frac{b^2}{c+a} + \frac{c^2}{a+b} \geq \frac{a^2}{a+b} + \frac{b^2}{b+c} + \frac{c^2}{c+a}.$$

Now add and use

$$\frac{b^2+c^2}{b+c} \geq \frac{b+c}{2} \quad \text{etc.}$$

11. By two applications of part (c) of example 6.9 on page 76,

$$\left(a^4 + b^4 + c^4 + d^4\right)(a+b+c+d)^2$$
$$\geq \left(a^3 + b^3 + c^3 + d^3\right)\left(a^2 + b^2 + c^2 + d^2\right)(a+b+c+d)$$
$$\geq \left(a^2 + b^2 + c^2 + d^2\right)^3.$$

Exercise 6c

1. We have to prove that $m_{-5}^4 \geq m_{-4}^5$. Now

$$m_{-5}^4 \geq m_{-4}m_{-1}m_{-5}^3 \geq m_{-4}^2 m_{-2}m_{-5}^2 \geq m_{-4}^3 m_{-3}m_{-5} \geq m_{-4}^5.$$

2. If $a = e^{\theta}$ and $b = e^{-\theta}$, the inequality is equivalent to

$$\left(\frac{a^{n+1} + b^{n+1}}{2}\right)^n \geq \left(\frac{a^n + b^n}{n}\right)^{n+1};$$

then use theorem 6.9 on page 80.

3. The generalisations of the two forms of Hölder's inequality given on page 81 are as follows:

(i) Suppose there are t sequences of n positive terms (a_k), (b_k), ..., (t_k), and that α, β, ..., τ are t positive rational numbers such that $\alpha + \beta + \cdots + \tau = 1$ then

$$a_1^{\alpha}b_1^{\beta} \cdots t_1^{\tau} + a_2^{\alpha}b_2^{\beta} \cdots t_2^{\tau} + \cdots + a_n^{\alpha}b_n^{\beta} \cdots t_n^{\tau}$$
$$\leq (a_1 + \cdots + a_n)^{\alpha}(b_1 + \cdots + b_n)^{\beta} \cdots (t_1 + \cdots + t_n)^{\tau}.$$

(ii) Suppose $(x_k), (y_k), \ldots, (w_k)$ are t sequences of n positive terms and $p, q, \ldots, s$ are t positive quantities such that

$$\frac{1}{p} + \frac{1}{q} + \cdots + \frac{1}{s} = 1,$$

then

$$x_1 y_1 \cdots w_1 + \cdots + x_n y_n \cdots w_n$$
$$\leq \left(x_1^p + \cdots + x_n^p\right)^{\frac{1}{p}} \left(y_1^q + \cdots + y_n^q\right)^{\frac{1}{q}} \cdots \left(w_1^s + \cdots + w_n^s\right)^{\frac{1}{s}}.$$

The proof in each case is the same as in example 6.10, example 6.11 and theorem 6.10 (on page 81) except that there are now t sequences rather than two.

4. Use the result of question 3(i) with $n = 2$ and $t = n$, the n sequences being $(1, a_1), (1, a_2), \ldots, (1, a_n)$ and

$$\alpha = \beta = \cdots = \tau = \frac{1}{n}.$$

We then have

$$(1 + a_1)^{\frac{1}{n}} (1 + a_2)^{\frac{1}{n}} \cdots (1 + a_n)^{\frac{1}{n}} \geq 1 + (a_1 a_2 \cdots a_n)^{\frac{1}{n}}$$
$$= 1 + g,$$

which on taking nth powers is what is required to prove.

Compare this proof with that of the same result in question 2 of exercise 3c.

5. Use the result of question 4 with $n = 4$ to show

$$\left\{\left(1 + \frac{1}{x}\right)\left(1 + \frac{1}{y}\right)\left(1 + \frac{1}{z}\right)\left(1 + \frac{1}{w}\right)\right\}^{\frac{1}{4}} \geq 1 + \frac{1}{(xyzw)^{\frac{1}{4}}}.$$

Now, by AM-GM, since $x + y + z + w = 1$ we have $(xyzw)^{\frac{1}{4}} \leq \frac{1}{4}$ so that

$$1 + \frac{1}{(xyzw)^{\frac{1}{4}}} \geq 5,$$

with equality if $x = y = z = w = \frac{1}{4}$.

6. Let

$$T^2 = (a_1 + b_1 + \cdots + t_1)^2 + (a_2 + b_2 + \cdots + t_2)^2 + \cdots$$
$$+ (a_n + b_n + \cdots + t_n)^2$$

$$= a_1(a_1 + b_1 + \cdots + t_1) + a_2(a_2 + b_2 + \cdots + t_2) + \cdots$$
$$+ a_n(a_n + b_n + \cdots + t_n)$$
$$+ b_1(a_1 + b_1 + \cdots + t_1) + b_2(a_2 + b_2 + \cdots + t_2) + \cdots$$
$$+ b_n(a_n + b_n + \cdots + t_n)$$

$$\vdots$$

$$+ t_1(a_1 + b_1 + \cdots + t_1) + t_2(a_2 + b_2 + \cdots + t_2) + \cdots$$
$$+ t_n(a_n + b_n + \cdots + t_n).$$

Applying the Cauchy-Schwarz inequality (or Hölder's inequality with $p = q = 2$) in many places we obtain

$$T^2 \le (a_1^2 + a_2^2 + \cdots + a_n^2)^{\frac{1}{2}} T + (b_1^2 + b_2^2 + \cdots + b_n^2)^{\frac{1}{2}} T + \cdots$$
$$+ (t_1^2 + t_2^2 + \cdots + t_n^2)^{\frac{1}{2}} T,$$

which provides the required result.

Can you also see why this inequality follows from the triangle inequality in n dimensions mentioned on page 43?

Harder See whether you can adapt the above proof, using Hölder's inequality with positive rational numbers p, q satisfying

$$\frac{1}{p} + \frac{1}{q} = 1,$$

to show the more general form of Minkowski's inequality:

$$(a_1^p + a_2^p + \cdots + a_n^p)^{\frac{1}{p}} + (b_1^p + b_2^p + \cdots + b_n^p)^{\frac{1}{p}} + \cdots$$
$$+ (t_1^p + t_2^p + \cdots + t_n^p)^{\frac{1}{p}}$$
$$\ge \{(a_1 + b_1 + \cdots + t_1)^p + (a_2 + b_2 + \cdots + t_2)^p + \cdots$$
$$+ (a_n + b_n + \cdots + t_n)^p\}^{\frac{1}{p}}.$$

Exercise 6d

1. (a) This comes from $[n, 0, \ldots, 0] \geq [1, 1, \ldots, 1]$ since

$$[n, 0, \ldots, 0] = (n-1)!(x_1^n + x_2^n + \cdots + x_n^n)$$
$$\text{and} \quad [1, 1, \ldots, 1] = n!(x_1 x_2 \cdots x_n).$$

   (b) This comes from $[2, 0, \ldots, 0] \geq [1, 1, 0, \ldots, 0]$ since

$$[2, 0, \ldots, 0] = (n-1)!(x_1^2 + x_2^2 + \cdots + x_n^2)$$
$$\text{and} \quad [1, 1, 0, \ldots, 0] = (n-2)! \sum_{i \neq j} x_i x_j.$$

2. (a) Put $x_1 = x_2 = \cdots = x_n = x > 0$ to get $x^{a_1 + \cdots + a_n} \geq x^{b_1 + \cdots + b_n}$ for all $x > 0$, forcing $a_1 + \cdots + a_n = b_1 + \cdots + b_n$. Then put $x_1 = x_2 = \cdots = x_i = x > 0$, $x_{i+1} = \cdots = x_n = 1$ and consider leading terms to see that $a_1 + \cdots + a_i \geq b_1 + \cdots + b_i$.

   (b) If $(a_1, a_2, \ldots, a_n) \neq (b_1, b_2, \ldots, b_n)$, look closely at the induction step in the proof of Muirhead's theorem to see that, for equality, $x_i = x_{i+1} = x_j$ and $x_1 = x_2 = \cdots = x_{j-1} = x_{j+1} = \cdots = x_k$ so that all the xs are equal.

3. Lengthy but routine algebra shows that the inequality to be proved is equivalent to

$$27[4, 2, 0] + 27[3, 3, 0] \geq 5[4, 1, 1] + 19[2, 2, 2] + 30[3, 2, 1],$$

   which follows from $[4, 2, 0] \geq [4, 1, 1], [2, 2, 2], [3, 2, 1]$ and $[3, 3, 0] \geq [3, 2, 1]$.

4. Multiplying by $a^2 b^2 c^2$ and expanding gives

$$a^4 b^2 + a^2 b^4 + b^4 c^2 + b^2 c^4 + a^4 c^2 + a^2 c^4 \geq$$
$$2\left(a^{\frac{8}{3}} b^{\frac{5}{3}} c^{\frac{5}{3}} + a^{\frac{5}{3}} b^{\frac{8}{3}} c^{\frac{5}{3}} + a^{\frac{5}{3}} b^{\frac{5}{3}} c^{\frac{8}{3}}\right),$$

   which follows from $[4, 2, 0] \geq \left[\frac{8}{3}, \frac{5}{3}, \frac{5}{3}\right]$.

5. Multiply out, using $16s(s-a)(s-b)(s-c) = 2\sum a^2 b^2 - \sum a^4$, to show that the required inequality is equivalent to $2\sum a^4 b^4 \leq \sum a^6 b^2$, which is immediate from $[6, 2, 0] \geq [4, 4, 0]$.

6. This expands to

$$4\left(x^4 + y^4 + z^4 + x^3 + y^3 + z^3\right)$$
$$\geq 3(1 + x + y + z + xy + yz + zx + xyz),$$

that is,

$$4([4,0,0] + [3,0,0]) \geq [0,0,0] + 3[1,0,0] + 3[1,1,0] + [1,1,1].$$

Then use $xyz = 1$ as in example 6.14 on page 88 and combine:

$$[0,0,0] = \left[\tfrac{4}{3}, \tfrac{4}{3}, \tfrac{4}{3}\right] \leq [4,0,0]$$
$$[1,0,0] = [2,1,1] \leq [4,0,0]$$
$$[1,1,0] = \left[\tfrac{4}{3}, \tfrac{4}{3}, \tfrac{4}{3}\right] \leq [3,0,0]$$
$$[1,1,1] \leq [3,0,0].$$

7. Multiplying out shows that the required inequality is equivalent to

$$[9,0,0] + 4[7,5,0] + [5,2,2] + [5,5,5]$$
$$\geq [6,0,0] + [5,5,2] + 2[5,4,0] + 2[4,2,0] + [2,2,2].$$

Then use $xyz \geq 1$ as in example 6.14 to compare sides:

$$[9,0,0] \geq [7,1,1] \geq [6,0,0]$$
$$[7,5,0] \geq [5,5,2]$$
$$[7,5,0] \geq [6,5,1] \geq [5,4,0]$$
$$[5,5,5] \geq [2,2,2].$$

We are left with trying to show that $[7,5,0] + [5,2,2] \geq 2[4,2,0]$ or the weaker result $[6,5,1] + [5,2,2] \geq 2[4,2,0]$. This suggests using $a + b \geq 2\sqrt{ab}$, which, applied term-wise, gives $[6,5,1] + [5,2,2] \geq 2\left[\tfrac{11}{2}, \tfrac{7}{2}, \tfrac{3}{2}\right] \geq 2[4,2,0]$.

Exercise 7a

1. The function $f(x) = 3x^4 + 8x^3 - 66x^2 - 144x + 567$ has a maximum at $(-1, 640)$ and minima at $(-4, 343)$ and $(3, 0)$. If we put $x = y + 3$, we obtain $g(y) = 3y^2 \left(\left(y + \frac{22}{3} \right)^2 + \frac{20}{9} \right)$ and deduce the same results without using calculus.

2. In the range $-1 < x < 1$, there is a minimum at $\left(\frac{1}{3}, 9 \right)$ and the function tends to infinity at both asymptotes. When $x > 1$, there is a maximum at $(3, 1)$. Alternatively, use the approach in example 1.10 on page 7.

3. The function $f(x) = \frac{x^4}{(x^2+1)^3}$ is even, with maxima at $\left(\pm 1, \frac{4}{27} \right)$ and a minimum at the origin, and tends to zero from above as $x \to \pm\infty$.

4. The function $f(x) = \frac{6x+8}{(x^2+1)}$ has a minimum at $(-3, -1)$ and a maximum at $\left(\frac{1}{3}, 9 \right)$ and is asymptotic to the x−axis. Alternatively, use the approach in example 1.10 on page 7.

5. There is a maximum when $x = \frac{\sqrt{5}-1}{2}$, which is a root of the equation $x^2 + x - 1 = 0$.

6. $f(x) = \frac{3\sin x}{2+\cos x}$ is an odd periodic function with an infinite number of maxima and minima. We need only consider the interval $-\pi \leq x \leq \pi$, where there is a minimum at $\left(-\frac{2\pi}{3}, -\sqrt{3} \right)$ and maximum at $\left(\frac{2\pi}{3}, \sqrt{3} \right)$.

7. Let $b^2 = k^2 ac$, where $k > 1$ since otherwise the inequality is trivial. Then put $x^2 = a^5$ and $y^2 = c^5$. Then

$$a^5 + b^5 + c^5 - 5abc(b^2 - ac) = x^2 + k^5 xy + y^2 - 5xyk(k^2 - 1)$$
$$= x^2 + k(k^4 - 5k^2 + 5)xy + y^2.$$

Let $f(k) = k(k^4 - 5k^2 + 5)$ with domain $k > 1$. Show this has a minimum of -2 when $k = \frac{1+\sqrt{5}}{2}$. Hence

$$a^5 + b^5 + c^5 - 5abc(b^2 - ac) \geq x^2 - 2xy + y^2 \geq 0$$

and we have equality when $b^2 = \left(\frac{3+\sqrt{5}}{2} \right) ac$.

Exercise 7b

1. Let $f(x) = \sin x - x \cos x$. Then $f(0) = 0$ and $f'(x) = x \sin x > 0$ for $0 < x < \pi$. Hence $\sin x > x \cos x$ for $0 < x < \pi$.

2. Let
$$f_n(x) = e^x - \left(1 + x + \frac{x^2}{2!} + \cdots + \frac{x^n}{n!}\right).$$
We have $f'_n(x) = f_{n-1}$, so since $f_0(x) = e^x - 1 > 0$ for $x > 0$ it follows by induction that $f_n(x) > 0$ for all $x > 0$.

3. Let $f(x) = \dfrac{\tan x}{x}$. We have
$$f'(x) = \frac{x - \sin x \cos x}{x^2 \cos^2 x}$$
and since $2x > \sin 2x$ for $x > 0$ it follows that $f'(x) > 0$ for $0 < x < \frac{\pi}{2}$. Hence
$$\frac{\tan x}{x} > \frac{\tan u}{u}$$
for $0 < u \le x < \frac{\pi}{2}$.

4. Let $f(x) = \dfrac{\sin x}{x}$. We have
$$f'(x) = \frac{x \cos x - \sin x}{x^2} < 0$$
for $0 < x < \frac{\pi}{2}$ by question 1. It follows that
$$\frac{\sin x}{x} \le \frac{\sin u}{u}$$
for $0 < u \le x < \frac{\pi}{2}$.

5. Consider the function $f(x) = 2x \ln x - (x^2 - 1)$. We have
$$f'(x) = 2 \ln x + 2 - 2x \quad \text{and} \quad f''(x) = \frac{2}{x} - 2.$$
We have $f'(1) = 0$ and $f''(x) > 0$ for $0 < x < 1$ and $f''(x) < 0$ for $x > 1$. It follows that $f'(x) < 0$ for $0 < x < 1$ and for $x > 1$.
Hence $f(x) \ge 0$ for $0 < x < 1$ and $f(x) \le 0$ for $x > 1$. Hence
$$\frac{x \ln x}{x^2 - 1} \le \frac{1}{2}$$
for $x > 0$, $x \ne 1$.

Exercise 7c

1. Consider $g(x) = \cos \pi x + 2x - 1$. We have $g(0) = g(\frac{1}{2}) = 0$ and

$$g'(x) = -\pi \sin \pi x + 2.$$

Note that $g'(0) = 2$ and $g'(\frac{1}{2}) = 2 - \pi < 0$. Also

$$g''(x) = -\pi^2 \cos \pi x < 0$$

for $0 \le x < \frac{1}{2}$, so $g(x)$ is concave for $0 < x < \frac{1}{2}$. It follows that $g(x) \ge 0$ over the entire interval and is strictly greater than zero for $0 < x < \frac{1}{2}$. Now let

$$f(x) = \frac{1}{\pi} \sin \pi x - x + x^2.$$

Since $f'(x) = g(x)$ and $f(0) = 0$ it follows by theorem 7.2 and the symmetry of $f(x)$ about $x = \frac{1}{2}$ that $f(x) > 0$ for $0 < x < 1$.

2. Consider the function

$$h(y) = \sin \frac{\pi y}{2} - \sqrt{2y}$$

where $0 \le y \le \frac{1}{2}$. Now $h(0) = h(\frac{1}{2}) = 0$. Also

$$h'(y) = \frac{\pi}{2} \cos \frac{\pi y}{2} - \sqrt{2}$$

$$\text{and} \quad h''(y) = -\pi^2 \sin \frac{\pi y}{2},$$

so that $h'(0) > 0$ and $h''(y) < 0$ for $0 < y < \frac{1}{2}$. Hence $h(y)$ is concave and so $h(y) \ge 0$ for $0 \le y \le \frac{1}{2}$, with equality if, and only if, $y = 0$ or $y = \frac{1}{2}$. Squaring, we obtain

$$\sin^2 \frac{\pi y}{2} \ge 2y^2$$

for $-\frac{1}{2} \le y \le \frac{1}{2}$ or $1 - 4y^2 \ge \cos \pi y$ for $-\frac{1}{2} \le y \le \frac{1}{2}$, with equality if (and only if) $y = -\frac{1}{2}, 0, \frac{1}{2}$.

Now put $x = y + \frac{1}{2}$ to obtain $4x(1 - x) \ge \sin \pi x$ for $0 \le x \le 1$, with equality if, and only if, $x = 0, \frac{1}{2}, 1$.

3. By the power means inequality for fractional indices we have

$$\frac{x^{\frac{1}{3}} + y^{\frac{1}{3}} + z^{\frac{1}{3}}}{3} \leq \left(\frac{x + y + z}{3}\right)^{\frac{1}{3}} = 2.$$

4. From the power means inequality for fractional indices

$$\tfrac{1}{3}\left(l^{\frac{5}{2}} + m^{\frac{5}{2}} + n^{\frac{5}{2}}\right) \geq \left(\frac{l + m + n}{3}\right)^{\frac{5}{2}}$$

and hence

$$3^{\frac{3}{2}}\left(l^{\frac{5}{2}} + m^{\frac{5}{2}} + n^{\frac{5}{2}}\right) \geq (l + m + n)^{\frac{5}{2}}$$
$$\geq (l + m + n)(l + m + n)^{\frac{3}{2}}$$
$$\geq 3^{\frac{3}{2}}(l + m + n)(lmn)^{\frac{1}{2}}.$$

Now

$$l^3(m + n) + m^3(n + l) + n^3(l + m) \geq 2l^3\sqrt{mn} + 2m^3\sqrt{nl} + 2n^3\sqrt{lm}$$
$$= 2(lmn)^{\frac{1}{2}}\left(l^{\frac{5}{2}} + m^{\frac{5}{2}} + n^{\frac{5}{2}}\right)$$
$$\geq 2lmn(l + m + n).$$

5. Let I be the incentre and L, M, N the feet of the perpendiculars from I on to the sides BC, CA, AB respectively. Let $BL = y$, $LC = z$, $CM = z$, $MA = x$, $AN = x$, $NB = y$. Let $\angle AIN = u$, $\angle BIL = v$, $\angle CIM = w$.

Then since AI bisects $\angle BAC$ etc. we have $0 < u, v, w < \frac{\pi}{2}$ and $u + v + w = \pi$. Let s be the semi-perimeter of triangle ABC. Then

$$\frac{s}{3} = \frac{x + y + z}{3} = \frac{\tan u + \tan v + \tan w}{3}$$

since the inradius is 1. But $\tan x$ is convex on $0 < x < \frac{\pi}{2}$ so

$$\frac{\tan u + \tan v + \tan w}{3} \geq \tan\left(\frac{u + v + w}{3}\right) = \tan\frac{\pi}{3} = \sqrt{3}.$$

Thus $s \geq 3\sqrt{3}$, with equality if, and only if, $u = v = w$, which is when the triangle is equilateral.

Exercise 7d

1. There is a minimum at the point $(2, -1)$.

2. There are minima at $(-1, -1)$ and $(1, 1)$ and a saddle point at $(0, 0)$.

3. There is a maximum at $(2, -3)$, a minimum at $(-2, 1)$ and saddle points at $(-2, -3)$ and $(-2, 1)$.

4. There is a maximum at $(1, 0)$ and a saddle point at $(-1, 0)$.

5. There is a maximum at $(1, 2)$ and a minimum at $(-\frac{1}{3}, -\frac{2}{3})$.

Exercise 7e

1. By using the standard technique, we obtain $\lambda x^2 = 4\lambda y^2 = 9\lambda z^2 = 1$. Hence $\lambda = 4$ and since $x, y, z > 0$ we have $(x, y, z) = (\frac{1}{2}, \frac{1}{4}, \frac{1}{6})$. Now let $x = \frac{1}{2} + u$, $y = \frac{1}{4} + v$, $z = \frac{1}{6} + w$, where, in order to satisfy the condition, $u + 4v + 9w = 0$. Now, using the binomial theorem,

$$
\begin{aligned}
\frac{1}{x} + \frac{1}{y} + \frac{1}{z} &= 2(1 + 2u)^{-1} + 4(1 + 4v)^{-1} + 6(1 + 6w)^{-1} \\
&= 2(1 - 2u + 4u^2 + \cdots) + 4(1 - 4v + 16v^2 + \cdots) \\
&\qquad\qquad + 6(1 - 6w + 36w^2 + \cdots) \\
&= 12 - 4(u + 4v + 9w) + 8(u^2 + 8v^2 + 27w^2) + \cdots \\
&= 12 + 8(u^2 + 8v^2 + 27w^2) + \cdots \\
&\geq 12
\end{aligned}
$$

(for small u, v, w) and hence the stationary value 12 is a (local) minimum.

2. The usual technique yields a critical point $x = y = z = \frac{1}{a+b+c}$ with value $(a + b + c)^2$. Again we consider variations of u, v, w in x, y, z respectively, under the condition $au + bv + cw = 1$. Now we have

$$
\begin{aligned}
\frac{a}{x} + \frac{b}{y} + \frac{c}{z} = (a + b + c)\Big[&a\big(1 + (a + b + c)u\big)^{-1} \\
&+ b\big(1 + (a + b + c)v\big)^{-1} + c\big(1 + (a + b + c)w\big)^{-1}\Big]
\end{aligned}
$$

$$= (a+b+c)^2 \Big[1 - (au + bv + cw)$$
$$+ (a+b+c)(au^2 + bv^2 + cw^2) + \cdots \Big]$$
$$= (a+b+c)^2 \Big[1 + (a+b+c)(au^2 + bv^2 + cw^2) + \cdots \Big].$$

For small values of u, v, w, the expression in the square brackets is at least 1, and so the value $(a+b+c)^2$ is a local minimum.

3. Using the standard technique, we obtain $\lambda(x+y) = \lambda(y+z) = \lambda(z+x) = 1$. Hence we have $x = y = z$ and, because $x, y, z \geq 0$, their common value is $\sqrt{3}$. Now let $x = \sqrt{3} + u$, $y = \sqrt{3} + v$, $x = \sqrt{3} + w$, where $2\sqrt{3}\sum u + \sum uv = 0$. Hence

$$4\sqrt{3}\sum u + \left(\sum u\right)^2 - \sum u^2 = 0$$

and so, using the quadratic formula,

$$\sum u = -2\sqrt{3} \pm \sqrt{12 + \sum u^2}.$$

If we take the negative sign, then $\sum u < -4\sqrt{3}$, which contradicts the fact that u, v, w are small. Hence we take the positive sign, in which case we have $\sum u > 0$. It then follows that

$$x + y + z = 3\sqrt{3} + u + v + w \geq 3\sqrt{3},$$

so the critical point is a minimum.

4. The usual technique yields

$$2x - \lambda(y+z) = 0$$
$$10y - \lambda(z+x) = 0$$
$$16z - \lambda(x+y) = 0.$$

From these, we obtain $(2+\lambda)x = (10+\lambda)y = (16+\lambda)z = K$ (say), and substituting this back into the first equation gives us

$$\lambda^3 + 14\lambda^2 - 160 = 0,$$

that is,

$$(\lambda+4)(\lambda^2 + 10\lambda - 40) = 0.$$

The value $\lambda = -4$ gives us $(x,y,z) = \left(-\frac{K}{2}, \frac{K}{6}, \frac{K}{12}\right)$, and now the side condition yields $K = \pm 3$. Thus we have two stationary points $\left(-\frac{3}{2}, \frac{1}{2}, \frac{1}{4}\right)$ and $\left(\frac{3}{2}, -\frac{1}{2}, -\frac{1}{4}\right)$. Both of these give the same value of 4 for $x^2 + 5y^2 + 8z^2$, but we must now show that this is a minimum. So let $x = -\frac{3}{2} + u$, $y = \frac{1}{2} + v$, $z = \frac{1}{4} + w$, where the side condition requires that $\frac{1}{4}(3u - 5v - 4w) + uv + vw + wu = 0$. Then

$$x^2 + 5y^2 + 8z^2$$
$$= 4 + (-3u + 5v + 4w) + \left(u^2 + 5v^2 + 8w^2\right)$$
$$= 4 + \left(u^2 + 5v^2 + 8w^2\right) + uv + vw + wu$$
$$= 4 + \frac{1}{2}\left((u+v)^2 + (v+w)^2 + (w+u)^2\right) + 4v^2 + 7w^2$$
$$\geq 0$$

so there is, indeed, a minimum value at these two stationary points.

5. There are four critical points, namely $(1,1)$, $(-1,-1)$, $(\sqrt{5}, -\sqrt{5})$ and $(-\sqrt{5}, \sqrt{5})$. Now the usual technique shows that

$$(1+u)(1+v) = (-1+u)(-1+v) = 1 - \tfrac{3}{10}(u-v)^2,$$

so the first two points are maxima, and

$$\left(\sqrt{5}+u\right)\left(\sqrt{5}+v\right) = \left(-\sqrt{5}+u\right)\left(-\sqrt{5}+v\right) = -5 + \tfrac{3}{2}(u+v)^2,$$

so the second two points are minima.

Exercise 8a

1. By the AM-GM inequality, $4 = \frac{ab+bc+ca}{3} \geq \sqrt[3]{abc}$, so $abc \leq 8$, with equality if, and only if, $a = b = c = 2$. Also $abc = 2+a+b+c \geq 2+3\sqrt[3]{abc}$, using the AM-GM inequality again, so, if $u = \sqrt[3]{abc}$, then $u^3 - 3u + 2 \geq 0$. But $u^3 - 3u + 2 = (u-2)\left((u+1)^2 + 3\right)$ and so $u \geq 2$ and $abc = 8$. It follows that the only solution is $a = b = c = 2$.

2. Let a, b, c, d be the roots of $x^4 - px^3 + qx - r = 0$. If $a = b = c = d = 0$ the result is trivial, and if not, $\sum a^2 > 0$. Show that this implies that $p > 0$, and find expressions in terms of p, q, r for $\sum a^3$ and $\sum a^5$.

3. By means of the substitution $x = t - \frac{1}{2}$, reduce the cubic to $t^3 - \frac{27}{4}t + \frac{13+2k}{4} = 0$ and apply (8.1) on page 113 to obtain $-7 \leq k \leq 20$.

4. First create a cubic with the roots $(\alpha, \beta, \gamma) = \left(\frac{a}{b}, \frac{b}{c}, \frac{c}{a}\right)$. We have $\sum \alpha = 3$, $\sum \alpha\beta = p$ and $\alpha\beta\gamma = 1$, so the cubic is $x^3 - 3x^2 + px - 1 = 0$ and we have to maximise the value of p. Using the substitution $x = t + 1$, reduce the cubic to $t^3 + (p-3)t + (p-3) = 0$ and apply (8.1) to obtain $(p-3)^2(4p+15) \leq 0$. Now p cannot be 3 since then the cubic would be a perfect cube with three roots equal to 1, which would imply that $a = b = c = 1$ and this is excluded. Hence $p \leq -\frac{15}{4}$, and it can be checked that this bound is achievable when $(a, b, c) = (2, -4, 8)$.

   It can actually be shown that whenever a, b, c are integers and $\frac{a}{b} + \frac{b}{c} + \frac{c}{a} = 3$ then abc is a perfect cube

5. First create a quartic with the roots $(\alpha, \beta, \gamma, \delta) = \left(\frac{a}{b}, \frac{b}{c}, \frac{c}{d}, \frac{d}{a}\right)$. We have

$$\sum \alpha = 4$$
$$\sum \alpha\beta = 2 + \frac{a}{c} + \frac{c}{a} + \frac{b}{d} + \frac{d}{b} = 2 + p$$
$$\sum \alpha\beta\gamma = \frac{a}{d} + \frac{d}{c} + \frac{c}{b} + \frac{b}{a}$$
$$\alpha\beta\gamma\delta = 1,$$

but now we can use the $ac = bd$ condition to show that $\sum \alpha\beta\gamma = 4$. Our task is to maximise p. Hence $x^4 - 4x^3 + (2+p)x^2 - 4x + 1 = 0$, which can be rewritten as $(x-1)^4 = (4-p)x^2$. If $2+p = 6$, then the quartic is $(x-1)^4 = 0$ and $a = b = c = d$, which is not the case.

Writing $4 - p = k^2$, for $k > 0$, we see that the equation becomes $x^2 - (2 \pm \sqrt{k})x + 1 = 0$, and both of these equations have real solutions if, and only if, $(2 \pm \sqrt{k})^2 \geq 4$ and so $k \geq 4$ and $p \leq 12$. This maximum is achievable when, for example,

$$(a, b, c, d) = (3 + 2\sqrt{2}, 1, -1, -3 - 2\sqrt{2}).$$

6. Let a, b, c be the roots of the cubic $x^3 - 6x^2 + 9x - r = 0$. By making the substitution $x = t + 2$, this can be reduced to $t^3 - 3t + (2 - r) = 0$ and now (8.1) implies that $0 \leq r \leq 4$, and, equivalently, $\left|\frac{r-2}{2}\right| \leq 1$. Now let $t = 2\cos\theta$ and use the formula $\cos 3\theta = 4\cos^3\theta - 3\cos\theta$ to yield the equation $\cos 3\theta = \frac{r-2}{2} = \cos\alpha$. Hence $3\theta = 2k\pi \pm \alpha$ and so the three roots are $2\cos\frac{2\pi - \alpha}{3}$, $2\cos\frac{\alpha}{3}$ and $2\cos\frac{2\pi + \alpha}{3}$. But these three angles are $\frac{2\pi}{3}$ apart, so we may choose them so that one lies in each of the ranges $\left(-\pi, -\frac{\pi}{3}\right)$, $\left(-\frac{\pi}{3}, \frac{\pi}{3}\right)$ and $\left(\frac{\pi}{3}, \pi\right)$ and hence the roots of $t^3 - 3t + (2 - r) = 0$ lie in the ranges $(-2, -1)$, $(-1, 1)$ and $(1, 2)$, one root to each range. It follows that the roots of the original cubic lie in the ranges $(0, 2)$, $(2, 3)$ and $(3, 4)$, one root to each range.

Exercise 8b

1. $6p_2^2 = 54$, so $p_2 = 3$. Now

$$p_1 = \frac{\sum a}{4} \geq p_2 = 3.$$

Hence the minimum value of $\sum a$ is 12, when $a = b = c = d = 3$. Also $3 = p_2 \geq p_4 = (abcd)^{\frac{1}{4}}$. Hence the maximum value of $abcd$ is 81, when $a = b = c = d = 3$.

2. We have

$$p_1 = \frac{\sum a}{4},$$

$$p_2^2 = \frac{\sum ab}{6} = 9,$$

$$p_3^3 = \frac{\sum abc}{4}.$$

Now $p_2^4 \geq p_1 p_3^3$ by lemma 8.1 on page 116. Hence

$$81 \geq \tfrac{1}{16} \sum a \sum abc$$

from which the result follows.

3. $\left(\sqrt{a} + \sqrt{b}\right)^2 = a + b + 2\sqrt{ab} = 2(p_1 + p_2)$ and $\sqrt{ab} = p_2$, so the equation is

$$x^2 - \sqrt{2(p_1 + p_2)}\, x + p_2 = 0.$$

Hence

$$\left(\frac{\sqrt{a} + \sqrt{b}}{2}\right)^2 = \frac{p_1 + p_2}{2} \leq p_1 = \frac{a + b}{2}$$

since $p_1 \geq p_2$.

4. The necessity is proved in lemma 8.1 on page 116. The sufficiency is school algebra and is a result of the formula for solving quadratic equations, $x = p_1 \pm \sqrt{p_1^2 - p_2^2}$. Clearly the roots coincide if, and only if, $p_1 = p_2$.

Exercise 9a

1. $AB < AP + BP$ by the triangle inequality. Now add two similar inequalities for BC and CA.

2. Labelling the vertices $ABCD$ in order, we have $AC < AB + BC$ and $AC < AD + DC$. Using a similar inequality for BD gives the first required inequality.

   For the other inequality, let X be the intersection of the diagonals. Then $AB < AX + BX$ and add three similar inequalities.

3. Rotate the trapezium through $180°$ about the midpoint of DC to create a parallelogram.

4. The result is trivial if $AC = BC$. So assume $BC > AC$ and produce CD to X so that triangle CXA is similar to triangle CBD. Now use ratios.

5. Assume first that A and B are on the same side of $\mathcal{L}$, with B closer to $\mathcal{L}$ than A. Extend AB to meet $\mathcal{L}$ at X. By considering another point on $\mathcal{L}$ and applying the triangle inequality, show that X is the point we are seeking.

   If A and B are on opposite sides, again with B closer than A, let B_1 be the reflection of B in $\mathcal{L}$ and let AB_1 meet $\mathcal{L}$ at X; again use the triangle inequality to show that X is the required point.

   Finally, we must consider the case where A and B are equidistant from $\mathcal{L}$ and on opposite sides of it. Define B_1 as before. If B_1 and A are coincident, then X can be anywhere on $\mathcal{L}$ since $AX = BX$. If not, then $AX - BX < AB_1$ and it approaches AB_1 asymptotically as X travels along $\mathcal{L}$.

6. (a) Let N be the point on BC such that AMN is a straight line. Now use the triangle inequality for triangles MNB and ANC.

   (b) Apply (a) three times.

Exercise 9b

1. For the left-hand inequality put $a = m + n$, $b = n + \ell$, $c = \ell + m$, with $\ell, m, n > 0$. The inequality transforms to the sum of three

inequalities like

$$\frac{1}{m} + \frac{1}{n} \geq \frac{4}{m+n}.$$

For the the right-hand inequality just clear fractions and apply AM-GM to six terms of the form a^2b, b^2a, or use theorem 3.2 on page 28

2. The right-hand side is (2.1) on page 10. The left-hand side follows from $a^2 < a(b+c)$ and two similar inequalities.

3. From question 2 we have $k \leq 2$. Putting $a = m+n$, $b = n+\ell$, $c = \ell + m$, the difference between the left-hand side and right-hand side is

$$(k-2)\sum m^2 + (3k-2)\sum mn,$$

which is negative for $k < 2$ when ℓ is large and m, n are small. So $k = 2$.

4. Using the standard substitution, as in problem 3, this reduces to the known inequality of example 5.1 on page 55

$$\ell^3 + m^3 + n^3 + 3lmn \geq \ell^2 m + m^2 n + n^2 \ell + \ell m^2 + mn^2 + n\ell^2.$$

5. The standard substitution reduces this to the inequality

$$\ell^3(m+n) + m^3(n+\ell) + n^3(\ell+m) \geq 2\ell mn(\ell + m + n).$$

Now by the AM-GM inequality we have both $\ell^3 m + \ell m^3 \geq 2\ell^2 m^2$ etc., and $\ell^2 m^2 + \ell^2 n^2 \geq 2\ell^2 mn$ etc.

6. The standard substitution reduces this to proving, for ℓ, m, $n > 0$ that

$$\ell^2 m + m^2 n + n^2 \ell + \ell m^2 + mn^2 + n\ell^2 + 2\ell mn \geq 8\ell mn > 0.$$

Now use the AM-GM inequality.

7. (a) Use

$$[ABC] = \frac{abc}{4R} = \frac{r(a+b+c)}{2}$$

to give

$$\frac{abc}{2Rr} = a + b + c \geq 3(abc)^{\frac{1}{3}},$$

which yields the desired result.

(b) Use $4R[ABC] = abc$ in (a) to give $[ABC]^2 \geq \frac{27}{2}Rr^3$.

(c) This follows from $[ABC] = \frac{1}{2}r(a + b + c)$ and (b).

8. From Heron's formula $r = 1$ implies $s = (s - a)(s - b)(s - c)$. The AM-GM inequality gives

$$\frac{s}{3} = \frac{(s-a) + (s-b) + (s-c)}{3} \geq s^{\frac{1}{3}}$$

and hence $s \geq 3\sqrt{3} > 5$.

9. In the given expression replace z by $-x - y$ and collect like terms, then use the cosine rule to obtain

$$2\left\{(bx + ay\cos C)^2 + (ay\sin C)^2\right\} \geq 0.$$

Exercise 9c

1. This follows at once from result 9.6 on page 130.

2. $a^2 + b^2 + c^2 = 4R^2(3 - \cos^2 A - \cos^2 B - \cos^2 C)$. The inequality now follows from example 9.10.

3. When the triangle has an obtuse angle, this result is trivial, so we shall assume that it is acute-angled.

    Use the cosine rule to show that the inequality is equivalent to

$$(b + c - a)^2(c + a - b)^2(a + b - c)^2$$
$$\geq (b^2 + c^2 - a^2)(c^2 + a^2 - b^2)(a^2 + b^2 - c^2).$$

Now

$$
\begin{aligned}
(a - b + c)^2(a + b - c)^2 &- (a^2 - b^2 + c^2)(a^2 + b^2 - c^2) \\
&= [a^2 - (b-c)^2]^2 - [a^4 - (b^2 - c^2)^2] \\
&= (b-c)^4 - 2a^2(b-c)^2 + (b-c)^2(b+c)^2 \\
&= (b-c)^2[(b-c)^2 - 2a^2 + (b+c)^2] \\
&= 2(b-c)^2(b^2 + c^2 - a^2),
\end{aligned}
$$

which is positive in this case. Hence we have three inequalities of the form

$$(a - b + c)^2(a + b - c)^2 \geq (a^2 - b^2 + c^2)(a^2 + b^2 - c^2)$$

and these can be multiplied together to yield the desired result.

4. Use the fact that $AH = 2R \cos A$ to reduce this to result 9.5(ii) on page 130.

5. Use the sine and cosine rules to show that $\cot B - \cot C = \frac{3}{2\sin A}$. Hence the minimum value is $\frac{3}{2}$ when $A = 90°$ and the triangle has sides $a : b : c = \sqrt{5} : 2 : 1$.

6. Let $x = \tan A$, $y = \tan B$, $z = \tan C$ then from result 9.5(i) we have

$$\frac{1}{yz} + \frac{1}{zx} + \frac{1}{xy} = 1.$$

Since $x, y, z > 0$ we can use theorem 3.2 on page 28 for

$$(\sqrt{yz}, \sqrt{zx}, \sqrt{xy}) \quad \text{and} \quad \left(\frac{1}{\sqrt{yz}}, \frac{1}{\sqrt{zx}}, \frac{1}{\sqrt{xy}}\right)$$

to obtain $yz + zx + xy \geq 9$. Now

$$\cos A = -\cos(B + C) = \sin B \sin C - \cos B \cos C$$

so that

$$\frac{\cos A}{\cos B \cos C} = yz - 1$$

and the result follows by adding.

7. In the range $0 < \theta < 45°$, $\tan^2 \theta$ is convex, so we can use Jensen's inequality (theorem 7.3 on page 97) to give

$$\tfrac{1}{3}(\tan^2 x + \tan^2 y + \tan^2 z) \geq \tan^2\left(\frac{x + y + z}{3}\right) = \tfrac{1}{3}.$$

and hence the left-hand inequality. For the right-hand inequality, note that

$$\tan x \tan y + \tan y \tan z + \tan z \tan x = \tan x \tan y + \frac{\tan y + \tan x}{\tan(x + y)}$$

$$= \tan x \tan y + (1 - \tan x \tan y)$$

$$= 1$$

since $x + y + z = 90°$. Now, letting $T = \tan^2 x + \tan^2 y + \tan^2 z$, we have

$$(\tan x + \tan y + \tan z)^2 = \tan^2 x + \tan^2 y + \tan^2 z + 2 = T + 2.$$

Now since $x, y, z < 45°$ we have $T < \tan x + \tan y + \tan z$, and so $T^2 < T + 2$. Hence $T < 2$.

8. Let C be the largest angle, then certainly $45° < C < 90°$. The required inequality is equivalent to proving

$$2 \cos \tfrac{1}{2}(A - B)\left(\cos \tfrac{1}{2}C - \sin \tfrac{1}{2}C \right) + (\sin C - \cos C) > 0.$$

Since $C > 45°$ we have $\sin C > \cos C$, and since $\tfrac{1}{2}C < 45°$ we have $\cos \tfrac{1}{2}C > \sin \tfrac{1}{2}C$, and hence the result.

9. Let H be the orthocentre and D, E, F the feet of the altitudes. Let $\angle ECH = \theta$. Then

$$CD + CE = CH \cos\theta + CH \cos(C - \theta)$$
$$\leq 2CH \cos \tfrac{1}{2}C$$
$$= 4R \cos C \cos \tfrac{1}{2}C.$$

Adding together two similar inequalities produces the result.

10. If a, b, c are not the sides of a triangle, then the left-hand side is negative and the inequality is trivial. If they are, let the semi-perimeter be s. Clearly $s = 1$, so we can multiply the left-hand side by s^3 so as to make the inequality homogeneous. Hence we have to prove that

$$64s^3(s - a)(s - b)(s - c) \leq 27a^2b^2c^2.$$

Now we use result 9.2 and result 9.3 on pages 127–128 to transform this to $64s^2[ABC]^2 \leq 27 \times 16R^2[ABC]^2$ or $(a + b + c)^2 \leq 27R^2$, and then the sine rule reduces this to $\sin A + \sin B + \sin C \leq \tfrac{3}{2}\sqrt{3}$. This is result 9.8(i) on page 131.

Exercise 9d

1. From example 9.14 on page 137 the length AU of the internal bisector of angle A is given by

$$AU^2 = \frac{bc(b + c - a)(b + c + a)}{(b + c)^2}.$$

The inequality now follows, using $b + c > a$ and $bc \leq \frac{1}{4}(b+c)^2$.

The inequality also follows from exercise 9a question 4 on page 122 and the AM-GM inequality.

2. We have

$$PC = BQ = \frac{ba}{b+c}$$

$$\text{and} \quad BP = QC = \frac{ca}{b+c}.$$

Using the cosine rule on triangles APC and APB we find

$$bc(b+c) = \frac{a^2bc}{b+c} + (b+c)(AP)^2.$$

Similarly

$$b^3 + c^3 = \frac{a^2bc}{b+c} + (b+c)(AQ)^2.$$

Subtracting yields the result

$$(AQ)^2 = (AP)^2 + (b-c)^2,$$

which shows that $AQ \geq AP$, with equality if, and only if, triangle ABC is isosceles with $b = c$.

3. The radius of circle BOC is easily shown to be $\frac{1}{2}R \sec A$ and since $\angle DBO = 90° + C - B$ it follows that $OD = R \sec A \cos(B - C)$. The required inequality now follows from

$$\cos(A - B)\cos(B - C)\cos(C - A) \geq 8\cos A \cos B \cos C.$$

Because $\sin 2A, \sin 2B > 0$, by AM-GM we have

$$\sin 2A + \sin 2B \geq 2\sqrt{\sin 2A \sin 2B},$$

with equality when $A = B$. Hence

$$\sin C \cos(A - B) \geq \sqrt{\sin 2A \sin 2B}$$

since $\sin(A + B) = \sin C$.

Multiplying this and two similar results, we get

$$\sin C \cos(A - B) \times \sin A \cos(B - C) \times \sin B \cos(C - A)$$
$$\geq \sin 2A \sin 2B \sin 2C$$
$$= 8 \sin A \cos A \sin B \cos B \sin C \cos C.$$

The result now follows since $\sin A, \sin B, \sin C > 0$. Equality occurs when $A = B = C$, that is, when the triangle is equilateral.

4. By the alternate segment theorem, $\angle CYX = \angle YZX$ and, by external angles of a cyclic quadrilateral, $\angle YZX = \angle YRP$, so PR is parallel to AC. Since the same is true for the other two sides the triangles ABC and PQR are homothetic, so they have a centre of similitude. This homothety also maps the circumcircle of PQR to that of ABC. Note that the former is the nine-point circle of XYZ, and the circumcircle of XYZ is the incircle of ABC. If the circumradii of these three circles are ρ, r and R, then $\rho = \frac{1}{2}r \leq \frac{1}{4}R$, and so the scale factor of the homothety is at most $\frac{1}{4}$. Since it takes the triangle PQR to ABC the result follows.

5. Let P be the point where the incircle touches AB and let XQ be a diameter of the circumcircle. Show that triangles API and QBX are similar, and hence that $\frac{PI}{BX} = \frac{AI}{QX}$ so that $AI \times BX = PI \times QX = 2Rr$. Also show that $IX = BX$. It follows that $AI \times IX = BI \times IY = CI \times IZ = 2Rr$. Therefore the required inequality is equivalent to $(AI)^2(BI)^2(CI)^2 \leq 8R^3r^3$. Now $AI = r \operatorname{cosec} \frac{1}{2}A$ etc., and a standard result is

$$r = 4R \sin \tfrac{1}{2}A \sin \tfrac{1}{2}B \sin \tfrac{1}{2}C.$$

The required inequality is therefore reduced to the standard result $\sin \frac{1}{2}A \sin \frac{1}{2}B \sin \frac{1}{2}C \leq \frac{1}{8}$.

6. Let A_1 be the midpoint of BC. By Apollonius's theorem

$$AA_1^2 = \ell^2 = \tfrac{1}{4}(2b^2 + 2c^2 - a^2).$$

Let the centre of the circle through A touching BC at A_1 be O_1. Then if $\angle AA_1C = \theta$ we have $\angle A_1O_1A = 2\theta$ and since $O_1A_1 = O_1A$ we have $\ell = 2R_1 \sin \theta$. Now, using the sine rule for triangle AA_1C, we have

$$\ell = \frac{b \sin C}{\sin \theta}.$$

It follows that

$$R_1 = \frac{\ell^2}{2b \sin C}$$

and hence

$$\frac{R_1}{a} = \frac{R(2b^2 + c^2 - a^2)}{4abc}.$$

Adding in similar expressions for $\dfrac{R_2}{b}$ and $\dfrac{R_3}{c}$ we have

$$\frac{R_1}{a} + \frac{R_2}{b} + \frac{R_3}{c} = \frac{3R(a^2 + b^2 + c^2)}{4abc}.$$

By the Cauchy-Schwarz inequality the square of this is

$$\leq (R_1^2 + R_2^2 + R_3^2)\left(\frac{1}{a^2} + \frac{1}{b^2} + \frac{1}{c^2}\right).$$

Hence

$$R_1^2 + R_2^2 + R_3^2 \geq \frac{9R^2(a^2 + b^2 + c^2)^2}{16(b^2c^2 + c^2a^2 + a^2b^2)} \geq \frac{27R^2}{16},$$

using (2.1) on page 10.

7. Using the notation of example 9.19 on page 142 we have the minimum when $\sin BPC : \sin CPA : \sin APB = x : y : z$. This means that P must satisfy $[BPC] = [CPA] = [APB]$, and so P coincides with the centroid G.

8. The minimum is when P satisfies

$$\sin BPC : \sin CPA : \sin APB = a : b : c$$

which implies $\angle BPC = 180° - A$, $\angle CPA = 180° - B$, $\angle APB = 180° - C$, so that P coincides with the orthocentre H.

Exercise 9e

1. Let the areal coordinates of P be (ℓ, m, n). Then since $[BMC] = [BPC] = \ell$ and since M lies on AC the areal coordinates of M are

$(\ell, 0, m+n)$, and, similarly, L is $(0, \ell+m, n)$ and N is $(n+\ell, m, 0)$. Hence the expression to be maximised is

$$\frac{n}{\ell+m} \times \frac{\ell}{m+n} \times \frac{m}{n+\ell} = \frac{\ell m n}{(m+n)(n+\ell)(\ell+m)},$$

and, by the argument in example 9.21 on page 148, this has a maximum value of $\frac{1}{8}$ when P is at the centroid of the triangle.

2. Use theorem 9.1(i) on page 147 and result 9.5 on page 130. Since the areal coordinates of H are $(\tan A, \tan B, \tan C)$ it follows that

$$\tan A(PA)^2 + \tan B(PB)^2 + \tan C(PC)^2$$
$$= \tan A(HA)^2 + \tan B(HB)^2 + \tan C(HC)^2$$
$$+ \tan A \tan B \tan C(PH)^2.$$

The result now follows since all of the tangents are positive when triangle ABC is acute, and precisely one is negative when triangle ABC is obtuse.

The stationary value in each case is $8R^2 \sin A \sin B \sin C$ since $AH = 2R \cos A$ etc.

3. The normalised areal coordinates of D are

$$\left(-1, \frac{2\sin B \cos C}{\sin A}, \frac{2\sin C \cos B}{\sin A}\right)$$

and those of E and F are found by cyclic change of A, B, C. The ratio $\frac{[DEF]}{[ABC]}$ is given by the determinant whose rows are the coordinates of D, E, F. When evaluated, using result 9.6 on page 130, this ratio comes to $3 + 8\cos A \cos B \cos C$. Now from example 9.10 on page 133 we have

$$\cos A \cos B \cos C \leq \tfrac{1}{8}$$

so

$$\frac{[DEF]}{[ABC]} \leq 4.$$

4. We find that $AG^2 = \frac{1}{9}(2b^2 + 2c^2 - a^2)$, using the distance formula on page 147. Now the normalised areal coordinates of S are

$$\frac{1}{a^2 + b^2 + c^2}(a^2, b^2, c^2),$$

so the displacement

$$\mathbf{AS} = \frac{1}{a^2 + b^2 + c^2}\left(-(b^2 + c^2),\ b^2,\ c^2\right).$$

Using the distance formula on page 147 we find that

$$\frac{AS}{AG} = \frac{3bc}{a^2 + b^2 + c^2}$$

and the inequality holds since $ab + bc + ca \leq a^2 + b^2 + c^2$ from (2.1) on page 10.

5. Use theorem 9.1(i) with K at G. The points P are the ends of the diameter containing G since these are the points where PG is a maximum or a minimum.

Bibliography

[1] A. D. Gardiner and C. J. Bradley. *Plane Euclidean Geometry: Theory and Practice*. United Kingdom Mathematics Trust, 2005.

[2] Ross Honsberger. *Episodes in nineteenth and twentieth century Euclidean geometry*. New Mathematical Library. Mathematical Association of America, 1995.

[3] Hojoo Lee. Topics in inequalities, 2009. Available from: `http://book.vnmath.com/2009/05/topics-in-inequalities-hojoo-lee.html`.

[4] Gerry Leversha. *Crossing the Bridge*. United Kingdom Mathematics Trust, 2008.

[5] Bill Richardson, editor. *Yearbooks*. United Kingdom Mathematics Trust, 1999–. Available from: `http://www.mathcomp.leeds.ac.uk/publications/index.php?type=Yearbook`.

Index